Advanced Placement
U.S. History 2
Twentieth-Century Challenges
1914–1996

Mary Anne Kovacs
Roberta J. Leach
Douglas E. Miller
John C. Ritter

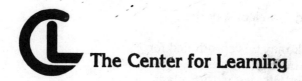
The Center for Learning

Mary Anne Kovacs, who earned her M.A. at the Bread Loaf School of English at Middlebury College, Vermont, is experienced as a curriculum director for the Center's language arts series and as a secondary English teacher. She is also author and coauthor of curriculum units in both the language arts and novel/drama series.

Roberta J. Leach was a social studies teacher, who earned her doctorate in history at Carnegie Mellon University. She has conducted A.P. U.S. history workshops. She is coauthor of eleven Center for Learning curriculum guides in social studies.

Douglas E. Miller earned his M.A. at San Jose State University, California. He was reading specialist, high school teacher, and social studies department chairperson. He has also served as editor of the *California Social Studies Review*. Currently, he is working with The American Promise.

John Ritter, who earned his M.S. at Western Oregon State College, has experience teaching at a maximum security institution. He has also taught social studies and English as a second language at the community college level.

The Publishing Team
Rose Schaffer, M.A., President/Chief Executive Officer
Bernadette Vetter, M.A., Vice President
Lora Murphy, M.A., Vice President, Social Studies Division
Amy Richards, M.A., Editor

Cover Design
Krina K. Walsh, B.S.I.D.

List of credits found on Acknowledgments page beginning on 233.

ISBN 1-56077-486-X

Contents

	Page	Handouts
Introduction	v	
Part 1: Between the Wars	1	
1. Defending Neutral Rights	3	1
2. The Treaty of Versailles—Wilson's Big Disappointment	9	2, 3
3. Women's Suffrage	15	4
4. Prohibition—The Noble Experiment	19	5, 6
5. Literature of the Twenties	25	7
6. Isolation—Fact or Revisionist Battleground?	29	8
7. The Twenties at Bay	33	9
8. Causes of the Great Depression	37	10
9. The "Okie" Experience and *The Grapes of Wrath*	41	11
10. The New Deal—Documents Question	49	12
11. The New Deal—A Writer's Forum	57	13
12. Isolation and Neutrality in the 1930s	61	14
13. Axis Partners—Clouds of War	65	15
14. Pearl Harbor—Interpretations of History	71	16
15. Japanese-American Internment	79	17
16. The United States and the Holocaust	87	18, 19
17. World War II Conferences	95	20
Part 2: The Postwar World—Adjusting to Change	103	
18. Cold War Revisited	105	21
19. The Truman Doctrine	109	22
20. McCarthyism and the Climate of Fear	117	23
21. Korean Inquiry	121	24
22. Economic Recovery after World War II	125	25
23. The New Frontier and Great Society	131	26
24. Vietnam—A Reappraisal	137	27

25. The Black Revolution—Where Do We Go from Here? 141 28

26. Women's Rights—A Chronicle of Reform 145 29

27. Native Americans—A Forgotten Minority 149 30

28. The Crimes of Watergate 157 31

29. Evaluating Recent Presidents .... 167 .... 32, 33

30. Social History and Contemporary Art 177 34

Part 3: The Grand Review—Mastering American History ... 181

31. Continuity and Change in American History 183 35

32. Turning Points in American History 187 36

33. Remember Your Ps and Qs—
    Presidential Promises and Quotable Quotations 193 37

34. Where in the U.S.A. Did It Happen, Carmen? 199 38

35. The Power of the Printed Word 205 39

36. Points of Conflict—The Focus of History 211 40

37. Our Inheritance—A Legacy of Reform 217 41

38. The Secretary of State Hall of Fame .... 221 .... 42, 43

39. The Individual in History 227 44

40. The Confidence Builder—Tackling the Essay 229 45

Introduction

Advanced Placement U.S. History 2 encourages students to process content actively rather than record data passively. Accordingly, lessons emphasize careful reading, exact writing, perceptive evaluation, and divergent thinking. These are the necessary skills students must develop as they challenge the thematic questions commonly found in advanced placement exams. Being able to synthesize historical fact in order to understand and value present reality is the promise and the measure of this book.

We realize that preparation for an advanced placement exam is an enormous undertaking for both teacher and student. There is so little time to create lessons that exhilarate and delight, as well as instruct. For that reason, we have included exercises that not only help students practice for the exam, but also provide enrichment activities that urge students to use their reason as well as their memories. Students interpret historical evidence, assume historical roles, and challenge historical generalizations. In short, the lessons reflect the concept that learning history involves pursuit of truth on the basis of evidence with the need for objective tolerance in that pursuit.

The lessons are designed to supplement an advanced placement course. (For basic American history lessons, see The Center for Learning U.S. History series.) A document-based question and several essays from previous exams are included. A foreign policy and secretary of state exercise involves cooperative research while reviewing nineteenth-century and twentieth-century American history. In each case, the student is asked to explore the past for its relevance to the present.

The lessons stress controversial issues and purposely avoid the dullness of homogenized opinion. They ask students to make their own interpretations of historical evidence and recognize the need to readjust their pictures of the past as an increasing amount of historical fact becomes known. Admitting that much of the evidence is uncertain, incomplete, or inconclusive, the exercises caution students not to go beyond what evidence will bear. Thus considered, students learn a history which teaches that a subjective view is a valuable tool.

Pupils mature as they acknowledge that there are many questions for which there is no single correct answer. These lessons reinforce the precept that opinions as well as facts must be subjected to the test of evidence and argument. In that spirit, we address the inquisitiveness of the advanced placement student.

Assignments and Evaluation

These lessons are intended for use in high school courses in *Advanced Placement U.S. History*. They are not designed to accompany a specific textbook.

Homework assignments are included in two ways, depending on their nature as either background or follow-up material. Handouts, classroom activities, and suggested assignments provide numerous tools for student evaluation. The introduction to each section lists basic questions students should be able to answer after completion of individual lessons.

Goals

This approach to the teaching of *Advanced Placement U.S. History* is based on these assumptions:

1. History is an evolutionary and revolutionary process. An accurate historical perspective necessitates analysis of cause-effect relationships.

2. An understanding of history's recurring themes enlightens the students' perspective on specific events.

3. History records efforts of people and nations to solve problems and improve circumstances. An understanding of the past enhances people's wisdom in confronting current and future situations.

4. An advanced study of history requires multiple critical thinking skills.

Objectives

1. To give students a conceptual knowledge of American history

2. To enable students to analyze historical materials independently and cooperatively

3. To enable students to exercise high-level thinking skills in analyzing historical developments and in drawing conclusions

4. To improve students' essay writing skills

5. To foster students' development of personal values in responding to history

Using the Course Materials

Advanced Placement U.S. History 2, 1914–1996, deals with events from World War I to the present and includes an extensive review section to prepare students for the Advanced Placement examination. It presupposes an understanding of previous American history, which is the subject of *Advanced Placement U.S. History 1*. This manual includes forty detailed lesson plans and a variety of student handouts. Many lessons easily lend themselves to expansion over several days of class.

Student handouts are intended both as in-class work and as homework. Although they are intended for distribution to students, some may be used effectively as transparencies for overhead projection. The lessons suggest ways of using the handouts and answers to questions. The lessons are flexible, allowing adjustment according to specific educational goals, students' needs, and availability of materials and equipment.

Using the Cross-Reference Chart

The cross-reference chart facilitates evaluation of the lessons and the book as a whole. It provides an analysis of the unit's incorporation of major themes and concepts. The chart also details the lessons' development of specific critical thinking skills.

Themes

1. A democratic society encourages but does not insure equality of opportunity and equality before the law.

2. Conflict can be resolved by compromise and change; otherwise it may lead to violence.

3. Individuals and groups tend to interpret historical events in terms of their own experiences, values, and points of view.

4. The more complex society becomes, the greater is the need for effective leadership, interaction, and interdependence.

5. Power can be used to achieve both constructive and destructive ends.

6. Through government and other organizations, society modifies and regulates the market economy in an effort to achieve economic justice, stability, freedom, and growth.

7. There exist time lags between the occurrence of a problem and identification of it, as well as between recognition and a possible solution.

8. Arts and literature generally reflect society.

Concepts

1. Immigration
2. Migration
3. Imperialism
4. Expansionism
5. Isolationism
6. Internationalism
7. Reform
8. Liberalism
9. Conservatism
10. Prosperity
11. Depression
12. Inflation
13. Deflation
14. Feminism
15. Prohibition
16. Technology
17. Foreign policy
18. Domestic program
19. Collective bargaining
20. Supply and demand
21. Sphere of influence
22. Change
23. Civil rights/Equal rights
24. Detente
25. Racism/Social Darwinism
26. Cold War
27. McCarthyism
28. Civil disobedience/Dissent
29. Black Power
30. Leadership

Critical Thinking Skills

1. Drawing conclusions from reading

2. Distinguishing between fact and opinion

3. Recognizing bias and stereotyping

4. Defining relationships among categories of information

5. Identifying relevant material

6. Interpreting various forms of print and nonprint materials

7. Using appropriate criteria to analyze topics

8. Recognizing and analyzing cause-effect relationships

9. Posing "what if" situations, and showing likely effects on subsequent events

10. Asking perceptive questions

11. Recognizing instances in which diverse interpretations of factual material are valid

12. Challenging generalizations about history in the light of specific facts

13. Comparing and contrasting historical events and trends

14. Relating specific events to recurring themes in American history

15. Analyzing literature and the arts as models of interpreting history

16. Recognizing values implicit in a situation and issues that flow from them

17. Expressing conclusions in clear thesis statements

18. Writing well-developed sentences, paragraphs, and essays

19. Communicating ideas effectively through oral modes

20. Reading and listening for a variety of purposes

21. Arranging supportive data in chronological order and in order of importance

22. Utilizing library facilities to fulfill research needs

Cross-Reference Chart

Lesson	Themes	Concepts	Critical Thinking Skills
1	2, 3, 5, 7	6, 17	1, 4, 5, 8, 17, 18
2	4, 5	6, 17	1, 5, 8, 9, 10
3	1, 3, 5, 7	7, 14, 23	1, 2, 3, 5, 14, 16, 19
4	3, 7	7, 8, 15	3, 8, 16, 18, 19, 20
5	3, 8	1, 5, 15, 25	1, 15, 16, 17
6	2, 3	5, 6, 17	1, 2, 11, 12
7	1, 3, 7	10, 14, 18, 20	1, 5, 7, 12, 19, 22
8	6, 7	10, 18, 20	1, 5, 11, 17, 21
9	1, 2, 7, 8	2, 11, 16, 18, 20	1, 4, 7, 15, 16, 18
10	1, 2, 3, 4, 6, 7	7, 8, 9, 11, 18, 20	4, 5, 6, 7, 8, 11, 12, 18, 21
11	4, 6, 7	7, 10, 11, 18, 20	1, 4, 5, 7, 17, 18, 21
12	3, 4, 7	5, 6, 17, 21	1, 4, 7, 8, 14, 19, 21
13	2, 5, 7	3, 5, 6, 17, 21	1, 8, 9, 19
14	2, 5, 7	5, 6, 17, 21	1, 2, 11, 12, 19
15	1, 2, 3, 7	1, 18, 23, 25	1, 3, 8, 16, 18
16	1, 2, 3, 4, 7	1, 6, 11, 17, 25, 28	1, 2, 3, 5, 12, 16
17	1, 5, 7	6, 17, 21	1, 11, 13, 19
18	3, 5	6, 17, 21, 26	1, 11, 21, 22
19	2, 3, 5	6, 17, 21, 26	1, 2, 8, 11, 13
20	1, 3, 5	21, 23, 26, 27	1, 3, 9, 19, 20
21	1, 3, 5	6, 21, 23, 26, 27	1, 5, 12, 19, 22
22	2, 6, 7	10, 12, 16, 18, 19, 20	1, 4, 6, 7
23	1, 4	18	1, 5, 13, 18
24	3, 5, 7	6, 17, 21	1, 5, 8, 16
25	1, 2, 5	23, 25, 29	1, 2, 3, 5, 19, 22
26	1, 3, 7	7, 8, 9, 14, 23	5, 13, 20
27	1, 3, 5, 7	2, 7, 18, 23, 25	1, 2, 3, 8, 9, 12, 16
28	1, 5, 7	18, 23, 33	1, 2, 8, 11, 12, 16
29	4, 5, 7	12, 13, 17, 23, 24, 26, 30, 31	1, 2, 4, 7, 11, 14, 16
30	3, 8	7, 8	6, 8, 15, 16, 18
31	1, 2, 5, 7	1, 7, 17, 18, 19, 22	5, 8, 13, 14, 21
32	5, 7	17, 18, 22	5, 18, 21
33	1, 2, 3	17, 18	5, 14
34	1, 2, 3, 4, 5	17, 18, 22	5, 14, 20
35	7	17, 18, 22	5, 14, 21
36	2	17, 18, 22	5, 7, 21
37	1, 7	7, 14, 19, 22, 23	5, 14, 17, 19, 20, 22
38	2, 3, 5	5, 6, 17, 24, 26	1, 7, 12, 19, 20
39	4, 5	17, 18, 22, 30	1, 7, 21
40	1, 2, 5, 7	7, 8, 9, 13, 19, 20, 22	5, 8, 11, 12, 14, 18

Part 1
Between the Wars

While you may choose to divide the period from World War I to the end of World War II into smaller units for teaching and testing purposes, it is very useful to view the period as a whole. Such smaller units might include World War I, the prosperity of the 20s, the depression of the 30s, and World War II. Students need to see, however, that the World War I peace settlement led to World War II, that the United States' decision to reject League of Nations membership affected our diplomacy for a generation, and that economic forces unleashed in World War I had implications for the economy of the 20s and the causes of the depression that followed.

As a result of individual lessons in Part 1, students should be able to answer the following basic questions:

- What factors led the United States to enter World War I?

- What accounts for the Senate rejection of the Treaty of Versailles?

- Why did enactment of the Nineteenth Amendment take so long to accomplish?

- What accounts for the failure of Prohibition?

- How did literature of the 1920s reflect society at the time?

- Was United States' isolation in the 1920s fact or illusion?

- In what ways did events of the 20s lay the foundation for troublesome issues in the future?

- What caused the Great Depression?

- To what extent did the fictional account in *The Grapes of Wrath* mirror reality?

- To what extent is it accurate to label Franklin Roosevelt a liberal and Herbert Hoover a conservative?

- To what extent did the New Deal reflect a coherent economic philosophy?

- How did the United States become progressively involved in world affairs in the 1930s?

- Could the United States have avoided Pearl Harbor?

- To what extent did United States' foreign policy in the late 30s support FDR's "Quarantine" philosophy?

- To what extent were Americans sufficiently informed at the time to recognize how the internment of Japanese-Americans constituted a violation of their civil rights and posed a threat to everyone's constitutional rights?

- Why didn't the United States do more to support victims of the Holocaust?

- What accounts for the Cold War?

Lesson 1 Defending Neutral Rights

Lesson 2 The Treaty of Versailles—Wilson's Big Disappointment

Lesson 3 Women's Suffrage

Lesson 4 Prohibition—The Noble Experiment

Lesson 5 Literature of the Twenties

Lesson 6 Isolation—Fact or Revisionist Battleground?

Lesson 7 The Twenties at Bay

Lesson 8 Causes of the Great Depression

Lesson 9 The "Okie" Experience and *The Grapes of Wrath*

Lesson 10 The New Deal—Documents Question

Lesson 11 The New Deal—A Writer's Forum

Lesson 12 Isolation and Neutrality in the 1930s

Lesson 13 Axis Partners—Clouds of War

Lesson 14 Pearl Harbor—Interpretations of History

Lesson 15 Japanese-American Internment

Lesson 16 The United States and the Holocaust

Lesson 17 World War II Conferences

Lesson 1
Defending Neutral Rights

Objectives

- To explore the steps that led the United States to enter into World War I

- To recognize the importance of formulating a controlling idea or commitment prior to writing a paragraph or essay

- To learn content through the process of writing history

Notes to the Teacher

When war broke out in Europe in 1914, President Wilson recognized the difficulty of thinking logically when one's sympathies are aroused and, from the start, urged Americans to remain "impartial in thought as well as in action." In a nation with an Anglo-Saxon cultural heritage and millions of hyphenated Americans who traced their ancestry to both sides in the war, this strict neutrality proved impossible. Sympathy for Britain, Belgium, France, and their allies, coupled with increasing estrangement from Germany and her allies, eventually brought the United States into the war in 1917 on the side of the Allies.

This lesson can produce intensified student involvement through student writing. The more students critique and revise the steps outlined in the procedure, the more they will learn content and risk revising previous convictions. The lesson also shows an insight into the historical method as the writer processes evidence to a topic. A complete discussion supporting this approach can be found on Henry A. Giroux's *The Process of Writing History: Episodes in European History.*

Before the lesson, have students review the causes of World War I by reading a world history text that shows how the interrelationship of nationalism, imperialism, militarism, and balance of power politics brought Europe to war in 1914 after a century of relative peace. They then complete a reading that explains America's entry into this war. The writing activities in this lesson help students develop their own explanation for the United States' transition from neutrality to war.

Procedure

1. Introduce the lesson using materials in the Notes to the Teacher and have students complete part A of **Handout 1**.

2. Take time to review their responses to questions 1 and 2.

Suggested Responses:

1. a. Loans to belligerents—*As a neutral country, the United States expected to trade freely with both sides, but the fact that America had loaned the Allies nearly $1.5 billion and had only $8 million in loans outstanding to the Central Powers swayed sympathies and made Germany's efforts to cut trade seem particularly threatening.*

    b. Lusitania—*Despite Germany's warnings to Americans not to sail on merchant ships of countries with whom she was at war, Americans were still shocked by the sinking of the British ship and the loss of nearly 1200 individuals, including 128 Americans.*

    c. House-Grey Memorandum—*This note made clear to Britain that American moral sympathies were clearly on Britain's side.*

    d. Sussex Pledge—*After U.S. warnings, Germany pledged to respect the rules of international law regarding visit, search, and destruction of merchant vessels, if their enemy, the British, adhered to the same rules. Early in 1917, however, the Germans announced their intention to resume unrestricted submarine warfare.*

2. Strict accountability

    German espionage

    Arabic crisis

    Submarine warfare

    British propaganda

    German atrocities

    Wilson's peace note

Peace without victory

Zimmermann note

Russian Revolution

3. Group students into sets of five and have them read each others' paragraphs. Have them judge the best controlling ideas, looking for those that contain or support most of the available evidence. Write the five or six best ideas on the board. Have the class list the best supporting evidence for each of these statements.

4. Have students compare their explanations with President Wilson's rationale (part B of **Handout 1**) in his message to Congress asking for a declaration of war. (He stressed the importance of making the "world safe for democracy," bringing freedom to small nations, and creating a lasting peace.)

5. To conclude the lesson, have students complete part C of **Handout 1**. Take time to debrief their reasoning when the paragraphs are complete.

U.S. Involvement in World War I

Part A.

How did our defense of neutral rights eventually lead to our declaration of war?

1. How did each of the following pieces of evidence support eventual intervention in the war by the United States?

   a. Loans to belligerents

   b. Sinking of the *Lusitania*

   c. House-Grey Memorandum

   d. Sussex Pledge

2. List five to seven additional pieces of evidence supporting America's decision to declare war.

3. Develop a controlling idea suggesting how all or most of the ideas above help to answer the original question.

4. Using your controlling ideas as a topic sentence, on another piece of paper, write a paragraph that uses at least three above items as supporting evidence.

Part B.

Woodrow Wilson made the key decisions, as he had since 1914. Certain members of the Senate still sought to avert war by keeping American ships out of the war zone. The President, however, decided that he had the necessary authority to arm these merchant ships, giving them a chance at self-protection, and to send them out. Wilson agonized over the situation, believing that the war was almost intolerable, that it might do irreparable damage to American institutions. And yet he saw no way out. The only hope was that Germany would avoid sinking the ships of neutral powers and especially those of the United States. Wilson, in other words, was prepared to retreat from the *Sussex* pledge of 1916, so eager was he to avoid war. He did not adhere doggedly to an extreme interpretation of international law, as formerly believed.[1]

Gradually, events carried Wilson toward war. On February 25, the British turned over to him an intercepted note from the German foreign secretary, Arthur Zimmermann, proposing that in the event of war Mexico should attack the United States and receive in return her lost province north of the border. Americans were infuriated. At about the same time, the Russian revolution eliminated one of the moral problems in Wilson's mind by replacing a despotism among the Allies with the constitutional monarchy. (This government lasted only until November 1917, when Lenin and the communists came into power.)[2]

Identify the controlling idea in the following excerpt from Wilson's Speech before Congress, April 2, 1917.

It is a distressing and oppressive duty, Gentlemen of the Congress, which I have performed in thus addressing you. There are, it may be, many months of fiery trial and sacrifice ahead of us. It is a fearful thing to lead this great peaceful people into war, into the most terrible and disastrous of all wars, civilization itself seeming to be in the balance. But the right is more precious than peace, and we shall fight for the things which we have always carried nearest our hearts—for democracy, for the right of those who submit to authority to have a voice in their own Governments, for the rights and liberties of small nations, for a universal dominion of right by such a concert of free peoples as shall bring peace and safety to all nations and make the world itself at last free. To such a task we can dedicate our lives and our fortunes, everything that we are and everything that we have, with the pride of those who know that the day has come when America is privileged to spend her blood and her might for the principles that gave her birth and happiness and the peace which she has treasured. God helping her, she can do no other.[3]

[1] James Leonard Gates, *The United States, 1898–1924* (New York: McGraw-Hill, 1976), 193.

[2] Frank Friedel, *America in the Twentieth Century* (New York: Alfred A. Knopf, 1976), 102–103.

[3] Woodrow Wilson, as quoted in Arthur S. Link, *Woodrow Wilson and the Progressive Era* (New York: Harper and Brothers, 1954), 281–282.

Part C.

Imagine yourself as a United States citizen on the eve of our entry into World War I. On another piece of paper, in three paragraphs, write your reflections on the following:

Paragraph 1: The United States is fully justified in declaring war on Germany.

Paragraph 2: List attitudes that the following people might have towards your viewpoint. Then write a paragraph addressing one person from the list.

Theodore Roosevelt
Robert LaFollette
A priest in the Roman Catholic Church
A businessman engaged in trade with the Allies
A German American
Nicolai Lenin

A member of the Ku Klux Klan
Jane Addams
Andrew Carnegie
A member of the Socialist Party
Someone in the future

Paragraph 3: Repeat step two by writing to a second person on the list.

Conclusion: Look at your three paragraphs. Do they express similar ideas? If different, how would you revise the original premise in paragraph 1 to reflect your current thinking on the issue?

Lesson 2
The Treaty of Versailles—
Wilson's Big Disappointment

Objective

• To account for the defeat in the U.S. Senate of the Treaty of Versailles

Notes to the Teacher

In asking for a declaration of war in 1917, President Wilson vowed that it would be "a war to end all wars" and a war "to make the world safe for democracy." Wilson's idealism continued when he outlined his Fourteen Points to serve as the basis for a peace settlement. He expected opposition from the British, French, and Italian representatives at Versailles and was prepared to negotiate to save his cherished proposal for a League of Nations, designed to preserve peace in the future. He did not, however, expect strong and, indeed, insurmountable opposition from U.S. senators who had to ratify the treaty.

In this two-part lesson, students gain an understanding of three perspectives—those of Wilson, Reservationists who wanted changes in the League Covenant, and Irreconcilables who opposed U.S. entry into any international organization. Students write questions each might have wished to pose to the others and questions they might have expected from the opposition. With this background, students discuss how they might have responded to an advanced placement document-based question on the failure of Wilson to secure Senate approval for the Treaty of Versailles.

This document-based question is an important part of the Advanced Placement examination and a significant challenge for students. Students need repeated opportunities to attempt such questions prior to taking the test. In some cases, working through the process as a class activity may be more helpful to students than actually writing an essay. This document-based question fits well with the theme of the lesson. A recent College Board publication (Luther Spoehr and Alan Fraker, *Doing the DBQ: Advanced Placement U.S. History Teaching and Learning with the Document-Based Question.* New York: The College Board, 1995.) makes incorporation of document-based questions at other appropriate points in your curriculum very easy. The publication includes all document-based questions used on the Advanced Placement examination between 1973 and 1995, arranged in the sequence one might use in a chronological course in American history and supplemented with key notes to the teacher on possible approaches to each of the questions.

Procedure

1. Introduce the topic using material in the Notes to the Teacher.

2. Assign **Handout 2** for homework.

   Suggested Responses:

   1. *Wilson might ask Reservationists how they would dare to threaten chances for preserving the peace by opposing Article X or ask the Irreconcilables how the United States could avoid taking its rightful role of leadership in the world. Certainly he would have expected questions regarding his own failure to consult the majority Republicans during the writing of the treaty or his unwillingness to compromise during the ratification process.*

   2. *Reservationists might question Wilson about how to reconcile possible League involvement in cases of aggression with the provision in the Constitution giving Congress the exclusive right to declare war. They had concerns, too, about the possible League interference in domestic matters, such as tariffs and immigration policy, and about domination of the organization by Britain and her dominions. Wilson might have questioned the stalling techniques used by the Reservationists, for instance reading the whole treaty aloud in the Senate at a time when public support for ratification was high.*

9

3. *Irreconcilables might ask questions about allowing a foreign tribunal to Direct U.S. actions, abandoning our traditional isolation, or reducing armaments. Wilson would surely question the wisdom of their isolationism in the new circumstances of globalism.*

3. Reserve time in class to evaluate the questions and why some are more perceptive than others. After discussion of students' questions, assign **Handout 3**. Begin by discussing who the liberals and conservatives were. Liberals and conservatives here do not mean the same as liberals and conservatives in domestic policy-making but rather conservative in support of traditional isolationism or liberalism in recognizing a new role of U.S. leadership in the world. Have students record, on a grid, information that they know regarding the objections of the liberals and conservatives, as well as the ineptitude and stubbornness of Wilson, *before* they read the documents. They can then record additional ideas as they read.

4. Discuss possible theses. A number of explanations are plausible, depending on priorities students attach to various factors. Record what supportive evidence they have, both from their own background and from the documents.

Suggested Evidence, Handout 3:
Wilson

Failure to take key Republicans to Versailles for negotiating process

Unwillingness to compromise, particularly on Article X

Unskilled in art of politics, especially working with new Republican majority after midterm elections

Unfortunate and crippling stroke at key point in ratification debate

Liberals

Hostility to Wilson

Determined to get revenge for failure to consult them early in the treaty negotiations

Opposition to Article X

Fear of involvement on war without Congressional declaration of war

Possible League interference in tariff and immigration policies

Possible domination of League by Britain and her dominions

Violation of traditional isolationism

Failure of treaty to deal with troublesome issues of nationalism

Reservationists stalled interminably until public opinion cooled

Irreconcilables

Fear of foreign entanglements

Foreign control of military decision-making possible

Questioned using "war to prevent war"

5. Finally, ask students to write a possible conclusion summarizing their point and explaining its significance for the future of U.S. foreign relations.

The Treaty of Versailles—Wilson's Big Disappointment

At the conclusion of World War I, President Wilson headed the United States' delegation to the peace conference at Versailles. He anticipated that his Fourteen Points, perhaps with some modifications, would serve as the basis for the peace treaty. He faced considerable opposition from more vindictive European leaders, but he did manage to salvage at least part of his peace plan, most notably his cherished League of Nations.

More surprising than opposition from the British and French was the opposition he faced from the U.S. senators who had to approve the Treaty of Versailles. Both Reservationists, who approved U.S. membership in the League of Nations with some modifications in the provisions, and Irreconcilables, who wanted a return to traditional U.S. isolation, voiced strong objections. Substantive issues, as well as personality conflicts, caused problems. Assume that President Wilson had been able to sit down with leaders of the opposition forces for a face-to-face discussion of the issues. Write a series of questions that might have surfaced in that debate. Remember that perceptive questions can be influential in causing persons to change their positions or behavior. In each case, write *two* questions each might have wanted to ask the opponents and *one* question each might have expected to be asked.

President Wilson

1.

2.

3.

Senator Henry Cabot Lodge, Sr., Republican chairperson of the Senate Foreign Relations Committee and spokesperson for the Reservationists

1.

2.

3.

William Borah, spokesperson for the Irreconcilables

1.

2.

3.

The College Board
Advanced Placement Examination
United States History
Section II

Part A.

(Suggested writing time—40 minutes)

Percent of Section II score—50

The following question requires you to construct a coherent essay that integrates your interpretation of Documents A-I *and* your knowledge of the period referred to in the question. High scores will be earned only by essays that both cite key pieces of evidence from the documents and draw on outside knowledge of the period.

1. It was the strength of the opposition forces, both liberal and conservative, rather than the ineptitude and stubbornness of President Wilson that led to the Senate defeat of the Treaty of Versailles.

   Using the documents and your knowledge of the period 1917–1921, assess the validity of this statement.

Document A

The first proposition connected with the proposed league is that of a tribunal to settle the matters of controversy which may arise between the different nations.

Will anyone advocate that those matters which are of vital importance to our people shall be submitted to a tribunal created other than by our own people and give it an international army subject to its direction and control to enforce its decrees? I doubt if anyone will advocate that. . . . If you do not do so, Mr. President, what will your league amount to? . . .

In its last analysis the proposition is force to destroy force, conflict to prevent conflict, militarism to destroy militarism, war to prevent war. In its last analysis it must be that if it has any sanction behind its judgment at all. There is where the difficulty lies. . . .

Source: William Borah, Speech in the United States Senate, December 6, 1918.

Document B

Liberals all over the world have hoped that a war, which was so clearly the fruit of competition and imperialist and class-bound nationalism, would end in a peace which would moralize nationalism by releasing it from class bondage and exclusive ambitions. The Treaty of Versailles does not even try to satisfy these aspirations. Instead of expressing a great recuperative effort of the conscience of civilization, which for its own sins has sweated so much blood, it does much to intensify and nothing to heal the old and ugly dissensions.

Source: *The New Republic*, May 24, 1919.

Document C

When you read Article X, therefore, you will see that it is nothing but the inevitable, logical center of the whole system of the Covenant of the League of Nations, and I stand for it absolutely. If it should ever in any important respect be impaired, I would feel like asking the Secretary of War to get the boys who went across the water to fight, . . . and I would stand up before them and say, Boys, I told you before you went across the seas that this was a war against wars, and I did my best to fulfill the promise, but I am obliged to come to you in mortification and shame and say I have not been able to fulfill the promise. You are betrayed. You have fought for something that you did not get.

Source: Woodrow Wilson, Speech, September 5, 1919.

Document D

I take the liberty of urging upon you the desirability of accepting the reservations now passed. . . .

I have the belief that with the League once in motion it can within itself and from experience and public education develop such measures as will make it effective. I am impressed with the desperate necessity of early ratification.

The delays have already seriously imperiled the economic recuperation of Europe. In this we are vitally interested from every point of view. I believe that the Covenant will steadily lose ground in popular support if it is not put into constructive operation at once because the American public will not appreciate the saving values of the Covenant as distinguished from the wrongs imposed in the Treaty . . .

Source: Herbert Hoover to Woodrow Wilson, November 19, 1919.

Document E

Reprinted by permission: Tribune Media Services.

Document F

According to [the French] vision of the future, European history is to be a perpetual prize-fight, of which France has won this round, but of which this round is certainly not the last. . . . For Clemenceau made no pretense of considering himself bound by the Fourteen Points and left chiefly to others such concoctions as were necessary from time to time to save the scruples or the face of the President [Wilson].

. . . . The policy of reducing Germany to servitude for a generation, of degrading the lives of millions of human beings, and of depriving a whole nation of happiness should be abhorrent and detestable,—abhorrent and detestable, even if it were possible, even if it enriched ourselves, even if it did not sow the decay of the whole civilized life of Europe.

Source: John Maynard Keynes, *Economic Consequences of the Peace*, 1920.

Document G

This election is to be a genuine national referendum. . . .

The chief question that is put to you is, of course: Do you want your country's honor vindicated and the Treaty of Versailles ratified? Do you in particular approve of the League of Nations as organized and empowered in that treaty? And do you wish to see the United States play its responsible part in it? . . .

[The founders of the Government] thought of America as the light of the world as created to lead the world in the assertion of the rights of peoples and the rights of free nations. . . . This light the opponents of the League would quench.

Source: Woodrow Wilson, "Appeal to the Country," October 3, 1920.

Document H

Forty-one nations, including nearly every Negro and mulatto and colored government of the world, have met in Geneva and formed the assembly of the League of Nations. This is the most forward-looking event of the century. Because of the idiotic way in which the stubbornness of Woodrow Wilson and the political fortunes of the Republicans became involved, the United States was not represented. But despite its tumult and shouting this nation must join and join on the terms which the World lays down. The idea that we single-handed can dictate terms to the World or stay out of the World, is an idea born of the folly of fools.

Source: W.E.B. DuBois, "The League of Nations," *Crisis*, March, 1921.

Document I

The League of Nations afforded a wide difference of opinion in every group. The Woman's Peace Party held its annual meeting in Chicago in the spring of 1920 and found our Branches fairly divided upon the subject. . . . The difference of opinion was limited always as to the existing League and never for a moment did anyone doubt the need for continued effort to bring about an adequate international organization.

Source: Jane Addams, *Peace and Bread in time of War*, 1922.

Advanced Placement Examination, United States History, Section II, Part A (Princeton, New Jersey: Educational Testing Service, 1991).

Lesson 3
Women's Suffrage

Objectives

- To view feminism in a historical context

- To probe various factors in the fights for and against women's suffrage

Notes to the Teacher

This lesson enables students to trace the feminist movement in a historical context from colonial life to Prohibition. It also encourages students to probe implications of stances for and against women's suffrage. Depending on students' backgrounds, the discussion of part B of the handout may vary from extreme feminism to male chauvinism.

Before this lesson, have students read the material in their texts regarding women's suffrage and the Nineteenth Amendment.

Procedure

1. Have students read the introductory quotation on **Handout 4**. Ask why Carrie Chapman Catt made this statement. (*To accentuate the extensive effort that was necessary for such a seemingly simple adjustment.*) Point out that she traces the campaign to 1868, the year the Fourteenth Amendment was ratified. This amendment first introduced the word "male" to the Constitution.

2. Have students complete part A of the handout. Discuss responses.

   Suggested Responses:

   Colonial life—*hard physical labor, involvement of wives in their husband's work, some political voice*

   Revolutionary period—*support for military, some "free thinking," e.g., Abigail Adams*

   Antebellum South—*strict separation of men's and women's roles among aristocracy; exploitation of female slaves by white masters*

   Seneca Falls Convention, 1848—*originated by Elizabeth Cady Stanton, Lucretia Mott, and others; Declaration of Sentiments, based on Declaration of Independence, created agenda for change*

   Nineteenth century spheres—*men busy with the difficult and personally draining demands of business; "ladies" focused on the welfare of their husbands and children*

   Abolition and feminism—*share a conviction of citizenship that goes beyond white manhood; both emphasize the importance of equal rights, especially the right to vote; differences abound, one of them being the contrast between the largely illiterate African American population and numbers of educated white women; virtually all social institutions supported the concept of women's subservience.*

3. Have students complete part B of the handout.

4. Summarize class responses on an overhead or the board.

5. Conduct a classroom discussion based on students' opinions and supportive reasoning. You may need occasionally to play devil's advocate representing divergent attitudes.

   Sample Discussion Points:

   1. Equality of Quaker men and women in meetings; Quaker background of Lucretia Mott and Susan B. Anthony; Quaker role in society and reform

   2. Perception of need to consider African-American suffrage and women's suffrage as separate issues; omission of the word "sex"

   3. Reaction based on endemic racism; awareness of possibility of success in seeking reform; emphasis on importance of the right to vote—"Taxation without Representation"

   4. Extreme limitation of spheres for both sexes; consignment of women's interests to virtue, fashion, and home life; limitation of women's intellectual life; absolute dependence of wives and daughters

15

5. Feminism, like abolitionism, based on awareness of human rights; fear of effect women's freedom might have on family structure

6. May have speeded passage of Nineteenth Amendment but meant suffrage did not bring equality; relates to ongoing campaign for equality today

7. Opposition by powerful liquor lobby; growth in speaking and organizing abilities; support by others convinced of evil of drinking; destructive effect of drinking and drunkenness on the family and society

8. Supports traditional view of family— even forces family unity; contradicts traditional value of human freedom

9. Laws enforcing women's economic dependence; double standard of morality; need for someone to care for home and children; inability to share authority; belief that males are inherently "higher" than females

10. Evidence that women do not vote as a lobbying block; pluralism in thinking among both men and women; tendency for women to agree with their husband's positions

Extension Assignment

You may want to have students research, write, and report of the following topics:

- The split between Lucy Stone and Elizabeth Cady Stanton

- International Woman Suffrage Alliance

- League of Women Voters

- Woodrow Wilson and women's suffrage

- Strategies of Alice Paul

- Role of Anna Howard Shaw

- Civil War and women's roles

- Women's roles in Progressivism

- World War I and women's suffrage

- Development of coeducation

- Darwinism and feminism

- Role of Charlotte Perkins Gilman

- Roles of minority women in the feminist movement

- The flapper ideal

- Thinking of Margaret Sanger

- Women's roles and fashions

- Women's roles in World War II

- Feminism after World War II

The Long Road to Women's Suffrage

" . . . to get that word, male, out of the Constitution, cost the women of
the country 52 years of pauseless campaign; 56 state referendum campaigns; 480 legislative campaigns to get state suffrage amendments submitted; 47 state constitutional campaigns; 277 state party convention
campaigns; 30 national party convention campaigns to get suffrage planks
in the party platforms; 19 campaigns with 19 successive Congresses to
get the federal amendment submitted, and the final ratification campaign."[1]

Carrie Chapman Catt, on the Ratification of the Nineteenth Amendment

Part A.

From the Colonial Period to the ratification of the Nineteenth Amendment, many American
women demonstrated creativity, intelligence, and courage. Yet, despite the obvious achievements
of many and the selfless efforts of some, women did not receive rights of full citizenship until
after World War I.

Review your knowledge of women's roles in:

Colonial life

Revolutionary period

Antebellum South

Seneca Falls Convention

Nineteenth century "spheres" of men and women

Abolition and feminism

During the nineteenth century, the abolition movement and the movement toward female
equality were deeply entwined. Many of the great feminist leaders, such as Lucretia Mott,
Elizabeth Cady Stanton, Lucy Stone, and Susan B. Anthony, were deeply committed to emancipation of African Americans. What similarities do you see in the two causes? What differences
are evident?

Later, many feminists became involved in various temperance movements working for Prohibition. What connections do you see between these two movements?

[1] Keith Ian Polakoff, *Generations of Americans: A History of the United States* (New York: St. Martin's
Press, 1976), 541.

Part B.

Based on information from previous study and from your text, state your opinion on each of the following statements from "Thoroughly Agree" to "Thoroughly Disagree." Be prepared to explain and support your reasoning.

	Thoroughly Agree	Agree	Undecided	Disagree	Thoroughly Disagree
1. Women today owe a debt to Quaker philosophy for their freedom.					
2. The Fifteenth Amendment was an insult to American women.					
3. If African Americans had not received the right to vote, feminists would not have been so adamant in pursuit of women's suffrage.					
4. In the nineteenth-century concept of male and female "spheres," women actually had the better part.					
5. It is odd that any men were sympathetic to feminism.					
6. During the suffrage movement, women should not have put aside the equality theme to stress how they would use the vote to promote a better society.					
7. Feminist support for Prohibition did not affect women's success in seeking equal rights.					
8. Anti-feminism supports traditional values.					
9. Women's suffrage was delayed by white, male-dominated society's need for a system of slavery.					
10. The fact that American voting patterns reflected little change after 1920 indicates that women's suffrage was really not necessary.					

Lesson 4
Prohibition—The Noble Experiment

Objectives

- To examine the effects of Prohibition on the American people

- To explore cultural attitudes about Prohibition as a factor in its failure

Notes to the Teacher

This lesson on Prohibition consists of three parts. The first part asks students to answer questions concerning Prohibition. The second part focuses on several quotations from people of that era. The third part directs students to interview each other from a prescribed set of questions designed to lead to conclusions on the effect of Prohibition on the average person and society as a whole. To begin the third exercise, students should form pairs and discuss their answers to the first two exercises. One student should be designated an interviewer and the other the interviewee. Encourage them to be creative and dramatic and to conclude with a general discussion.

Before the class, have students read the material in their texts dealing with Prohibition.

Procedure

1. Have students complete **Handout 5**, part A. Conduct a discussion based on their answers.

   Suggested Responses, Part A:

   1. *Progressives and prohibitionists had often claimed that liquor was the root of all evil. To save families and children from destruction, it was necessary to stop the sale and manufacture of all alcoholic spirits.*

   2. *By the turn of the century, these organizations, working through the schools, press, politics, and churches, had succeeded in "drying up" five states. These groups were active, well organized, and had excellent publicity. They did much to further the cause of Prohibition.*

   3. *In view of dissatisfaction about the ease with which alcohol was imported from "wet" into "dry" zones and the inadequacy of local and federal enforcement machinery, people decided that if Prohibition did not work at the local level, then it had to be national.*

   4. *Ironically, women, who previously had been banished from the saloon, were now invited to frequent speak-easies. In this respect, women had greater "opportunity."*

   5. *Criminals were sometimes glamorized and treated as folk heroes, while the police were seen as dishonest, inept people who did not promote the public welfare.*

   6. *Prohibition fostered the development of other forms of leisure activities; since saloons and bars were closed, people, primarily men, were forced to develop other forms of social entertainment, e.g., taking a drive in a car, listening to the radio, attending sporting events, or going to the movies.*

   7. *They correlated Prohibition and individual freedom. Even the president violated the law.*

   8. *A wide variety of responses may emerge—e.g., increased crime, fostering of organized crime, need for bootlegging.*

2. Have students complete **Handout 5**, part B. Discuss student responses.

   Suggested Responses, Part B:

   1. *Prohibition as a moral cause involved the Protestant "moral community" cleaning up the corrupt city.*

   2. *An anti-prohibitionist (probably Irish Catholic) claims that since Jesus drank wine, Christians should be able to drink liquor.*

3. Mencken pokes fun at the "suffering" anti-prohibitionists longing for a drink.

4. "Wet" urban North vs. "dry" rural South conflict. It is important to note that the 1920 census had revealed for the first time a predominance of urban population. This explains the conflict between rural and urban values.

5. Prohibitionist fervor sought to rally voters in a "Save the Children" plea.

6. The quotation points out the dilemma of living with a law that is not respected. Much of society and many politicians scorned Prohibition.

3. Have students, working in pairs, prepare one or more of the interviews based on **Handout 6** and present them to the class.

4. After all the presentations, conclude the lesson by having students write one-page reaction essays summarizing their views of Prohibition's effect on society.

Extension Assignment

Ask students to compare and contrast, either orally or in written form, Prohibition with current United States laws on controlled substances.

Prohibition—The Noble Experiment

Part A.

To begin your study of the topic, answer the following questions on Prohibition.

1. Comment on the marriage of morality and Prohibition. How are the two issues intertwined?

2. Discuss the effect that these organizations had on Prohibition: the Women's Christian Temperance Union; the Anti-Saloon League; the Methodist Church.

3. Where did the demand for national Prohibition originate?

4. How did Prohibition affect the revolution in sexual standards?

5. Do you think Prohibition changed the attitude of people toward criminals? The police? Explain.

6. How did Prohibition encourage the creation of new forms of social activity?

7. Why did the American public refuse to regard violations of Prohibition as criminal enterprises?

8. How did Prohibition affect the moral fabric of America?

Part B.

State, in your own words, the main ideas in the following Prohibition quotations.

Quotation 1

"Prohibition permitted the Protestant countryside to coerce the newer Americans in the city. One 'dry' asserted: 'Our nation can only be saved by turning the pure stream of country sentiment and township morals to flush out the cesspools of cities and so save civilization from pollution.'"[1]

Quotation 2

"'The government which stands against the founder of Christianity cannot survive,' declared Senator Walsh of Massachusetts."[2]

Quotation 3

"The satirical essayist H.L. Mencken claimed that prohibition had caused suffering comparable only to that of the Black Death and the Thirty Years War."[3]

[1] Samuel Eliot Morison, et al., *A Concise History of the American Republic* (New York: Oxford University Press, 1977), 591.

[2] Morison, *A Concise History of the American Republic*, 591.

[3] Samuel Eliot Morison, et al., *The Growth of the American Republic, Volume 2* (New York: Oxford University Press, 1980), 438.

Quotation 4

"The wet city is trying to impose its will on the dry country. The wet North on the dry South!"[4]

Quotation 5

"If the Christian vote did not go to the polls, 'we shall see our towns and villages rum-ridden in the near future and a whole generation of our children destroyed.'"[5]

Quotation 6

"Twice a week he [Harding] sought to banish care by inviting his friends to the White House for poker parties. Liquor flowed freely at these affairs, for the President—like many other Americans—did not take prohibition seriously. The 'drys' got after him, however, and he finally confined his drinking to the family bedrooms."[6]

[4] Morison, *The Growth of the American Republic*, 439.

[5] Morison, *The Growth of the American Republic*, 440.

[6] Morison, *The Growth of the American Republic*, 440.

Prohibition Interviews

Interviewer

Put yourself into the guise of an inquisitive, probing reporter. Do not settle for answers that seem less than honest. Add original questions, if you wish, as you examine your subject's attitude toward Prohibition.

1. Are you in favor of Prohibition? Explain your position.

2. Do you favor free choice concerning liquor? Why, or why not?

3. Is liquor evil?

4. How effectively is the government enforcing Prohibition?

5. Does the government have the right to tell you what to eat or drink?

6. Do you have evidence that Prohibition is, in fact, increasing urban crime?

7. Do you obey the law strictly, or just when it is convenient?

8. Have you ever visited a speak-easy?

9. Do you think it is hard for most other people to live with Prohibition?

10. Will Prohibition last? Why do you think so?

Interviewee

In the interview, identify as closely as possible with your assigned 1920s character(s). Respond to the reporter's questions honestly and frankly.

1. **Horace C. Whitewash, retired county judge**—pious man, lives on a farm, takes long walks and reads Shakespeare

2. **Mrs. Clorida Barnswallow, a minister's wife**—age forty-two, three children, city dweller, likes to sew, paint, and putter in the garden

3. **Renardo Jones, freight hauler**—age thirty-eight, city dweller, hard worker, chews tobacco, attends local Baptist Church

4. **Tony Lucharese, bricklayer**—age twenty-six, five children, city dweller, likes to play pool

5. **Doug (Law and Order) Peterson, city dweller**—a police officer, age thirty-eight, active in local Moose Lodge

6. **Patrick O'Hanahan, store clerk**—age nineteen, will marry soon, still lives at home with mother and father, hard worker

7. **Sally McPherson, librarian**—age twenty-seven, attends local church, likes to paint and ride horses, active in civic improvement association

8. **Tom Bailey, unemployed**—age twenty-nine, does nothing, hangs around downtown area

9. **John C. Portus, city councilman**—active in local Methodist Church, two children, age forty-two

10. **Maryann Smythe, social worker**—lives in the city, no time for social recreation, active in WCTU (Women's Christian Temperance Union)

Lesson 5
Literature of the Twenties

Objective

* To analyze literature of the 1920s as reflections of the decade

Notes to the Teacher

Variously dubbed "the lost generation," "the Harlem Renaissance," and the "Jazz Age," the 1920s constitute a high point in American literary history. A glance at any American literature text suggests a litany of great names writing during this period.

Many intellectuals and artists of the decade tended toward disillusionment and alienation. Expatriation, especially in Paris, attracted many. Others gathered in New York's Greenwich Village or Harlem. Some expressed nostalgia for the rural America of an earlier era while others found much to criticize in values prevalent at the time. However, newcomers to the country gloried in possibilities unknown in the "Old Country."

In this lesson, students research the lives, works, and themes of several key writers of the decade. Taking the perspective of his or her assigned writer, each student then participates in a small group charged with the task of writing a thesis statement that accurately characterizes the intellectual mood of the 1920s, as it was reflected in the literature of the decade. Before this lesson, have students read the section in their textbooks about the 1920s.

Procedure

1. Divide the class into groups of five with one student in each group assigned to research each of the five authors identified in **Handout 7**. The assigned report should be completed as a homework assignment.

2. Begin class on the day of this lesson by having students share their completed research with others in their small groups so that each member has notes on each of the writers.

Suggested Responses:

1. *Fitzgerald, an aristocrat from Minnesota, was born to wealth and privilege, he served in World War I after attending Princeton.* The Great Gatsby *portrays postwar cynicism, disillusionment, and search for pleasure and forgetfulness. The novel illustrates themes of the decade such as organized crime, the free flow of liquor during Prohibition, the revolt against nineteenth-century attitudes, and materialism, as well as the racism of the decade.*

2. *Hemingway, an idealist from the midwest, joined the Ambulance Corps during World War I. Alienated after the war, he joined others of the "lost generation" as an expatriate in Paris.* The Sun Also Rises *illustrates various themes of the 1920s, including wild drinking, alienation, emphasis on the self and the present, revolt against the values of the nineteenth century, ambivalence toward Europe, and anti-Semitism.*

3. *Lewis, a Minnesota native, studied in the East before taking a position as a journalist in New York. Very much a product of the middle class, Lewis ridiculed the hypocrisy and misplaced values of the class he loved so much. In* Main Street, *he parodied middle-class, small-town life. In* Babbitt, *he ridiculed the materialism of a little man caught up in the striving to accumulate wealth. In later novels of the decade he satirized the clergy, the medical profession, mercantilists, and politicians as well.*

4. *Hughes, the most cosmopolitan of the writers of the Harlem Renaissance, was born in Missouri, attended high school in Cleveland, worked in Mexico, and traveled in Europe and Africa before settling in Harlem. The versatile rebel poet wrote in African-American vernacular and often brought the rhythm of jazz and blues into his writing. His works stressed the nobility of lowly walks of life, developed racial pride,*

walks of life, developed racial pride, contemplated the place of African-Americans in a white world, and wondered what would happen if African-Americans did not receive social justice soon. His writing helped boost the self-esteem of African-Americans and gained the attention of whites; both were necessary first steps before the Black Revolution of later decades.

5. *Yezierska, the daughter of poor Jewish immigrants from Russian Poland, wrote several novels popular in the 1920s. Her father was a Talmudic scholar, and the family of nine children struggled to survive in their new country. Yezierska wrote of the search for personal fulfillment within the traditional Jewish family structure in the "Land of Opportunity." Her own struggle for an education, economic independence, and a marriage based on love made her a forerunner of the women's liberation movement.*

3. After the reports, have each group develop a thesis that defines the character of the 1920s through its literature.

4. Reconvene the class as a whole to share and evaluate the thesis statements written by each group. Thesis statements will, of course, differ, but students may recognize that, in spite of the nostalgia for simpler values of the past and the emptiness and alienation of the war generation, there is a sense of African-American pride and immigrant determination that bodes well for a different and more vibrant society in the future.

The Literature of the 1920s

Prominent writers of the 1920s did much to illuminate the mood and philosophy of the decade. Your homework task is to research one of the following writers and his or her key work, as listed, in preparation for a short oral report to your group. In addition, if time permits, research other works written by the author as well.

a. F. Scott Fitzgerald (*The Great Gatsby*)

b. Ernest Hemingway (*The Sun Also Rises*)

c. Sinclair Lewis (*Main Street* and *Babbitt* in particular)

d. Langston Hughes (poetry, such as "The Negro Speaks of Rivers," "Negro," "Harlem," and *Weary Blues*)

e. Anzia Yezierska (*The Breadgivers*)

As you prepare your report, consider the following points:

1. What biographical data about the author helps to put his or her writing in historical context?

2. What themes are covered in the author's key work(s)? Try to convey to your audience a sense of the work(s) you are describing.

3. How do the writer's works help to characterize one aspect of American life in the 1920s?

Lesson 6
Isolation—
Fact or Revisionist Battleground?

Objective

- To review the foreign policy of the 1920s by actively testing some revisionist interpretations

Notes to the Teacher

Believing that the League of Nations was essential to preventing a repetition of the international anarchy that had led to World War I, President Wilson insisted that the Allies include the League Charter in the Treaty of Versailles. However, opposition at home, both from extreme isolationists and from more moderate reservationists, led the Senate to reject the Treaty of Versailles and, with it, U.S. membership in the League of Nations. Thus ended Wilson's dream of American leadership in his proposed organization to encourage disarmament and settle international disputes peaceably.

Many saw final rejection of the Treaty of Versailles as the signal for a return to America's usual peacetime isolation. This familiar story that during the 1920s the United States returned its former peacetime isolation persisted. This characterization has endured in spite of studies by Robert Freeman Smith,[1] William Appleman Williams,[2] Warren I. Cohen,[3] and L. Ethan Ellis.[4] Although this lesson is not primarily an analysis of revisionist historians, it does provide a vehicle for reviewing the diplomatic history of the period. Students test whether the United States was as interventionist and internationally minded as the above authorities contend, and more so than has been previously held.

Procedure

1. Introduce the lesson using material in the Notes to the Teacher.

2. Follow this introduction with a brief review of other traditional tenets of U.S. foreign policy. Ask students to what extent these earlier policies were, in fact, isolationist and help them explore the answer(s).

   a. Monroe Doctrine (1823 presidential statement warning European nations not to colonize further the American continents and suggesting that the United States would refrain from intervention in European affairs)

   b. Manifest Destiny (1844 slogan of James K. Polk that it would be the fate of the United States to expand its boundaries from the Atlantic to the Pacific)

   c. Open Door Policy (1899 circular note from Secretary of State John Hay to nations with spheres of influence in China that there should be equal trading opportunities for all nations in China; later extended to say it would be the policy of the United States to "preserve the territorial integrity of China")

   d. Roosevelt Corollary (1904 presidential extension—or perversion—of the Monroe Doctrine to suggest that in cases of "chronic wrongdoing," it might be necessary for the United States to intervene in Latin American countries to protect America's new interests in the area)

[1] Robert Freeman Smith, "American Foreign Relations, 1920–1942," Bernstein, Barton J., ed., *Towards a New Past* (New York: Random House, 1968), 232–262.

[2] William Appleman Williams, "The Legend of Isolationism in the 1920s" in Milton Pleasure, *The 1920s: Problems and Paradoxes* (Boston: Allyn and Bacon, Inc., 1969), 92–110.

[3] Warren I. Cohen, *The American Revisionists* (Chicago: University of Chicago Press, 1967).

[4] L. Ethan Ellis, *Republican Foreign Policy, 1921–1933* (New Brunswick: Rutgers University Press, 1968).

e. Dollar Diplomacy (President Taft's policy supporting American commercial enterprises abroad, particularly in Latin America and the Far East, with dollars rather than bullets)

3. Based on the foregoing discussion, ask students to write a foreign policy they would design based on our earlier policies. Proposals should include the following items:

a. Recognition of the Soviet Union, a communistic state

b. United States' policy toward disarmament

c. United States' reaction toward countries who refuse or cannot pay their war debts

d. United States' policy toward Latin America, especially Mexico

e. United States' responsibilities toward the League and the World Court, including preventing future wars

You may wish to frame the above items in questions, and then poll the students. Do they have difficulty maintaining consistency? Why, or why not? (This is an excellent metacognition exercise for students—to think about their thinking!)

4. Have students complete **Handout 8**. Then have them compare handout answers with their original hypotheses. Student answers should reflect a serious challenge to the theme of isolation.

Suggested Responses:

1. *The Senate found the provision, which was intended to encourage collective action in the event of aggression, particularly objectionable. Opponents regarded it as a threat to their role in declaring war; Wilson, on the other hand, regarded this provision as essential to the League's effectiveness. When the two sides were unable to reach a compromise, the Senate rejected the Treaty of Versailles, and, with it, Article X. This action appeared to some a return to isolation.*

2. *The Big Five nations, including the United States, Britain, Japan, France, and Italy, agreed to a ten-year moratorium on the building of large warships and agreed to maintain an established ratio of large warships, respectively. The idealistic and temporary expedient required the United States to do most of the scrapping of large vessels and included no provisions for enforcement. It did, however, appeal to many American taxpayers.*

3. *The United States called this conference to try to extend the ratio arranged at Washington to smaller vessels. This attempt failed completely and led quickly to naval expansion by the United States.*

4. *The Dawes Plan provided a U.S. loan to Germany to help that country establish an orderly payment of reparations to European Allies. The Young Plan reduced substantially the amount Germany was expected to pay. Both initiatives by the United States were intended to facilitate trade with Europe in order to protect the American economy.*

5. *This pact between France and the United States outlawed war "as an instrument of national policy." Although it was signed by most nations of the world, its lack of provision for enforcement led one historian to compare it to a "letter to Santa Claus."*

6. *These pacts committed major nations to respect each other's interests in the Pacific and reaffirm the Open Door in China.*

7. *This semi-official statement of the Undersecretary of State repudiated the interventionist slant of the Roosevelt Corollary and paved the way for the "Good Neighbor Policy" and improved opportunities for favorable trade relations with Latin America.*

5. To conclude the lesson, assign the proposition, "The foreign policy issue of the twenties was never isolation." Have students outline the evidence to support or reject the thesis. Then have students account for the differences of historical interpretation.

Sample Responses:

a. *We tend to believe the facts we hear first.*

b. *All the facts are not known at the time of the event.*

c. *Historians also have preconceived notions.*

d. *New discoveries challenge old assumptions.*

e. *People who opposed entry into the League were improperly labeled isolationist.*

f. *Isolationists got us into World War II.*

Ask students if it is important to challenge hasty or improperly drawn themes of history.

Sample Responses:

a. *It is difficult to make wise choices from an improperly drawn past.*

b. *It tends to propagate the myth of superiority to the past.*

c. *It breeds suspicion of foreign countries.*

Foreign Policy in the 1920s

For several decades our history books have taught us that the United States evaded its responsibilities after World War I. As evidence, authors stress that our repeated failures to join the League of Nations and our consequent withdrawal from world affairs formed a foreign policy of isolationism. Research each of the following events to learn this country's actions and the extent to which each suggests a return to isolation.

1. Ratification of the League Covenant, Article X

2. The Washington Conference, 1921

3. Geneva Conference, 1927

4. War Debts: The Dawes and Young Plans

5. Kellogg-Briand Peace Pact, 1928

6. Relations with Asia: The Four and Nine Power Pacts

7. The Caribbean: The Clark Memorandum, December 17, 1928

Lesson 7
The Twenties at Bay

Objectives
- To draw conclusions about the crucial significance of the twenties

- To challenge commonly-held notions of the twenties

Notes to the Teacher

To many Americans the twenties means Babe Ruth, Red Grange, Charles Lindbergh, the Dempsey-Tunney fight, jazz, talkies, Model T Fords, Prohibition, flappers, radio, and Mah Jong. It's possible that ordinary Americans make more associations with the twenties than with any other decade in our nation's history. In the popular mind the era has a style and mood all its own.

Professional historians, on the other hand, have difficulty grasping the lasting impact of the period. They note that the census of 1920 marked the first time that the country was predominantly urban. The decline of rural values certainly shaped events of the decade. Too, the materialism, intolerance, and corruption may have differed in degree from that of earlier periods. However, no historian has written the definitive account of the era's relationship to what came before and what followed.

This lesson challenges the commonly-held notion that the era of Fords and Flappers was simply fluff and nonsense. Students work in small groups to research key aspects of the twenties. In class they relate their research findings to major questions relating to the decade. To conclude the lesson, students try to outline an answer to an essay topic on the lasting impact of the period.

On the day before the lesson, distribute **Handout 9** and assign or allow students to choose one of the five areas for specialization. Stress the importance of research and the necessity of bringing sources to class. Possible references are provided at the conclusion of the teacher's section.

Procedure

1. Arrange students according to their assigned or selected areas. Assign the area question to the appropriate group. Allow students time to discuss the question, reach a consensus, and be able to support their conclusion.

Area Questions

One: Politics and Government—Were the twenties a retreat from Progressivism or an extension of reform?

Two: Economics—The twenties: A business person's paradise or an economic dirge?

Three: Cultural Clashes—Was this an age of unlawful protest or legal repression?

Four: Diplomacy and Foreign Affairs—Are the twenties best remembered as a period of isolation or one of internationalism?

Five: Mass Culture—Was the so-called "Jazz Age" characterized as *carefree or insecure?*

Sample Response: Economics

Expect students to conclude that during this period, government was captured by business; nonetheless allow them to range freely with their answers.

2. Have each group select a spokesperson to report findings to the class. Allow time for questioning.

3. For homework, require each group to present their findings in report form to be used as review by the class. Their sources should be included along with annotations.

4. To conclude the lesson, discuss possible theses, organization, evidence, and conclusions for the essay topic below:

Seldom has a generation given so little of permanent value and so much that was troublesome to the future. Assess the validity of this statement.

References

Sources commonly found in school libraries.

Allen, Frederick Lewis. *Only Yesterday*. New York: Harper and Bros., 1931.

Carter, Paul A. *The Twenties in America*. New York: Thomas Y. Crowell Company, 1968, 1–34.

Chaffee, Zachariah, Jr. *Free Speech in the United States*. Cambridge, Mass.: Harvard University Press, 1941.

Cott, Nancy F. *Grounding of American Feminism*. New Haven, CT: Yale University Press, 1989.

Dulles, Foster Rhea. *America's Rise to World Power, 1898–1954*. New York: Harper, 1955.

Handlin, Oscar. *Al Smith and His America*. Boston: Little, Brown, 1958.

Hicks, John D. *Republican Ascendancy, 1921–33*. New York: Harper, 1960.

Higham, John. *Strangers in the Land*. New York: Atheneum, 1965, 264–330.

Huggins, Nathan I. *Harlem Renaissance*. New York: Oxford University Press, 1971.

Leuchtenburg, William E. *The Perils of Prosperity, 1914–1932*. Chicago, Illinois: University Press, 1958.

Mowry, George E. *The Twenties: Fords, Flappers, and Fanatics*. Englewood Cliffs, N.J.: Princeton University Press, 1963.

Murray, Robert K. *The Harding Era*. Minneapolis, Minnesota: University of Minnesota Press, 1969.

Nash, Gerald D. *The Great Transition*. Boston, Massachusetts: Allyn and Bacon, Inc., 1971, 159–202.

Nash, Roderick. *The Nervous Generation: American Thought 1917–1930*. Chicago: Rand McNally and Co., 1970, 5–32.

Noggle, Burl. *Teapot Dome: Oil and Politics in the 1920s*. Louisiana: State University Press, 1962.

Schlesinger, Arthur S., Jr. *The Crisis of the Old Order*. Boston, Mass.: Houghton Mifflin, 1960.

Shannon, David A. *Between the Wars: America, 1919–1941*. Boston, Mass.: Houghton Mifflin, 1965.

Williams, William Appleton. *The Tragedy of American Diplomacy*. New York: Norton, 1988.

In addition, the sources below offer important historiographical interpretations of the era.

May, Henry F., "Shifting Perspectives on the 1920s," *Mississippi Valley Historical Review*, 43 (December, 1956), 405–427.

Hicks, John D., "Research Opportunities in the 1920s," *Historian* 25 (November, 1962), 1–13.

Noggle, Burl, "The Twenties: A New Historirgraphical Frontier," *Journal of American History*, 53 (September, 1966), 299–314.

Researching the Twenties

For homework, spend time researching information in your text, and do some general reading in outside sources. Prepare to discuss your area. Bring your sources with you.

Area One

Politics and Government

    a. The Harding, Coolidge, and Hoover administrations

    b. The Harding scandals and the Bonus Bill veto

    c. The effects of the Nineteenth Amendment on society

    d. Hoover and the Hawley-Smoot Tariff

Area Two

Economics

    a. Influence of Henry Ford

    b. The agricultural problem and labor unrest

    c. The growth of mass production

    d. Prosperity and innovation

Area Three

Cultural Clashes

    a. Red Scare and Palmer Raids

    b. Immigration restriction versus Golden Door

    c. Traditional moral values versus modernists—Prohibition/Scopes Trial

    d. New woman versus Victorian values

    e. Race relations/Ku Klux Klan/Garveyism

    f. Urbanism vs. Suburbanism/Migration of African-Americans

Area Four

Diplomacy and Foreign Affairs

    a. Role of U.S. in disarmament conferences

    b. Dawes and Young Plans for reparations

    c. Relations with Mexico and Latin America

    d. Kellogg–Briand Peace Pact

Area Five

Mass Culture

    a. Harlem Renaissance/jazz

    b. Lost Generation

    c. Creation of mass culture by radio, movies, and popular magazines

    d. Increased leisure time/professional sports, amusement parks, national parks

Lesson 8
Causes of the Great Depression

Objective

- To gain an understanding of the multiple causes of the Depression

Notes to the Teacher

Teaching a lesson on the causes of the Great Depression offers an opportunity to focus on basic economic concepts. Students need to recognize that many interrelated factors, both domestic and foreign, played a role in causing the worst depression in America's history. The nation's increasingly large urban population meant that this depression brought unprecedented depths of despair.

Students begin by creating a time line of events related to the outbreak of the Depression. They then cite evidence from their time line to illustrate various factors recognized as valid causes of the Depression. After rank ordering these causes, students write their own thesis on what caused the Depression and then write a short essay explaining at least three factors that might have slowed, halted, or reversed the economic disaster.

Procedure

1. Introduce the topic using material in the Notes to the Teacher.

2. Write the following terms on the board, and ask students to define them: speculation, overproduction, underconsumption, buying on margin, tariff, capital, credit, and stock market crash.

3. Direct students to use their texts and other sources to construct time lines relative to the causes of the Great Depression. (See page 38 for sample time line.)

4. Divide the class into small groups and have students complete **Handout 10**, part A.

5. Conduct a discussion based on the handout to have students determine the class's top three Depression causes. Have the class critique several of the thesis statements.

6. Have students complete part B of **Handout 10**. You may wish to use these essays for evaluation purposes. They serve as the basis for class discussion. Possible answers include lowering the tariff when supplies accumulated, introducing "New Deal-type" legislation at a much earlier time, or introducing banking and stock market controls much earlier.

Sample Time Line:

3 August	1923—Coolidge is sworn in as president
13 August	1923—U.S. Steel inaugurates 8-hour day
18 March	1924—Soldiers' Bonus bill
26 February	1926—Revenue Act becomes law
11 February	1927—McNary-Haugen bill
2 February	1929—Federal Reserve Board forbids its member banks to make loan to anyone who wants to buy stock on margin
4 March	1929—Hoover becomes president
15 June	1929—Congress passes Agricultural Marketing bill
22 October	1929—President of New York's National City Bank states "I know of nothing fundamentally wrong with the Stock Market"
23 October	1929—Steady decline in stock market; signs of panic in New York Stock Exchange
24 October	1929—Black Thursday; collapse of New York Stock Exchange; 13,000,000 shares sold
29 October	1929—Black Tuesday—it's too late!
13 November	1929—$30,000,000,000 lost in value of stocks on New York Exchange; Chicago Market collapses
31 December	1929—Hoover delivers his annual message to Congress and declares that confidence in Nation's business has now been restored
2 January	1930—Economy sinking; prices falling; national income collapsing; unemployment at 4 million; Hoover meets with Congressional leaders to discuss public works plan
31 March	1930—Congress adopts Public Buildings Act
4 April	1930—Congress votes 300 million to build state roads
4 June	1930—Hawley-Smoot Tariff bill passed
October	1930—Unemployment at 4,500,000; Hoover says Federal government must remain aloof
2 December	1930—Hoover recognizes problem and asks Congress for $150 million for constructing public works
11 December	1930—Bank of United States (a private New York bank with 60 branches and 400,000 depositors) closes; 1300 bank closures in one year
2 January	1931—5 million unemployed
27 February	1931—Congress overrides Hoover's veto and passes Bonus Loan bill
3 March	1931—Hoover vetoes Muscle Shoals bill
22 July	1931—Kansas farmers produce a bumper crop of wheat; prices collapse
October	1931—827 more United States banks close
27 February	1932—Glass-Steagall Banking Act
21 July	1932—Hoover signs Relief and Reconstruction Act
22 July	1932—Federal Home Loan Bank Act
8 November	1932—Roosevelt wins election; 13 million are unemployed

Name_____
Date_____

Causes of the Depression

Part A.

Below are eleven recognized causes of the Great Depression. In your groups, first brainstorm evidence from your time line or textbook to support each of the possible causes of the Depression. Second, rank in order the following causes of the Depression, with *1* representing the strongest factor and *11* the weakest.

_____a. Maldistribution of income and purchasing power

_____b. Overexpansion of agricultural production

_____c. Overproduction of industry

_____d. Automation

_____e. Unregulated banking practices

_____f. American tariff policy

_____g. Impact of European and world economy

_____h. Monopolistic pricing

_____i. Philosophy and policies of the Hoover administration

_____j. Overexpansion of credit

_____k. Stock market speculation and crash

Write a thesis showing how your three or four most important causes are related.

Part B.

To conclude the lesson, identify three points at which some specific intervention might have slowed, halted, or reversed the Depression. Write a short essay defending your selections.

Lesson 9
The "Okie" Experience and
The Grapes of Wrath

Objectives

- To analyze factors in the creation of the Dust Bowl

- To develop insights into a novel whose author strove to depict reality in his fictional account of Okie migrant life in California during the Depression

Notes to the Teacher

The literary classic, *The Grapes of Wrath*, portrays the "Okie" experience of the 1930s, from the parched southwestern plains to migrant labor camps in California. Steinbeck's novel sympathizes with the migrants, stressing their essential dignity. The villains are the bankers, landowners, salesmen, and California growers. Ideally, advanced placement students read the novel either in history or English class. If this is not possible, you may wish to show the film version, analyze a sound filmstrip analysis of the novel, or use the Woody Guthrie folk song, "Tom Joad" to convey a sense of the story.

This lesson focuses on causes of the agricultural crisis that precipitated the migration of Okies to California. Students analyze agricultural statistics and interpret their significance in causing the agricultural disaster of the Depression years. To conclude the lesson, they write short essays relating *The Grapes of Wrath* to one of several themes in the history of the period.

Procedure

1. Point out that the effects of the collapse of the stock market and the Great Depression were compounded by an agricultural disaster in the southwestern plains. Emphasize that this disaster was caused by a combination of human errors and natural causes.

2. Have students complete part A of **Handout 11**.

Suggested Responses, Part A:

1. a. *Rise in cost with World War I; fall with Depression; decline in prices below 1910 level (Point out that rise from 1931 to 1933 is positive only for those who have wheat to sell.)*

   b. *Evident revolution of agriculture by motorized farming; capacity to cultivate broad areas quickly*

   c. *Increased commitment to/dependence on wheat farming*

2. *Higher prices stimulated increased production for greater profit. Tractors facilitated increased production. Increased production resulted in greater supply, hence lower prices. Lower prices stimulated increased production for an adequate income, which, however, ultimately only reduced total income.*

3. Have students complete part B of the handout.

Suggested Responses, Part B:

1. *Drought conditions prevailed, with generally about 50 percent of average precipitation. Unless irrigation methods were available, the crops were bound to fail. (Point out that high winds in an area like this could lead to near-desert characteristics, such as sandstorms.)*

2. *Farmers had a bumper crop but made less money for it.*

3. *Levels of production and income were severely depressed. The 1936 harvest acreage was about 20 percent that of 1930; yield about 10 percent of that in 1930; market value about 15 percent of that in 1930; and total farm income less than 30 percent of that in 1930.*

4. Have students complete part C of the handout.

Suggested Responses:

Barren acreage, dust storms, tractors, eviction of tenant farmers, mass migrations

Point out that Oklahoma's huge population loss led to rise of the term "Okie" to designate all migrants from the Southwest

5. Have students read part D and conduct a discussion based on questions 1 to 4.

Suggested Responses:

1. *Sympathy, pity, anger against the "system"*

2. *By sharing their experiences*

3. *Difficulty in achieving true perspective; need to integrate data very quickly; immediacy of bias*

4. *The use of Okies as migrant laborers, the lack of adequate government regulation of many camps, the below subsistence wages, and the squelching of protests on the part of migrant workers all mirror the Okie experience in the novel.*

6. To conclude the lesson, ask students to write short essays relating *The Grapes of Wrath* to one of the following themes:

   • Necessity of federal intervention in local affairs

   • Technological changes in agriculture

   • Plight of migrant laborers

   • Gap between the affluent and the poor

   • Responsibility for social problems

   • Causes and patterns of American mobility

   Have students share their ideas on these topics.

The Dust Bowl

Part A.

Study the charts below. Use the information provided to answer the questions that follow. Be prepared to discuss your responses.

The Dust Bowl: Sections of Colorado, Kansas, New Mexico, Oklahoma, and Texas

	1910	1917	1929	1931	1933
Price of wheat per bushel in Dust Bowl	$ .91	$2.06	$ .99	$ .34	$ .71

	1915	1920	1925	1930	1933
Number of tractors in southwestern Kansas	286	1,333	3,501	9,727	11,655

	1915	1920	1925	1931	
Percent of land in wheat in southwestern Kansas	9.9%	13.6%	17.8%	38%	

1. Describe the trends in

   a. wheat prices

   b. tractor farming

   c. wheat planting

2. How do the three correlate?

Part B.

Haskell County, Kansas	1930	1931	1932	1933	1934	1935	1936
Inches of precipitation	24.3	12.5	16.5	11.2	11.0	12.0	12.8
Acres of winter wheat harvested	171,280	181,525	47,552	17,900	78,997	47,390	34,215
Yield in bushels	1,712,800	3,448,975	332,864	89,500	394,985	189,560	171,075
Market value of wheat	$1,061,936	$1,034,693	$99,859	$71,600	$343,637	$181,978	$181,340
Total farm income	$1,411,028	$1,279,355	$330,436	$420,105	$513,390	$549,757	$421,244

1. Rainfall in 1930 was about average. How would you describe the succeeding years?

   Describe the effects you would expect in an agricultural region.

2. Analyze the statistics about the harvest of 1931.

3. Contrast the statistics for 1930 with those for 1936.

Part C.

"In '34 I had I reckon four renters and I didn't make anything. I bought tractors on the money the government give me and get shet o' [rid of] my renters. You'll find it everywhere all over the country thataway. I did everything the government said—except keep my renters. The renters have been having it this way ever since the government came in. They've got their choice—California or WPA."

". . . the dust storms that swept across the southern plains in the 1930s created the most severe environmental catastrophe in the entire history of the white man on this continent . . . Not even the Depression was more devastating economically."

"Across the nation the only states that had fewer residents at the end of the decade than at the beginning were all on the plains. South Dakota's drop was the highest rate in the country, at 7.2 percent followed by North Dakota, Kansas, and Oklahoma. In net loss through migration—outflow minus inflow—Oklahoma was the easy leader: 440,000. . . . Almost a million plains people left their farms in the first half of the decade, and 2.5 million left after 1935. Not all were dusted out, but all were uprooted— a generation of human tumbleweeds, cut loose from the soil."[1]

The opening chapters of *The Grapes of Wrath* deal with life in the Dust Bowl. What historical facts does the novel reflect?

---

[1] Sources: Hurt, Douglas R. *The Dust Bowl: An Agricultural and Social History*. Chicago: Nelson-Hall, 1981 and Worster, Donald. *Dust Bowl: The Southern Plains in the 1930s*. New York: Oxford University Press, 1979, 24, 48–49, 58.

Part D.

The Grapes of Wrath and the "Okie" Migrants

August 1936	*San Francisco News* asked a young California writer, John Steinbeck, to investigate and report on migrant conditions in California. He visited various Hoovervilles and the Arvin Sanitary Camp, also called Weedpatch. There he met the capable and compassionate camp manager, Tom Collins.
September 1936	Steinbeck visited Weedpatch again.
October 1936	*San Francisco News* printed Steinbeck's articles.
October 1937	Accompanied by Tom Collins, Steinbeck took a trip to research the migrant experience by actually living it.
February 1938	In a letter to a friend, Steinbeck wrote:

"I must go to Visalia. Four thousand families, drowned out of their tents are really starving to death. . . . The newspapers won't touch the stuff but they will under my byline. The locals are fighting the government bringing in food and medicine. I'm going to try to break the story hard enough so that food and drugs can get moving. Shame and a hatred of publicity will do the job to the miserable local bankers. . . ."[2]

March 1938	In a letter after another trip, Steinbeck wrote:

"It is the most heartbreaking thing in the world . . . I break myself every time I go out because the argument that one person's effort can't really do anything doesn't seem to apply when you come on a bunch of starving children and you have a little money . . . I want to put a tag of shame on the greedy bastards who are responsible for this but I can best do it through newspapers."[3]

Later, he commented:

"I'm trying to write history while it is happening and I don't want to be wrong."[4]

May–December 1938	Steinbeck wrote *The Grapes of Wrath*.

1. Describe John Steinbeck's attitude toward the migrants.

---

[2] Jackson J. Benson, *The True Adventures of John Steinbeck* (New York: The Viking Press, 1984), 368.

[3] Benson, 370–371.

[4] Benson, 375.

2. How did he prepare himself to write about the migrants' lives?

3. Why is it difficult to "write history while it is happening?"

4. How accurately does *The Grapes of Wrath* reflect this description of the Okie experience?

> "The large growers . . . were glad to see this new labor pool arrive. They had over 200 commercial crops on their farms, most of them needing hand labor for brief periods: peaches and prunes, lemons and oranges, lettuce and asparagus, cotton and flax, all to be picked and boxed or baled. Their former supply of cheap Mexican workers had been cut off in 1929 by immigrant restrictions . . . Most of the farms provided temporary lodging—tents or rude cabins—but with only three state inspectors and 8,000 camps to inspect, the quarters were bound to be generally poor. Any family entering this stoop-and-pick life could expect to work about half the year and earn $350 to $450, only 50 per cent of what the California Relief Administration estimated to be a subsistence level. It was take it or leave it; strikes for higher wages were squelched and radical organizers beaten, shot, and jailed. With only 175,000 workers needed at peak seasons and at least two or three desperate migrants for every job, the growers could name the terms."[5]

---

[5] Donald Worster, *Dust Bowl: The Southern Plains in the 1930s* (New York: Oxford University Press, 1979), 52–53.

Lesson 10
The New Deal—Documents Question

Objectives

- To analyze a document-based question from a previous Advanced Placement examination

- To practice the question under test conditions

Notes to the Teacher

If your class period permits, you might assign the question comparing and contrasting the early statements of Hoover and Roosevelt to be written in class. If you wish, discuss the definition of conservatism and liberalism either on that day or the previous day. The short but useful definitions by Clinton Rossiter are included for your convenience.

This exercise comes best after a thorough study of the Hoover administration and the first four years of the New Deal. The question itself challenges the misconception that Roosevelt was an unqualified liberal and Hoover was a well-defined conservative. The solution hinges on students' abilities to incorporate the willingness to use federal power into the definitions of liberalism and conservatism.

Procedure

1. Discuss definitions of liberalism and conservatism. Ask for students' conception before sharing Rossiter's definition or your own.

   Liberalism, the stickiest word in the political dictionary, is the attitude of those who are reasonably satisfied with their way of life yet believe that they can improve upon it substantially without betraying its ideals or wrecking its institutions. The liberal tries to adopt a balanced view of the social process, but when he faces a showdown over some thoughtful plan to improve the lot of men, he will choose change over stability, experiment over continuity, the future over the past. In short, he is optimistic rather than pessimistic about the possibilities of reform.

   Conservatism is committed to a discriminating defense of the social order against change and reform. The conservative knows that change is the rule of life among men and societies, but he insists that it be sure-footed and respectful of the past. He is pessimistic, though not always darkly so, about the possibilities of reform, and his natural preferences are for stability over change, continuity over experiment, the past over the future. The essential difference between conservatism and liberalism is one of mood and bias. No line separates one camp from the other, but somewhere between them stands a man who is at once the most liberal of conservatives and most conservative of liberals. In genuine liberals there is a strain of conservatism, in genuine conservatives a strain of liberalism; and all men, even extreme radicals, can act conservatively when their own interests are under attack.[1]

2. Distribute **Handout 12** and allow forty minutes for completion. Alert students that they are to read the question carefully and spend enough time classifying the documents before writing their answers.

   Suggested Analysis:

   ### Document A

   - *Hoover defines liberalism as a countervailing force against bureaucracy, thereby allowing for political equality, free speech, free assembly, free press, and equality of opportunity.*

   - *He suggests that industry dominated by any power-group and public utilities that are unregulated deny the qualities of a liberal society.*

   ### Document B

   - *Hoover's definition of liberalism does not call for risky or expanded government projects.*

   - *Views depression as one of those unavoidable cycles*

[1] Clinton Rossiter, *Conservatism In America* (New York, New York: Alfred A. Knopf, 1956), 12–13.

- *Stresses voluntary help in a liberal society with government acting as one of these agencies*

Document C

- *Hoover introduces the idea that increased government aid to the hungry will discourage the larger and more significant local, state, voluntary, and corporate aid.*

- *He expresses his faith that enough is being done.*

- *He continues to present evidence of the aid already given by the government.*

Document D

- *Hoover is shown holding fast to capital while Congress, business, and the people are in danger of the same fate as Europe.*

- *The cartoon suggests that Hoover is trying to combat the Depression but is using the wrong methods.*

- *It also suggests that by playing politics and using improper tactics, the Democrats gain an advantage.*

Document E

- *In a campaign speech, Roosevelt criticized Hoover's financial policy from the conservative point of view.*

  a. *too much federal control*

  b. *deficits too high*

  c. *cost of government too high*

  d. *budget out of balance*

- *Roosevelt promises to remedy the above defects.*

Document F

- *Both presidents go into deficit spending.*

- *Public debt doubles from 1933 to 1941.*

- *Government expenditures increase steadily.*

- *Budget is never balanced.*

- *Federal spending reduced in 1937–1938.*

Document G

- *Where Hoover blames the danger of too much government for inequities, Roosevelt*

sees injustice arising from private or free enterprise.

- *Defense liberalism as that change agent which will protect institutions in spite of conservative intransigence.*

Document H

- *Roosevelt announces a new agenda based on need.*

- *Implies that there is a need for more federal help*

3. If your students have relatively little experience with document-based questions, you may wish to offer a few suggestions to help them with one of the challenges of the Advanced Placement examination.

   1. Since half of the score comes from outside data supplied by the student, it is useful for students to record relevant data that they know before reading the documents. Many students find a format such as the outline here useful.

	Hoover	**Roosevelt**
Conservative		
Liberal		

   2. Successful students typically spend approximately fifteen to twenty minutes planning and reading documents prior to writing the essay.

   3. It is important in an essay such as this to make clear one's definition of *liberal* and *conservative*.

   4. It is not necessary to refer to documents by letter in the essay, but it *is* important to use the information in the documents to address the question rather than merely summarize the documents in a "laundry list."

   5. A strong thesis is key to developing an effective essay.

   6. Giving evidence of understanding the context of the times strengthens any essay.

   7. Effective essays conclude with an attempt to draw a conclusion or show the long-range significance of the topic rather than merely summarizing the evidence.

Roosevelt and Hoover—A Document-Based Question

This question appeared in the 1984 Advanced Placement examination in American History. The suggested writing time was 40 minutes.

The following question requires you to construct a coherent essay that integrates your interpretation of Documents A–H *and* your knowledge of the period referred to in the question. In your essay, you should strive to support your assertions both by citing key pieces of evidence from the documents and by drawing on your knowledge of the period.

President Franklin D. Roosevelt is commonly thought of as a liberal and President Herbert C. Hoover as a conservative. To what extent are these characterizations valid?

Document A

"It is a false liberalism that interprets itself into the government operation of commercial business. Every step of bureaucratizing of the business of our country poisons the very roots of liberalism—that is, political equality, free speech, free assembly, free press, and equality of opportunity. It is the road not to more liberty, but to less liberty. Liberalism should be found not striving to spread bureaucracy but striving to set bounds to it. . . .

"I do not wish to be misunderstood in this statement. I am defining a general policy. It does not mean that our government is to part with one iota of its national resources without complete protection to the public interest. . . .

"Nor do I wish to be misinterpreted as believing that the United States is free-for-all and devil take the hindmost. The very essence of equality of opportunity and of American individualism is that there shall be no domination by any group or combination in this republic, whether it be business or political. On the contrary, it demands economic justice as well as political and social justice. It is no system of laissez faire. . . .

"Years ago the Republican administration established the principle that such evils could be corrected by regulation. It developed methods by which abuses could be prevented while the full value of industrial progress could be retained for the public. It insisted upon the principle that when great public utilities were clothed with the security of partial monopoly, whether it be railways, power plants, telephones, or what not, then there must be the fullest and most complete control of rates, services, and finances by government or local agencies. It declared that these businesses must be conducted with glass pockets. . . ."

Source: Candidate Herbert Hoover, speech, New York, New York
(October 22, 1928)

Document B

" . . . Economic depression cannot be cured by legislative action or executive pronouncement. . . . The best contribution of government lies in encouragement of this voluntary cooperation in the community. The government—national, state, and local—can join with the community in such programs and do its part.

"As a contribution to the situation the federal government is engaged upon the greatest program of waterway, harbor, flood control, public building, highway, and airway improvement in all our history. This, together with loans to merchant shipbuilders, improvement of the navy and in military aviation, and other construction work of the government will exceed $520,000,000 for this fiscal year. This compares with $253,000,000 in the fiscal year 1928. The construction works already authorized and the continuation of policies in government aid will require a continual expenditure upwards of half a billion dollars annually.

"I favor still further temporary expansion of these activities in aid to unemployment during this winter. The Congress will, however, have presented to it numbers of projects, some of them under the guise of, rather than the reality of, their usefulness in the increase of employment during the depression. There are certain common-sense limitations upon any expansions of construction work. The government must not undertake works that are not of sound economic purpose and that have not been subject to searching technical investigation, and which have not been given adequate consideration by the Congress. The volume of construction work in the Government is already at the maximum limit warranted by financial prudence as a continuing policy."

Source: President Herbert Hoover, second annual message to Congress
(December 2, 1930)

Document C

"It is not an issue as to whether people shall go hungry or cold in the United States. It is solely a question of the best method by which hunger and cold shall be prevented. . . .

"And there is a practical problem in all this. The help being daily extended by neighbors, by local and national agencies, by municipalities, by industry and a great multitude of organizations throughout the country today is many times any appropriation yet proposed. The opening of the doors of the federal treasury is likely to stifle this giving and thus destroy far more resources than the proposed charity from the government. . . .

"To reinforce this work at the opening of Congress, I recommend large appropriations for loans to rehabilitate agriculture from the drought and provision of further large sums for public works and construction in the drought territory, which would give employment in further relief to the whole situation . . . to increase federal construction work from a rate of about $275,000,000 a year prior to the depression to a rate now of over $750,000,000 a year. . . .

"I have indeed spent much of my life in fighting hardship and starvation both abroad and in the Southern States. I do not feel that I should be charged with lack of human sympathy for those who suffer. . . .

"I am willing to pledge myself that if the time should ever come that the voluntary agencies of the country together with the local and state governments are unable to find resources with which to prevent hunger and suffering in my country, I will ask the aid of every resource of the federal government because I would no more see starvation amongst our countrymen than would any senator or congressman. I have faith in the American people that such a day will not come."

Source: President Hoover, statement to the press (February 3, 1931)

Document D

Source: J.N. ("Ding") Darling in the
Des Moines Register (December 18, 1931).

Document E

"For over two years our federal government has experienced unprecedented deficits, in spite of increased taxes. . . .

". . . you can never expect any important economy from this [Hoover] administration. It is committed to the idea that we ought to center control of everything in Washington as rapidly as possible—federal control. That was the idea that increased the cost of government by a billion dollars in four years. . . .

". . . I shall approach the problem of carrying out the plain precept of our party, which is to reduce the cost of current federal government operations by 25 percent. . . .

"In accordance with this fundamental policy it is necessary to eliminate from federal budget-making during this emergency all new items except such as relate to direct relief of unemployment. . . .

"I have sought to make two things clear: first that we can make savings by reorganization of existing departments, by eliminating functions, by abolishing many of those innumerable boards and those commissions . . . to total many hundreds and thousands of dollars a year.

"Second, I hope that it will not be necessary to increase the present scale of taxes. . . .

"The above two categorical statements are aimed at a definite balancing of the budget. At the same time, let me repeat from now to election day so that every man, woman, and child in the United States will know what I mean: if starvation and dire need on the part of any of our citizens make necessary the appropriation of additional funds which would keep the budget out of balance, I shall not hesitate to tell the American people the full truth and ask them to authorize the expenditure of that additional amount. . . ."

Source: Candidate Franklin D. Roosevelt, speech, Pittsburgh, Pennsylvania
(October 19, 1932)

Document F
United States Government Finances, 1929–1941
(in billions of dollars)

Fiscal Year	Expenditures	Surplus (+) or Deficit (-)	Total Public Debt
1929	$3.127	$0.734	$16.9
1930	3.320	0.738	16.2
1931	3.577	-0.462	16.8
1932	4.659	-2.735	19.5
1933	4.598	-2.602	22.5
1934	6.645	-3.630	27.1
1935	6.497	-2.791	28.7
1936	8.422	-4.425	33.8
1937	7.733	-2.777	36.4
1938	6.765	-1.177	37.2
1939	8.841	-3.862	40.4
1940	9.589	-2.710	43.0
1941	13.980	-4.778	44.0

Source: U.S. Bureau of the Census, *Historical Statistics of the United States,
Colonial Times to 1970, Bicentennial Edition, Part 2* (1975).

Document G

" . . . Who is there in America who believes that we can run the risk of turning back our government to the old leadership which brought it to the brink of 1933? Out of the strains and stresses of these years we have come to see that the true conservative is the man who has a real concern for injustices and takes thought against the day of reckoning. The true conservative seeks to protect the system of private property and free enterprise by correcting such injustices and inequalities as arise from it. The most serious threat to our institutions comes from those who refuse to face the need for change. Liberalism becomes the protection for the far-sighted conservative.

"Never has a nation made greater strides in the safeguarding of democracy than we have made during the past three years. Wise and prudent men—intelligent conservatives—have long known that in a changing world worthy institutions can be conserved only by adjusting them to the changing time. In the words of the great essayist, 'The voice of great events is proclaiming to us. Reform if you would preserve.'

"I am that kind of conservative because I am that kind of liberal."

Source: President Franklin D. Roosevelt, speech, Syracuse, New York
(September 29, 1936)

Document H

". . . We are celebrating the 1936 victory. That was not a final victory. It was a victory whereby our party won further opportunity to lead in the solution of the pressing problems that perplex our generation. Whether we shall celebrate in 1938, 1940, and in 1944, as we celebrate tonight, will deservedly depend upon whether the party continues on its course and solves those problems.

"And if I have aught to say it will continue on its course and it will solve those problems. . . .

"Here is one-third of a nation ill-nourished, ill-clad, ill-housed—NOW!

"Here are thousands upon thousands of farmers wondering whether next year's price will meet their mortgage interest—NOW!

"Here are thousands upon thousands of men and women laboring for long hours in factories for inadequate pay—NOW!

"Here are thousands upon thousands of children who should be at school, working in mines and mills—NOW!

"Here are strikes more far-reaching than we have ever known, costing millions of dollars—NOW!

"Here are spring floods threatening to roll again down our river valleys—NOW!

"Here is the Dust Bowl beginning to blow again—NOW!

"If we would keep the faith with those who had faith in us, if we would make democracy succeed, I say we must act—NOW!"

Source: President Franklin D. Roosevelt, speech, Washington, D.C.
(March 4, 1937)

Advanced Placement Examination (Princeton, New Jersey: Educational Testing Service, 1984).

Lesson 11
The New Deal—A Writer's Forum

Objectives
- To practice writing an essay on a previous advanced placement question on the New Deal

- To improve first drafts by creating essay standards

Notes to the Teacher
This lesson provides an opportunity to involve students in the writing-grading process while practicing an essay question on key aspects of the New Deal. The procedure contains a common scheme for classifying New Deal legislation and encourages students to devise two other schemes of their own. The prewriting activity, writing assignment, grading activity, and revision process provide activities and material for several days of classwork.

Procedure
1. Distribute part A of **Handout 13** and assign it for homework. Announce that this material will be critical to success on a writing activity to follow. Point out, too, that a review of notes on economic aspects of Progressivism and the 1920s will be helpful.

Suggested Responses, Part A:
1. a. Emergency Banking Relief Act *backed up Roosevelt's emergency closing of banks to determine their solvency.*

   b. CCC *employed young men to plant trees, construct dams, and complete other conservation projects.*

   c. FERA *gave immediate aid to the starving.*

   d. AAA *aimed to raise farm prices by reducing acreage in cultivation and paying farm subsidies for lost acreage.*

e. TVA *developed the Tennessee Valley region by building dams to generate hydroelectric power, providing an inland waterway system, and creating lakes for recreation.*

f. HOLC *tried to prevent farm foreclosures.*

g. NIRA *planned industry standards to put people back to work at decent jobs and under decent working conditions to stimulate purchasing power and thus production.*

h. PWA *tried to create jobs building bridges, highways, dams, and power plants.*

i. FDIC *guaranteed bank deposits in an effort to prevent runs on banks.*

j. CWA *created jobs building roads, parks, schools, and airports; helped fix up run-down neighborhoods; and cleared and cleaned up wastelands.*

k. FHA *insured loans to homeowners for home repairs or mortgages.*

l. SEC *regulated stock exchanges.*

m. Resettlement Administration *aided farmers in moving from worn-out lands to more fertile areas.*

n. WPA *created jobs in building; sponsored artists, scholars, photographers, and writers; and promoted research into local history.*

o. Wagner Act *regulated and protected unions and their right to bargain collectively.*

p. Social Security *provided unemployment insurance; retirement benefits; and disability payments to workers and aided widows and dependent children in the event of a worker's death.*

q. Soil Conservation Act *raised farm prices by curtailing production through soil conservation programs.*

r. Fair Labor Standards Act *set maximum hours and minimum wages and prohibited most child labor.*

2. Relief—*Emergency Banking Relief Act, FERA, CCC, CWA, PWA, and WPA*

   Recovery—*AAA, NIRA, TVA, HOLC, Resettlement Administration, Soil Conservation Act*

   Reform—*FDIC, SEC, Social Security, FHA, Wagner Act, FLSA*

3. *Students might also categorize them for their political impact in creating a new Democratic coalition or whether or not the programs became permanent features of the American system. Students will see other possibilities.*

2. In class on the following day, distribute **Handout 13**, part B and assign questions equally. Have students write their responses under test conditions.

3. To follow up the essay portion, reassign the questions so that groups have new subjects. Have them research the new topics and discuss possible theses and evidence in class, or assign the topic for homework. They are to prepare for the role of examiner by finding evidence which must be included in a good essay.

4. Distribute the essays (completed in procedure 2) to the proper groups of examiners. Have the examiners read the essays and evaluate them. Ask them to help the writers by preparing written responses to the following essay standards:

   a. Is there a clearly expressed thesis statement?

   b. Does the writer put the topic in historical context?

   c. Has the writer responded to the thesis statement?

   d. Does the evidence go beyond the topic?

   e. Is there enough evidence?

   f. If not, what evidence could be added?

   g. Does the conclusion go beyond a simple summary to explain the long-range importance of the topic?

   h. What was best about the answer?

   When the students finish, have them return the essays to their owners for revision. (The revisions then could be given to the teacher for further comment or grading.)

New Deal Reforms

Part A.

Complete the following activity in preparation for a writing activity on key reforms of the New Deal.

1. Identify the major purpose of each of the agencies created by the act of Congress.

2. Categorize New Deal reforms according to a common scheme by labeling each as Relief, Recovery, or Reform. In other words, did the measure bring immediate assistance to those in dire need, help to restore the economy to health, or aim to prevent a similar disastrous depression in the future?

3. Devise at least two additional schemes for categorizing the New Deal programs. Be prepared to justify your classifications.

	First 100 Days		**Purpose**
a.	Emergency Banking Relief Act	March 9, 1933	_____
b.	Civilian Conservation Corps (CCC)	March 31, 1933	_____
c.	Federal Emergency Relief Administration (FERA)	May 12, 1933	_____
d.	Agricultural Adjustment Act (AAA)	May 12, 1933	_____
e.	Tennessee Valley Authority (TVA)	May 18, 1933	_____
f.	Home Owner's Refinancing Act (HOLC)	June 13, 1933	_____
g.	National Industrial Recovery Act (NIRA)	June 16, 1933	_____
h.	Public Works Administration (PWA)	June 16, 1933	_____
i.	Glass-Steagall Banking Reform Act (FDIC)	June 16, 1933	_____

New Deal Measures from 1933–1939

j.	Civil Works Administration (CWA)	November 9, 1933	_____
k.	National Housing Act (FHA)	June 28, 1934	_____
l.	Authorization for Securities and Exchange Commission (SEC)	June 6, 1934	_____
m.	Resettlement Administration	April 30, 1935	_____
n.	Works Progress Administration (WPA)	May 6, 1935	_____
o.	Wagner Act (NLRB—National Labor Relations Board)	July 5, 1935	_____
p.	Social Security Act	August 14, 1935	_____
q.	Soil Conservation Act	February 29, 1936	_____
r.	Fair Labor Standards Act (FLSA)	June 25, 1938	_____

Part B.

New Deal Essay Questions

1. Roosevelt's New Deal differed from Hoover's administration in that the New Deal was willing to use government power to adjust the contending claims of major interest groups. Assess the validity of this generalization.

2. To what extent did the measures of the New Deal reflect a coherent economic philosophy?

3. The New Deal did not radically alter American business, but conserved and protected it. Assess the validity of this statement.

4. Despite superficial similarities, the domestic programs of the New Deal constituted a fundamental departure from those of the Progressive Era. Assess the validity of this generalization.

5. The New Deal secured the support of labor and agriculture after 1932 as the Republican party had secured the support of industry and commerce since 1920—with special-interest programs giving financial aid, legal privileges, and other types of assistance. Assess the validity of this statement, giving attention to both periods (1920–32 and 1932–40).

Lesson 12
Isolation and Neutrality in the 1930s

Objectives

- To review U.S. foreign policy from 1929–1939

- To role-play the decision-making process that went into formulating the foreign policy of that time

Notes to the Teacher

After the Senate's rejection of League of Nations membership, the United States vacillated between a return to isolation and exploring possibilities of peace through international cooperation. During the 1920s new immigration restrictions, high tariffs, and rejection of World Court membership all suggested a "return to normalcy," or isolation in foreign policy. However, the country assumed a new peacetime diplomatic posture when it participated in the Washington and London Naval conferences, cooperated with several League of Nations agencies, and signed international pacts such as the Kellogg-Briand Pact.

While the foreign policy of the 1920s has frequently been incorrectly labeled as isolationist, recent scholarship concedes that isolationism aptly characterizes the 1930s. Various labels such as, "The Isolationist Impulse." "Storm-Cellar Isolation," and "The Lessons of the Thirties" are found in studies. Nearly all suggest that the isolationist mood was based on extreme disillusionment with the failure of Versailles.

Students construct a foreign policy time line for the 1930s and then participate in a role-playing activity developing an appropriate foreign policy following the German invasion of Poland in 1939. To conclude the lesson, students contrast their own policy with the actual foreign policy position of the United States at the time.

Procedure

1. Introduce the lesson using material in the Notes to the Teacher.

2. Direct students to use their text or other sources to construct a time line that includes the significant United States foreign policy decisions from the Kellogg-Briand Peace Pact of July 24, 1929, to the German invasion of Poland, September 1, 1939. Instruct students to use only those items that explain how the United States tried to keep out of war. The time line can be constructed in groups, pairs, or individually. (See sample time line on page 63.)

3. Explain that while time lines appear as a simple sequence of events, their placement and relationship tell a story. If students have conscientiously chosen events that explain our isolationist mood to remain isolationist or at least removed from foreign affairs, they have part of the story.

4. Ask students to reexamine their time lines in order to detect trends. If necessary, ask:

   a. Was the League able to halt aggression?

   b. How did the United States treat Central and South America?

   c. Were we becoming more isolationist?

   d. What was the purpose of our neutrality laws?

   e. What effect did the Nye Investigation have on our neutrality laws?

   f. How had America's neutrality affected other countries?

5. Have students complete **Handout 14**. After 15 or 20 minutes, group students and tell them to compare their answers and reconcile differences. Then select a representative from each group and have them simulate a staff meeting to plan policy, including both Europe and the Far East.

6. To conclude the lesson, discuss the following points:

    a. Show students the synopsis of the November 4, 1939, Neutrality Act. Have them compare their proposed policy and discuss differences.

    b. Ask students if the planners could have predicted Pearl Harbor. Were there indicators that the Japanese would take such a gamble?

    c. In order to recommend wise policy, what knowledge must a planner possess? (Possible responses include a sense of the past; the story behind each event; an ability to relate the past to the present and to see the future in the past.)

A Synopsis of the Neutrality Act of 1939

November 4, 1939

Purpose—To preserve neutrality

Proclamation—The President shall announce when he determines that a state of war exists between or among foreign states.

Commerce with above-named states

a. A strict embargo of American passengers and goods to these warring states shall be enforced. Fines and/or imprisonment will be imposed for violators.

b. American vessels may trade except in certain restricted areas.

Combat areas—The president shall name combat areas and forbid American travel thereto. Violators will suffer penalties.

Travel on vessels of belligerent states—All American travel on belligerent ships is forbidden.

Arming of merchant vessels—American merchant vessels will be unarmed, except for small arms deemed necessary for the preservation of discipline aboard vessels. They will not carry any armament, arms, ammunition, or implements of war.

Financial Transactions—It will be unlawful to exchange, purchase, or sell bonds or securities to any state named a belligerent. Loans are subject to the same proscription.

American republics—These restrictions will not apply to any American republic engaged in war against a non-American state, provided the American republic is not cooperating with a non-American state in such war.

National Munitions—All citizens are forbidden to receive or sell weapons or ammunition to belligerent states.

Repeals—This act repeals all previous neutrality acts but not its penalties.[1]

---

[1] Full text can be found in Henry Steele Commager, ed., *Documents of American History* (Englewood Cliffs, N.J.: Prentice-Hall, 1973), 600–604.

Sample Time Line:

Date	Event	Significance to the United States
1929 24 July	United States approved Kellogg-Briand	Outlaws war
1930 22 April	London Naval Treaty	Limits tonnage
1930 17 June	Hawley-Smoot Tariff	Tariff barrier
1931 18 September	Japan's march into Manchuria	United States does nothing
1932 7 January	Stimson Doctrine	Non-recognition
1932 9 July	United States refusal to cancel war	Their problems, not ours
1933 24 February	Japan walks out of League	No reprisals
1934 12 April	Nye Investigation	
1934 6 August	Marines leave Haiti	Munitions profits cause U.S. entry into war in 1917
1935 31 August	1st Neutrality Act	More attention at home
1935 9 December	Japan leaves 2nd London Naval Conference	Forbids arms to belligerents
1936 29 February	2nd Neutrality Act	Only England and the United States agree to limitations
1936 17 July	Spanish Civil War begins	No loans to belligerents
1937 1 May	3rd Neutrality Act	United States does not intervene
1937 5 October	F.D.R.'s Speech—Quarantine the Aggressors	Cash and Carry
1937 11 December	Italy's withdrawal from the League	Meets with disinterest
1938 30 December	Munich Pact	League takes no action
1938 24 December	Lima, Peru Conference	Delays Hitler
1939 1 September	Germany invades Poland	Hemispheric solidarity

First Day on the Job

The time is late September 1939. In June you graduated from Harvey Mudd College, where you received a Ph.D. in Political Science. Your father, a wealthy executive with McDonnell-Douglas, has used his influence to get you a job in the Planning Division of the Department of State. That group is still reeling from Hitler's surprise invasion of Poland and many of your new colleagues seem confused. You have been chosen to bring some fresh ideas and new insight into their discussions. Your first task is to review American foreign policy from around the time of the Kellogg-Briand Peace Pact up to the present. Your father's influence, plus your studies at college, have convinced you of the following:

1. World War I was a mistake.

2. Germany was not solely to blame for the war.

3. A policy of neutrality should keep us out of war, not get us into one.

4. Greedy profiteers were influential in the U.S. decision to enter World War I.

5. It is difficult to negotiate with countries who refuse to pay their war debts.

After reviewing U.S. foreign policy since 1919 and its impact on other countries, you go on to make recommendations about the following topics:

1. Should the United States support any country or bloc of countries?

2. If yes to the above, what countries should we support and to what extent? (Make at least three recommendations.)

3. If no to the above, how do we improve our present policy of neutrality?

    a. Should it remain the same?

    b. Should we become less involved?

    c. Should we become more involved?

4. President Roosevelt and Congress are presently considering new neutrality legislation. Write your recommendations for such laws and be prepared to defend their implications.

5. What should be our long-range goals?

6. How should we meet the threat of Japan?

Lesson 13
Axis Partners—Clouds of War

Objective
- To consider what the possible effects would have been if our leaders had made different choices in international incidents prior to Pearl Harbor

Notes to the Teacher
This lesson emphasizes skills in recognizing cause-effect relationship. Students discuss the implications of FDR's quarantine policy in relationship to specific international incidents. They then hypothesize, validate, and speculate about the events.

Procedure
1. Have students read the directions on **Handout 15**, part A. Review directions as necessary.

2. Divide the class into small groups, with each member addressing one of the scenarios described. Then have group members pool results. For each event, students will find (a) positive action was required; (b) earlier United States' involvement; possibly, earlier termination of the war.

3. Regroup the class so that students work with others who focused on the same scenario. Have each group discuss the appropriate question from the question list in part B of **Handout 15**.

4. Have groups report their conclusions to the class.

5. Conclude the lesson by having students assess the validity of the following statement: President Roosevelt's Quarantine Speech was not a prescribed course of action but a sounding board to elicit public opinion on U.S. intervention in world conflicts.

Applications of FDR's "Quarantine Speech"

Part A.

Franklin Delano Roosevelt, in his sensational "Quarantine Speech" on October 5, 1937, in Chicago, stated that the troublesome nations (Japan, Germany, and Italy) should be quarantined to preserve peace. Denouncing the dictators, he declared, "The peace, the freedom, and the security of 90 percent of the population of the world is being jeopardized by the remaining 10 percent, who are threatening a breakdown of all international order and law. Surely the 90 percent who want to live in peace under the law and in accordance with moral standards that have received almost universal acceptance through the centuries, can and must find some way to make their will prevail. . . . There must be positive endeavors to preserve peace."

Following are several factual scenarios. For each, consider these questions: (a) In the light of the speech, what would you have expected FDR to do? (b) What would have resulted?

Scenario 1: The Panay Incident

The Japanese invasion of China was meanwhile degenerating into an orgy of lust and loot. At various times American citizens, male and female, were subjected to slapping and stripping by arrogant Nipponese soldiers. Some American schools and hospitals were damaged by aerial bombers, despite the huge American flags painted on their roofs.

The most sensational incident of all came on December 12, 1937, when Japanese aviators bombed and sank a United States gunboat, the *Panay*, on the Yangtze River in broad daylight. Two men were killed and some thirty wounded; escaping survivors were repeatedly machine-gunned. The vessel was so plainly marked and the visibility was so clear that the incident could hardly have resulted from mistaken identity. One plausible explanation was that hot-headed Japanese officers, defying the Tokyo government, had thus vented their contempt for Yankees.

The American people were shocked by this wanton attack, which also involved the destruction of three Standard Oil tankers. Cartoonists represented the Japanese ambassador as saying, "So sorry—excuse please," while the bodies of mangled American sailors lay about. Washington promptly demanded apologies, reparation, and adequate precautions against the repetition of such an outrage.

The Tokyo Foreign Office, put in a bad light by irresponsible military men, made haste to tender the most profound apologies and pay full monetary reparation—$2,214,007.36. Thousands of Japanese subjects attempted to make amends through private gifts. In these circumstances, the crisis quickly blew over.[1]

a.

b.

[1] Thomas A. Bailey, *A Diplomatic History of the American People* (Englewood Cliffs, N.J.: Prentice Hall, 1980), 705.

Scenario 2: The Finnish Interlude

When war erupted in 1939, many Americans assumed that the conflict would follow the familiar pattern of 1914–1918. The supposedly impregnable concrete Maginot Line on France's eastern border would hold Hitler at bay. The strangling noose of Britain's blockade would slowly choke Germany into starvation, and Berlin would be forced to sue for peace, as in 1918.

But surprises were speedily forthcoming. German mechanized divisions speedily overran Poland, while Stalin came in for his prearranged share of the loot. Yet the lesson of the Polish preview meant little to the Allied countries. They went ahead with their business-as-usual plans for waging the conflict, while the bored journalists wrote disgustedly of the "phony war."

Unexpected excitement developed late in 1939 over the Finnish crisis. Joseph Stalin, not trusting his dictator-accomplice Adolph Hitler, sought to secure from Finland certain strategic areas that would enable him to bolster his defenses against Germany. "Brave little Finland" resolutely refused the proffered exchange of territory. Late in November, 1939, the Soviet Union spurned Washington's offer of good offices and assaulted its tiny neighbor. Russian aircraft, in defiance of an appeal from Roosevelt, heavily bombed civilian centers.[2]

a.

b.

Scenario 3: The Robin Moor Sinking

Then, on May 21, 1941, the American merchantman *Robin Moor* was torpedoed and shelled in the South Atlantic by a German submarine. This was the first United States vessel of any kind to be deliberately sunk by German hands, either in or out of the war zones. American public opinion was shocked and angered, even though no lives were lost. Senator Carter Glass of Virginia expressed the views of countless interventionists when he cried, "I think we ought to go over there and shoot hell out of every U-boat."

Hitler's spokesmen defended the sinking by alleging that the *Robin Moor* was carrying contraband of war to Britain's South Africa. Yet the Germans, in forcing the passengers and crew into small boats hundreds of miles from land, had not made provision for their safety in accordance with international law and the London protocol of 1936, which Berlin had freely signed. Roosevelt angrily denounced this act of "piracy," but Germany rejected his claims for damages. Washington in retaliation "froze" all German and Italian assets in the United States, and ordered all German and Italian consulates, as hotbeds of subversive activity, to be closed. Berlin and Rome retaliated in kind.

[2] *Ibid.*, 712–713.

The *Robin Moor* opened a new chapter in German-American relations. Until then, Washington had little justification for complaint against the Germans, as far as America's specific rights were concerned. But it had much reason to complain of Hitler's ruthless attacks on the community of nations, of which the United States was a leading member. On purely legalistic grounds, Berlin had much better grounds for protest against America's unneutral aid to the Allies than America had for complaint against Germany's infractions of America's rights. The lend-lease act widened the breach irreparably. The United States was now a virtual cobelligerent of the Allies. Hitler, with bitter memories of America's role in terminating World War I, did not wish to provoke a showdown yet. But henceforth the German submarine commanders, pursuant to orders, could hardly be expected to refrain from defending themselves against American destroyers escorting lend-lease supplies to Britain.[3]

a.

b.

Scenario 4: Aid to Russia

Hitler's fateful attack on the "Mongol halfwits" of Russia wrought a revolution in American opinion. Stalin—the cynical, self-seeking, iron-fisted aggressor—suddenly became a most welcome ally of those nations who were seeking to halt Hitlerism. President Roosevelt promptly issued promises of aid to Moscow, and soon made some military supplies available. In about four months, after investigating Stalin's capacity to resist, he provided the first installments of lend-lease assistance to Russia that ultimately totalled a staggering $11 billion.

No less astonishing was the reversal of American opinion regarding Finland. Alleging prior attacks, Russia reopened war with her, and the Finns, forced into bad company, fought back with Hitler's help. Many of the same Americans who had applauded Finnish victories the year before were now hoping for Russian victories, while Washington vainly tried to persuade Finland to drop out of the war. The Berlin press screamed "criminal intervention" and "Jewish impudence."

The American people, especially diehard conservatives, were not altogether happy over "Bloody Joe" Stalin, their new ally. If Russia won, they asked, would not communism, which was as bad as Nazism, engulf all Europe? Would Stalin prove to be a co-operative associate at the peace table? Roman Catholic and other religious denominations were deeply disturbed by the long-continuing persecutions directed against the Greek Orthodox Church in Russia. "I have no more confidence in Stalin," presciently

[3] *Ibid.*, 724–725.

declared Archbishop Curley of Baltimore, "that I have in Hitler." American isolationists saw in the unexpected boon of a Russo-German was additional evidence that the two dictators should be allowed to slit each other's throats on the frozen wastes of Russia. The democratic world would then emerge strong and triumphant.[4]

a.

b.

Scenario 5: The Economic Crackdown on Japan

The restraining hand of Uncle Sam may have held Japan back from the riches of the Dutch East Indies in the summer of 1940, but not from those of French Indo-China. In September, 1940, Tokyo put the screws on the Hitler-dominated French government and extorted strategic bases in northern Indo-China. Secretary Hull roundly condemned this fresh act of aggression, and Washington retaliated by agreeing to lend China an additional $25 million.[5]

a.

b.

Scenario 6: Last-Ditch Negotiations with Tokyo

The efforts of the diplomats to halt war-mad Nippon with words continued to be futile. At the Atlantic Conference in August, 1941, Roosevelt and Churchill had worked out a threatening protest against Japanese aggression, but Washington later presented it to Tokyo in a watered-down form. The next month, September, 1941, hope sprang anew when the conciliatory Prince Konoye, the Japanese Premier, indicated a willingness to meet with Roosevelt in a Pacific conference, perhaps at Honolulu. But the

[4] *Ibid.*, 726–727.

[5] *Ibid.*, 733–734.

President, fearing that the Japanese were plotting a propaganda victory by placing the onus for a diplomatic breakdown on America, insisted on specific concessions in advance. Konoye, suspecting that the news of such commitments would leak out and destroy him, was unwilling or unable to yield. The proposal for a conference was dropped, the Konoye ministry fell the next month, and a militaristic group, ominously headed by the unsmiling and truculent General Tojo ("The Razor"), took over. The drift toward war continued with seeming inevitability.[6]

a.

b.

Part B.

In your new group, circle the appropriate question from the question list below. Then discuss the following points regarding your proposed "What If."

a. What issues would this action have raised?

b. What additional information would you want to know to determine whether or not it would have been a sound policy?

c. What would have been likely consequences of the proposed action?

d. What alternative actions would have been possible?

e. What policy would you have recommended in the situation? How would you justify your choice?

Question List

1. What if FDR had sent the fleet to the Yangtze River and landed troops in China?

2. What if FDR had viewed Russia's invasion of Finland as an act of war and immediately ordered the Air Force to supply the Finnish army?

3. What if FDR had declared war on Germany for sinking the *Robin Moor*?

4. What if FDR had not offered aid to the Soviet Union?

5. What if FDR had approved Japan's action?

6. What if Prince Konoye and FDR had met at Honolulu and reached an agreement?

[6] *Ibid.*, 734–735.

Lesson 14
Pearl Harbor—
Interpretations of History

Objective
- To understand that the complex facts surrounding an event may lead to widely differing interpretations

Notes to the Teacher
Many Americans first learned of the early morning surprise attack on Pearl Harbor on December 7, 1941, when news bulletins interrupted broadcast of professional football games that Sunday afternoon. To them, the unthinkable had happened—this country, so long protected by wide oceans, had suffered a direct attack. The death toll exceeded 2300, and nearly 2000 more suffered injuries. If Americans had hoped to remain aloof from the wars in Europe and the Far East, the events of that day shattered their dreams. On the following day, President Franklin Roosevelt asked for and received a declaration of war against Japan. Within days, Japan's European allies, Germany and Italy, declared war on the United States.

Interpretations of the causes of the Pearl Harbor attack differ widely:

1. FDR planned and executed a cover-up of data to allow Japan to attack. This act would draw America out of her isolationist mood and allow FDR to aid Britain and the other allies overtly. He may have had a part in ordering the aircraft carriers out to sea for maneuvers away from Pearl Harbor.

2. It was good fortune for Japan. All the conditions were right: weather, timing, etc.

3. It resulted from failure of U.S. Intelligence.

4. The United States ignored the warnings of its allies. Even Peru warned the United States ambassador to Japan six months before the Pearl Harbor attack regarding Japan's plans.

Students read four different interpretations of the devastating event. They are asked to draw their own conclusions regarding responsibility for the event and identify five "lessons" the government and military should have learned from the disaster of Pearl Harbor.

Procedure
1. Have the class complete **Handout 16**, part A.

   Suggested Responses, Part A:

   Minority Report—*high authorities in Washington and the commanders in the field*

   Theobald—*FDR*

   Nohlstetter—*no one cause*

   Prange—*"a puzzle with no single answer"*

2. Conduct a discussion based on the following questions.

   a. Which source do you trust? Why?

   b. How do you relate these explanations to the information in your text?

   c. Use your text to assess Theobald's Lincoln analogy.

   d. To what extent was FDR culpable?

   e. If FDR is deemed responsible for Pearl Harbor, what effect will that have on his reputation in history? Explain your answer.

3. To conclude the lesson, have students work in small groups to complete part B. Discuss their conclusions in a large-group discussion. Groups may focus on quite specific suggestions or view the event in the broader context of American diplomacy in general. Exposure to different perspectives of complex events helps students to expand their own concept of what it means to "think historically."

Analyzing Conflicting Evidence

Part A.

For each of the documents, answer the following question: Who or what was responsible for the surprise attack at Pearl Harbor?

Investigation of the Pearl Harbor Attack
[Minority Report]

. . . [572] Exhaustive attention has been given to the military aspects of the events leading up to Pearl Harbor and an invaluable record has been compiled for future students of the situation.

A far less complete record has been written of its diplomatic aspects and here there is the most urgent need of further exploration in justice to the future generations of Americans who may learn here a little of the lessons for which America has paid so great a price.

How to avoid war and how to turn war—if it finally comes—to serve the cause of human progress is the challenge to diplomacy today as yesterday. Here, too, much cannot be known regarding all the petty episodes that finally add up to war. No war comes in a moment. War is the sum of many minor decisions and some that are major. In this diplomatic aspect the Pearl Harbor investigation has sadly failed to live up to the lofty prospectus with which it was launched.

In the light of these facts and the foregoing conclusions, the charge that the "country" is to blame for what happened at Pearl Harbor cannot be sustained.

Conclusion:

In our opinion, the evidence before this Committee indicates that the tragedy at Pearl Harbor was primarily a failure of men and not of laws or powers to do the necessary things, and carry out the vested responsibilities. No legislation could have cured such defects of official judgment, management, cooperation, and action as were displayed by authorities and agents of the United States in connection with the events that culminated in the catastrophe at Pearl Harbor on December 7, 1941.

This demonstrates the weakness of depending on the political head of the Government to bring about the necessary coordination of the activities of the military branch, particularly in the area of intelligence, and unification of command. The major lesson to be learned is that this coordination should be accomplished in advance of a crisis.

Summary of Responsibilities

Having examined the whole record made before the Joint Committee and having analyzed the same in the foregoing Conclusions of Fact and Responsibility, we find the evidence supports the following final and ultimate conclusion:

The failure of Pearl Harbor to be fully alerted and prepared for defense rested upon the proper discharge of two sets of *interdependent* responsibilities: (1) the responsibilities of high authorities in Washington; and (2) the responsibilities of the commanders in the field in charge of the fleet and of the naval base. . . .

The evidence clearly shows that these two areas of responsibilities were inseparably essential to each other in the defense of Hawaii. The commanders in the field could not have prepared or been ready successfully to meet the hostile attack at Hawaii without indispensable information, matériel, trained manpower, and clear orders from Washington. Washington could not be certain that Hawaii was in readiness without the alert and active cooperation of the commanders on the spot.

The failure to perform the responsibilities indispensably essential to the defense of Pearl Harbor rests upon the following civil and military authorities:

FRANKLIN D. ROOSEVELT—President of the United States and Commander in Chief of the Army and Navy.

HENRY L. STIMSON—Secretary of War.

FRANK KNOX—Secretary of the Navy.

GEORGE C. MARSHALL—General, Chief of Staff of the Army.

HAROLD R. STARK—Admiral, Chief of Naval Operations.

LEONARD T. GEROW—Major General, Assistant Chief of Staff of War Plans Division.

The failure to perform the responsibilities in Hawaii rests upon the military commanders:

WALTER C. SHORT—Major General, Commanding General, Hawaiian Department.

HUSBAND E. KIMMEL—Rear Admiral, Commander in Chief of the Pacific Fleet.

Both in Washington and in Hawaii there were numerous and serious failures of men in the lower civil and military echelons to perform their duties and discharge their responsibilities. These are too numerous to be treated in detail and individually named.[1]

In the spring of 1940, Denmark, Norway, Holland, Belgium and France were conquered by Germany, and throughout the remainder of that year Great Britain's situation was so desperate that many expected her collapse early in the ensuing year. Fortunately, however, the Axis powers turned East in 1941 to conquer Greece and to attack Russia.

There is every reason to believe that when France was overcome President Roosevelt became convinced the United States must fight beside Great Britain, while the latter was still an active belligerent, or later sustain the fight alone, as the last democratic stronghold in a Nazi world. Never, however, had the country been less prepared for war, both psychologically and physically. Isolationism was a dominant philosophy throughout the land, and the armed forces were weak and consequently unready.

The United States not only had to become an active participant in democracy's fight as quickly as possible, but a people, completely united in support of the war effort, had to be brought into the arena. But, how could the country be made to fight? Only a cataclysmic happening could move Congress to enact a declaration of war; and that action would not guarantee that the nation's response would be the completely united support which victory has always demanded. This was the President's problem, and his solution was based upon the simple fact that, while it takes two to make a fight, either one may start it.

As the people of this country were so strongly opposed to war, one of the Axis powers must be forced to involve the United States, and in such a way as to arouse the American people to wholehearted belief in the necessity of fighting. This would require drastic action, and the decision was unquestionably a difficult one for the President to make.

[1] Paul Burtness and Warren U. Roin, *The Puzzle of Pearl Harbor* (Evanston, Ill.: Peterson & Co., 1962), 228–229.

In this connection, it should be remembered that Japan, Germany, and Italy signed the Tripartite Treaty on September 28, 1940, by which the three nations agreed to make common cause against any nation, not then a participant in the European war or the Sino-Japanese conflict, which attacked one of the signatories.

Thereafter, the fact that war with Japan meant war with Germany and Italy played an important part in President Roosevelt's diplomatic strategy. Throughout the approach to war and during the fighting, the primary U.S. objective was the defeat of Germany.

To implement the solution of his problem, the President: (1) instituted a successful campaign to correct the Nation's military unpreparedness; (2) offered Germany repeated provocations, by violations of neutrality and diplomatic usage; (3) applied ever-increasing diplomatic-economic pressure upon Japan, which reached its sustained climax on July 25, 1941, when the United States, Great Britain, and the Netherlands stopped their trade with Japan and subjected her to almost complete economic encirclement; (4) made mutual commitments with the British Prime Minister at Newfoundland in August, 1941, which promised mutual support in the event that the United States, Great Britain, or a third country not then at war were attacked by Japan in the Pacific; (5) terminated the Washington conference with the note of November 26, 1941, which gave Japan no choice but surrender or war; (6) retained a weak Pacific Fleet in Hawaiian waters, despite contrary naval advice, where it served only one diplomatic purpose, an invitation to a Japanese surprise attack; (7) furthered that surprise by causing the Hawaiian Commanders to be denied invaluable information from decoded Japanese dispatches concerning the rapid approach of the war and the strong probability that the attack would be directed at Pearl Harbor.

This denial of information was a vital feature of enticing a Japanese surprise attack upon Pearl Harbor. If Admiral Kimmel and General Short had been given the knowledge possessed by the Washington authorities, the Hawaiian Commands would have been alerted against an overseas attack. The Pacific Fleet would have kept the sea during the first days of December, 1941, until the issue of peace or war had been decided. With the highly effective Japanese espionage in Hawaii, this would have caused Tokyo to cancel the surprise attack.

The problem which faced Lincoln during March of 1861 was identical in principle—to unite the sentiment of the North behind the policy of compelling the seceded Southern states by force of arms to return to the Union. For a month after his inauguration, he made no move, and then South Carolina's insistent demands for the surrender of Fort Sumter gave him the answer to his problem. He refused to surrender the fort, and dispatched a fleet to reprovision it. South Carolina then fired the first shots of the Civil War. Pearl Harbor was President Roosevelt's Fort Sumter.

[Diplomatically, President Roosevelt's strategy of luring Japan to war by unremitting and ever-increasing diplomatic-economic pressure, and by simultaneously building our Fleet in Hawaii as an invitation to a surprise attack, was a complete success. Militarily, our ship and personnel losses mark December 7, 1941, as the day of tragic defeat. One is forced to conclude that the anxiety to have Japan, beyond all possibility of dispute, commit the first act of war, caused the President and his civilian advisers to disregard the military advice which would somewhat have cushioned the blow.] The President, before the event, probably envisaged a *Panay* incident of somewhat larger proportions. Despite the fact that the attack laid the foundation for complete victory, a terrific price was paid. . . .[2]

[2] Robert A. Theobald, *The Final Secret of Pearl Harbor* (Old Greenwich, CT: Devin-Adair Publishers, 1954), 2–5.

On the basis of this rapid recapitulation of the highlights in the signal picture, it is apparent that our decisionmakers had at hand an impressive amount of information on the enemy. They did not have the complete list of targets, since none of the last-minute estimates included Pearl Harbor. They did not know the exact hour and date for opening the attack. They did not have an accurate knowledge of Japanese capabilities or of Japanese ability to accept very high risks. The crucial question then, we repeat, is, If we could enumerate accurately the British and Dutch targets and give credence to a Japanese attack against them either on November 30 or December 7, why were we not expecting a specific danger to *ourselves*? And by the word "expecting," we mean expecting in the sense of taking specific alert actions to meet the contingencies of attack by land, sea, or air.

There are several answers for this question that have become apparent in the course of this study. First of all, it is much easier *after* the event to sort the relevant from the irrelevant signals. After the event, of course, a signal is always crystal clear; we can now see what disaster it was signaling, since the disaster has occurred. But before the event it is obscure and pregnant with conflicting meanings. It comes to the observer embedded in an atmosphere of "noise," *i.e.*, in the company of all sorts of information that is useless and irrelevant for predicting the particular disaster. For example, in Washington, Pearl Harbor signals were competing with a vast number of signals from the European theater. These European signals announced danger more frequently and more specifically than any coming from the Far East. The Far Eastern signals were also arriving at a center of decision were they had to compete with the prevailing belief that an unprotected offensive force acts as a deterrent rather than a target. In Honolulu they were competing not with signals from the European theater, but rather with a large number of signals announcing Japanese intentions and preparations to attack Soviet Russia rather than to move southward; here they were also competing with expectations of local sabotage prepared by previous alert situations.

In short, we failed to anticipate Pearl Harbor not for want of the relevant materials, but because of a plethora of irrelevant ones. Much of the appearance of wanton neglect that emerged in various investigations of the disaster resulted from the unconscious suppression of vast congeries of signs pointing in every direction except Pearl Harbor.[3]

How could the unthinkable have happened? How could a large Japanese fleet enter Hawaiian waters undetected? How could their aircraft have evaded the impersonal, all-seeing radarscope? How could an enemy pounce upon Pearl Harbor, widely believed to be impregnable? How could they successfully launch aerial torpedoes in its shallow waters? Where was American aerial reconnaissance? Why were the Hawaiian Air Force's planes lined up in plain sight on the aprons, perfect targets for Japanese bombing and strafing? How could officers of the stature of Kimmel and Short be caught by surprise?

Had United States intelligence services fallen flat on their faces, or had someone mishandled the available intelligence? Had information been available in the War and Navy departments that did not reach Short and Kimmel, respectively, and if so, whose fault was it?

[3] Roberta Nohlstetter, *Pearl Harbor: Warning and Decision* (Stanford, Calif.: Stanford University Press, 1962), 386–387.

It was no secret in 1941 that the Japanese had embarked upon a course of aggression and that Japanese-American relations were "friendly" only in the official sense of still maintaining diplomatic contacts. But could the whole tragedy have been avoided by a more creative, more flexible posture on the part of the U.S. State Department? Had American embargoes placed Japan in such a bind that it had no choice but to fight for its life? Did it really matter to the United States that Japan was a member of the Berlin-Rome-Tokyo Axis, that it was waging a bloody but undeclared war in China, that it obviously had designs upon French, Dutch, British, and perhaps American possessions in Southeast Asia? Had Secretary of State Cordell Hull offered Japan only terms so harsh that no sovereign nation could accept them?

Was Washington too preoccupied with the war in Europe and in the Atlantic? Had the transfer of a portion of Kimmel's ships to the Atlantic in the spring of 1941 so weakened the Pacific Fleet that Admiral Isoroku Yamamoto, Commander in Chief of Japan's Combined Fleet, dared to plan the Pearl Harbor attack and insist that it be carried out? Had Great Britain received materiel which should have remained in American arsenals? Had Hitler's attack on the Soviet Union further distracted American attention from the Japanese? For that matter, had the decision that the Philippines might, after all, be defensible, resulted in a denuding of the military forces in the Hawaiian Islands?

Had Congress fulfilled all its obligations? Could larger appropriations have been translated into a stronger defense in time to affect the issue? Should Congress have insisted upon investigating Japanese espionage in the United States? Would such an investigation have resulted in a recommendation to close the Japanese consulates, as the German had been closed, and would this measure have tightened security? And, as the American people elected their representatives to Congress, should the entire adult populace examine its individual and collective conscience?

Most disturbing of all, how much did the White House know about all this? Could it be possible that President Franklin D. Roosevelt, with his outspoken sympathy for embattled Britain, had a commitment to the British to go to war on their behalf? As no incident of sufficient importance to warrant a declaration of war on Germany had happened in the Atlantic, had Roosevelt egged on the Japanese to attack the United States? Did he know about the Pearl Harbor attack in advance and withhold information from Oahu's defenders to ensure that the Japanese would not abort the mission?

These and many other questions have plagued the American public from December 7, 1941, until this very day. Eight official investigations, culminating in an eight-month-long inquiry by a joint congressional committee, produced reams of testimony and documentation but could not come up with the clear-cut, foolproof answers that would have satisfied the American people. Nor could the investigators settle upon any single individual as solely responsible for the American debacle; therefore the public never had the satisfaction of being able to vent its wrath upon a readily identifiable villain. Too many strands were twisted into the cord of responsibility for any such happy ending. Today the story of American unreadiness at Pearl Harbor remains a puzzle with no single answer, a drama with no individual villain.[4]

[4] Gordon W. Prange, *Pearl Harbor: The Verdict of History* (New York: McGraw-Hill Book Co., 1986), XXXii–XXXiii.

Part B.

After World War I, historians tried to persuade government officials to base foreign policy on the "lessons" of our involvement in that war. The Neutrality Acts of the 1930s were one result. To conclude this lesson, reconsider the evidence regarding Pearl Harbor and write the five "lessons" you would have advised our government and military officials to apply after World War II to avoid similar disasters in the future.

1.

2.

3.

4.

5.

Lesson 15
Japanese-American Internment

Objectives
- To become acquainted with facts relevant to the forced evacuation and internment of Japanese-American citizens after Pearl Harbor

- To analyze and evaluate the thinking that led to the internment policy

Notes to the Teacher

Since the early 1890s, Japanese immigrants had joined those of other countries seeking economic opportunities in the United States. The newcomers exhibited a strong pattern of upward social mobility, practiced a philosophy not unlike the Puritan Work Ethic, and appeared to be models of patriotism. To many, they seemed to be ideal immigrants.

However, in the context of increasing tensions between the United States and Japan, the immigrants' distinct physical characteristics, coupled with their tendency to cluster in ethnic neighborhoods and maintain their old country's values and mores, made them seem suspect. The United States' internment of Japanese-Americans after the bombing of Pearl Harbor provides one of the saddest examples of American intolerance in our nation's history. Textbooks tend to avoid detailed treatment of this forced evacuation of over 100,000 Japanese-Americans from the West Coast during 1942.

This lesson provides materials to expand students' awareness of social, military, and political factors involved in establishing this policy. Students find evidence of racial prejudice, war hysteria, and failure of political leadership in dealing with this issue at the time. They then try to evaluate the extent to which sufficient information was available in the early 1940s for Americans to recognize the injustice of this policy.

Procedure
1. Introduce the topic using material in the Notes to the Teacher.

2. Divide students into small groups to complete **Handout 17**.

3. Discuss the evidence they compiled.

Suggested Responses:

Racial prejudice—*Prohibition on naturalizing Asians; determination to evacuate Japanese-American citizens, not just aliens; reluctance to apply evacuation/ internment procedures to DiMaggio family*

War hysteria—*Olson's fifth column suspicions; DeWitt's fears; Warren's comments*

Failure of political leadership—*Roosevelt's delegation of authority on West Coast; politicians' comments inciting people against Japanese; lack of attention to constitutional rights of citizens*

4. Emphasize that the issue in discussing the internment policy is not the aliens, but the American citizens who were deprived of their constitutional rights. Add that there has never been any evidence of Japanese-American sabotage during the war.

5. Point out that the Supreme Court decision in 1944 was not unanimous, and that the explications of the judges' decisions are somewhat contradictory. Ask what reasons might have made them reluctant to find internment illegal? (*war not over yet; need to preserve respect for executive authority and the military; problem of restitution; desire to preserve myth that United States can do no wrong*)

6. Ask the following question: How did you react to descriptions of the evacuation and internment of the Japanese-Americans during World War II? Encourage diverse responses.

7. Point out that the United States belatedly passed legislation in 1988 to provide limited compensation to survivors of the internment.

8. Conclude the lesson by having students write essays on the following question: To what extent was sufficient information available in the early 1940s to enable people generally to recognize the evacuation and internment of Japanese-Americans was an unjust consequence of racial prejudice, war hysteria, and failure of political leadership? Share and discuss completed essays.

Japanese-American Internment: Chronology

Study the following chronology, documents, and journalistic perspectives to compile evidence of racial prejudice, wartime hysteria, and a failure of political leadership, all factors which the 1980 Congressional Commission identified to explain the unjust, unconstitutional internment of Japanese-Americans during World War II.

1890	Significant numbers of Japanese begin to immigrate to the United States, especially Hawaii and West Coast.
1906	San Francisco School Board ordered segregation of Japanese-American students.
1907–1908	President Theodore Roosevelt's Gentlemen's Agreement with Japan limited Japanese immigration.
1913	California Alien Land Law prohibited non-American citizens from land ownership. (United States law prohibited Asians from naturalization.)
1919	Oriental Exclusion League in California conducted an extensive anti-Japanese campaign.
1921	The United States Supreme Court, in *Ozawa v. United States*, confirmed prohibition of Japanese naturalization.
1924	Immigration Act terminated Japanese immigration to United States.
1930	Nisei organized the patriotic Japanese-American Citizens League (JACL).
1941	*October-November*—Under President Franklin D. Roosevelt's orders,—Curtis B. Munson investigated and reported on Japanese-American loyalty to United States on West Coast and Hawaii.
	December 7—Japanese attacked Pearl Harbor.
	December 8—United States declared war on Japan.
	December 11—Chief of Staff George C. Marshall declared the Pacific Coast a "Theater of Operations."
	December 15—Secretary of the Navy Frank Knox claimed an active Japanese "fifth column" helped cause the disaster at Pearl Harbor.
1942	*January 3*—United States Army Major Karl Bendetsen called for registration, photographs, and fingerprints of all enemy aliens.
	February 11—President Roosevelt personally approved evacuation of Japanese-Americans in a phone conversation with Secretary of War Henry Stimson.
	February 19—President Roosevelt's Executive Order 9066 empowered military to designate and merge restricted military areas.
	February 20—Secretary Stimson delegated responsibility for evacuation to Lieutenant General John DeWitt.
	March 18—President Roosevelt created the War Relocation Authority (a civilian agency) to manage relocation centers and resettlement.
	August 7—Evacuation of Japanese-Americans from West Coast was complete.
1943	*January 28*—Secretary Stimson announced decision to recruit for a Japanese-American Combat Team.
1944	*January 20*—Secretary Stimson announced application of Selective Service System to Japanese-Americans.
	December 18—WRA announced closing of all relocation centers. United States Supreme Court endorsed legality of Japanese-American policy in *Korematsu v. United States*.
1945	*January 2*—West Coast restriction against Japanese-Americans ended.
1980	Congressional Commission reinvestigated and judged Executive Order 9066 to be unjustified.

Japanese-American Internment: Documents

"As interview after interview piled up, those bringing in results began to call it the same old tune . . . There is no Japanese 'problem' on the Coast. There will be no armed uprising of Japanese. There will undoubtedly be some sabotage financed by Japan and executed largely by imported agents."[1]

"The consensus of opinion is that there will be no racial uprising of the Japanese in Honolulu . . . The first generation, as on the Coast, are ideologically and culturally closest to Japan . . . it is considered that the big bulk of them will be loyal . . . The second generation is estimated as approximately ninety-eight percent loyal."[2]

From the Munson Report (November 1941)

". . . it is known that there are Japanese residents of California who have sought to aid the Japanese enemy by way of communicating information, or have shown indications of preparation for fifth column activities."[3]

From California Governor Culbert Olson (Speech, February 1942)

"There's a tremendous volume of public opinion now developing against the Japanese of all classes, that is aliens and non-aliens, to get them off the land . . . they want and they are bringing pressure on the government to move all the Japanese out. As a matter of fact, it's not being instigated or developed by people who are not thinking but by the best people of California . . . they feel that they are living in the midst of a lot of enemies. They don't trust the Japanese. . . ."[4]

From Lt. General DeWitt to Major Karl Bendetsen (Telephone, January 29, 1942)

". . . Any estimate of the situation indicates that the following are possible and probable enemy activities:

a. Naval attack on shipping in coastal waters;

b. Naval attack on coastal cities and vital installations;

c. Air raids on vital installations, particularly within two hundred miles of the coast;

d. Sabotage of vital installations throughout the Western Defense Command. Hostile Naval and air raids will be assisted by enemy agents signaling from the coastline . . . and by supplying and otherwise assisting enemy vessels by sabotage . . .

[1] Michi Weglyn, *Years of Infamy: The Untold Story of America's Concentration Camps* (New York: William Morrow and Company, 1976), 45.

[2] *Ibid.*, 47.

[3] Roger Daniels, *Concentration Camps USA: Japanese Americans and World War II* (New York: Holt, Rinehart and Winston, Inc., 1971), 60.

[4] *Ibid.*, 51.

I now recommend . . . that the Secretary of War provide for the exclusion from . . . military areas . . .

    a. Japanese aliens

    b. Japanese Americans citizens

    c. Alien enemies other than Japanese aliens

    d. Any and all other persons who are suspected . . . to be actual or potential saboteurs . . .

That the evacuation of classes (a), (b), and (c) from such military areas be initiated on a designated evacuation day and carried to completion as rapidly as practicable."[5]

> From Memorandum to Secretary Stimson from Lt. General DeWitt
> (February 13, 1942)

"Neither of the DiMaggio seniors is a citizen. They have reared nine children . . . eight of whom were born in the United States . . . Three of the boys are outstanding persons in the sports world. Joe who is with the Yanks . . . Dominic is with the Boston Red Sox . . . Vincent is with the Pittsburgh team. To evacuate [people like the DiMaggios] would . . . present . . . a serious situation. Many of the people affected by the existing order have boys and girls in the armed forces . . . it would be destructive and have a tendency to lower morale . . . if information should reach those in the armed forces that their relatives have been ordered to move out of this area because unfortunately they are not citizens."[6]

> From San Francisco Attorney Chauncey Tramutolo (Tolan Congressional
> Hearings, February–March 1942)

"Unfortunately [many] are of the opinion that because we have had no sabotage and no fifth column activities in this state . . . that means that none have been planned for us. But I take the view that this is the most ominous sign in our whole situation. It convinces me more than perhaps any other factor that the sabotage we are to get, the fifth column activities that we are to get, are timed just like Pearl Harbor was timed . . ."[7]

> From Earl Warren (Gubernatorial Candidate, 1942)

"The proposal of the War Department to organize a combat team consisting of legal American citizens of Japanese descent has my full approval. The new combat team will add to the nearly 5,000 loyal Americans of Japanese ancestry who are already serving in the armed forces for our country . . . No loyal citizens of the United States should be denied the democratic right to exercise the responsibilities of his citizenship, regardless of ancestry . . . A good American is one who is loyal to his country and to our creed of liberty and democracy."[8]

> From President Roosevelt to Secretary Stimson (Letter, February 1, 1943)

[5] Roger Daniels, *The Decision to Relocate the Japanese Americans* (Philadelphia: J.B. Lippincott Company, 1975), 110–111.

[6] Daniels, *Concentration Camps USA*, 75.

[7] Daniels, *Ibid.*, 76.

[8] Dillon S. Myer, *Uprooted Americans: The Japanese Americans and the War Relocation Authority During World War II* (Tucson: The University of Arizona Press, 1971), 313.

Journalistic Perspectives From the 1940s
Problems of the Japanese Migration

by Ernest K. Lindley

For the first time since the Indians were put on reservations, a racial group within the United States is being forced to migrate. All persons of Japanese blood are being removed from military zones on the Pacific Coast. They number 112,000 of whom three-fifths were born in the United States and therefore are American citizens.

The exodus has been ordered for two reasons: Federal and local officials feel incapable of distinguishing between loyal and disloyal persons of Japanese descent, and, in the event of attack, sabotage, or even further reverses in the Pacific, angry white people might wreak vengeance on the innocent as well as the guilty.

Against the decision, many arguments have been presented. The first is that rights of American citizens are being violated. To this the answer given is that citizenship is not a dividing line between loyalty and disloyalty to the United States, especially among a people who have not been assimilated socially. The second is that no similar emigration has been ordered from a much more vulnerable area—the Hawaiian Islands. It is pointed out also that not a single instance of sabotage by persons of Japanese lineage has been established in Hawaii.

The answer is twofold. The practical difficulties of such an exodus from Hawaii are almost insoluble; the absence of sabotage both in Hawaii and on the Pacific Coast is the surest sign that Japanese agents will go into action later. Cases are known in which Japanese officers have exiled themselves to other lands for years, posing as humble civilians in preparation for the supreme hour.

A third argument bites deep. Loyal Japanese-Americans would be of great value in espionage and propaganda work in the Far East.

The Japanese Government is trying to make this a racial war: that is implicit in the slogan: "Asia for the Asiatics." The United Nations cannot stand for white superiority—not with the Chinese, the Filipinos, and the Indians as their allies. Their battle cry must be "democracy," with all that it implies as to equality. As this argument goes, we are impairing the propaganda value of democracy and throwing away the services of loyal Japanese-Americans. German and Italian aliens are also being removed from certain military zones—but not American citizens of German and Italian descent.

The decision has been made, however. Responsible officials agree that it is probably wise. The best that can now be done is to make the migration as easy and fair as possible to the migrants. The President has set up a War Relocation Authority, headed by an able public official, Milton S. Eisenhower.

The first question is where to move the Japanese and how to employ them. Excepting some of the Colorado sugar-beet growers, private employers do not appear to want the migrants. And if scattered in private jobs, loyal Japanese-Americans might be exposed to vigilante action. The alternative is to segregate them in self-supporting communities or in camps engaged in public works. Small settlements will have to be created—and the possibility is being explored of having these communities produce war goods of types requiring hand work or only simple tools.

The other main problem is to protect the property of the emigrants. Instances have been reported in which they have been frightened into selling their possessions at sacrifice prices. The danger of racketeering is obvious. However, the Treasury has made the Federal Reserve Bank of San Francisco trustee, and the latter has set up local committees of three—representing the Federal Reserve Bank, the Farm Security Administration, and the Federal Security Agency—to help the Japanese, both aliens and citizens, in the sale, lease, or storage of property. This plan is said to be working well, and it may be left undisturbed by the Alien Property Custodian.

The transplantation is a severe test for Japanese whose loyalty now lies with us. At best it will leave wounds. These can be mollified if time is permitted for an orderly movement and if the property holdings of the emigrants are scrupulously protected. Unfortunately, the same military considerations which forced the decisions probably will require that it be executed in a hurry. The price is only too likely to be the permanent alienation of a group of citizens who, if intelligently handled, could be of unique aid in our war with the imperial militarists of their fatherland.

Newsweek, March 30, 1942, 26.

When Is a Jap?

Dillion S. Myer, director of the War Relocation Authority, sighed last week: "I would like to get out of this relocation thing tomorrow." For he had a tough problem on his hands: what to do about the 110,000 Japanese-Americans evacuated from the West Coast last year.

The ten relocation camps, established last spring and summer by the WRA in seven Western states on the President's order that Japanese-Americans be cleared out of the vital Pacific Coast area, have been the focus of controversy ever since. And so has the fate of the internees, of whom 65,400 are Nisei (American citizens by right of birth) and 5,680 Kibei (American-born but educated in Japan and mostly loyal to the emperor). The WRA was intended as an emergency setup, to care for the evacuees until they could be settled in jobs in other parts of the country. But movement from the Army-guarded and fence-enclosed tarpaper-barrack settlements has been slow.

By last week the reasons for that slowness had boiled up into an issue that involved some basic questions in the Japanese-American problem— and some plain racial hatred. The questions: Can any Japanese be trusted? How can the loyal be distinguished from the disloyal? News of the execution of our Tokyo raiders had aroused popular resentment and befogged the answers.

"Exposé": The streets of Cody and Powell, Wyo., close by the Heart Mountain relocation center, were empty of Japanese last week for the first time in months. The town councils had forbidden their appearance unless accompanied by military escort.

It all started when a Denver Post reporter visited a center and returned with Page 1 stories of waste and hoarding of rationed food. Among other things, he charged that the Japanese were being fed the almost forgotten luxury of bananas and alligator pears, and that rations were better than those in the Army. Actually the camp gets its food through the Army quartermaster, and residents have had bananas twice since the center was established last summer.

But the "expose" had its effect. Indignation in Denver and the whole West ran high over "coddling" of the internees. The War Manpower Commission, which had hoped to place thousands of Nisei in agriculture this year, voiced fear its program would bog down. As it was, about 4000 were employed permanently as communities in many parts of the country were refusing to put up with Nisei. And in time the government was shelling out $70,000,000 a year for the WRA and would probably spend $80,000,000 for 1944.

Further to complicate matters, in the pillared chamber of the Supreme Court last week charges were made that mass evacuation itself was unconstitutional. In the cases of Minoru Yasui, 26, and Gordon Hirabayashi, 24, both American-born of Japanese parents, who were convicted of violating a preinternment curfew order last year (Hirabayashi also refused to register for evacuation), attorneys charged that the evacuation order was void because it was without authority of Congress, that American citizens cannot be interned without a hearing under the due process and equal-protection clauses and that the military orders were void as no martial law had been declared.

To all this a Senate Military Affairs subcommittee, headed by Sen. Albert B. Chandler and just back from an investigating tour of the camps, thought it had the solution: abolish the camps. Last week Senator Chandler planned to submit to the President for action three recommendations: (1) Make all draft laws applicable to Japanese who are American citizens, (2) keep disloyal Japanese in regular internment camps for enemy aliens and (3) find jobs for loyal Japanese in areas where they will be acceptable.

But Chandler's program had its critics particularly on the Pacific Coast. For out of decades of experience with Japanese cut-rate laborers and farmers, Westerners have developed a hard core of suspicion and dislike for anything Japanese. With Lt. Gen. John L. DeWitt, head of the Western Defense Command, they feel that no matter what his citizenship "A Jap is a Jap." They don't like the idea of putting Japanese into our Army. Many threaten that if the Japanese return to the Coast they "will be buried" there. At defenders of the internees some hurl the epithet "Jap-lover."

As for the internees themselves, many were once eager to be free. But now that they can't know what to expect wherever they go, most want to stay in camp.

Newsweek, May 24, 1943, 33–34.

The Nisei Go Back

Mitsuye Endo is a loyal U.S. citizen, born 24 years ago in Sacramento. Her eyes happen to slant upward because her ancestors were Japanese. In 1942, when the U.S. Army uprooted 110,000 people of Japanese blood from their truck gardens and berry patches along the West Coast, Mitsuye Endo landed in a War Relocation center in Topaz, Utah.

This week the Supreme Court of the U.S. unanimously agreed that Citizen Endo—and, by implication, any other loyal Japanese-American—has a right to live where she pleases. Justice Frank Murphy denounced "the unconstitutional resort to racism inherent in the entire evacuation program." But the court, frankly avoiding a tough constitutional issue in wartime, almost contradicted itself.

Tackling the case of another relocated Japanese-American, the Justices ruled, 6-to-3, that the Army had the right to evacuate all Japanese and Nisei in a time of national emergency. Said the court: "Exclusion of large groups of citizens from their homes . . . is inconsistent with our basic Government institutions. But . . . hardships are part of war."

For almost two years, the right of the Government to shuffle citizens around at will had been a burning constitutional issue. But by the time the Supreme Court ruled this week, the question was academic. Day before, the Army had rescinded its mass evacuation order, told the loyal Japanese and Nisei they could return. Invasion, the Army explained, is no longer "a substantial possibility."

Interior Secretary Harold Ickes soothingly promised Westerners that there would be "no hasty mass movement" of returning evacuees. But the difficulties of readjustment loomed large enough to give pause to all citizens of good will. Problems had already cropped up:

In Hood River, Ore. (pop. 3,280), American Legionnaires daubed paint on their servicemen's honor roll to obliterate the names of 16 Nisei soldiers.

At Brawley, Calif., 3,500 citizens jammed onto the high-school athletic field for an anti-Japanese mass meeting, listening to an orator scream: "Do you want these yellow-bellied sneaks to return to Brawley?" The crowd roared: "No!"

In Parker, Ariz. (pop. 456), Andy Hale put a sign in his barbershop: "Japs Keep Out You Rats," ejected Raymond Matsuda, a Nisei veteran, wounded in Italy.

These were isolated instances, in small communities. But most of the U.S. Japanese on the West Coast lived in such small towns. And in the larger cities, the Hearst press kept up its anti-Japanese screams. California's Governor Warren, setting the tone for the vast majority of West Coast citizens, promised every effort to keep the return of the Nisei orderly.

Time, December 25, 1944, 14.

Lesson 16
The United States and the Holocaust

Objectives

- To analyze factors that retarded the United States' intervention on behalf of European Jews

- To consider international responsibility and its consequences relative to the Holocaust

Notes to the Teacher

This lesson assumes students' basic awareness of the Nazi program to annihilate European Jewry. Students are encouraged to consider various social, economic, and political factors in U.S. policy and actions regarding Germany's extermination program. Students begin by analyzing the *St. Louis* refugee incident in 1939. With this background, they then interpret U.S. Holocaust policy during the war and conclude by considering broader questions of our country's intervention in other nations' affairs.

Procedure

1. Write on the board the word *Holocaust*. Remind students that throughout the war the Nazis were pursuing a deliberate program to get rid of all Jews in Europe. Ask students to share what they know about the Holocaust. Write the word *genocide* on the board. Help students apply the word to the Holocaust.

2. Point out that since World War II, many people have criticized the United States and President Roosevelt, as well as other countries, groups, and individuals, for failing to intervene on behalf of European Jews.

3. Have students work in small groups on **Handout 18**.

   Suggested Responses:

   1. *Should the United States have admitted refugee children from the* St. Louis?

   2. *The legality of the case did not require admission; isolationism was a popular idea in the United States at the time; no compromise with American Jewish organizations had been reached; the United States was not adequately prepared for war.*

3. *Immigration laws/quotas; prejudice/ discrimination; refugees; asylum; human rights*

4. *Political realities, lack of preparation for war, no desire to antagonize Nazis*

5. *Admission might have cost political support; he could shift responsibility to Congress; Nazis could use this as excuse for initiating hostilities*

6. *Maintaining isolation when the United States was unprepared for war; his failure to end Great Depression also likely played a role*

7. *No action taken*

8. a. *Concentration camps and probably death*

   b. *May have cost Jewish support*

   c. *Support from isolationists and groups with an anti-Jewish bias*

   d. *Damage to characterization as humanitarian*

4. Have students work in small groups to complete **Handout 19**.

5. Conduct a discussion based on the handout questions. Emphasize that the issue of responsibility for the Holocaust is a complex one, as well as that the primary guilt can certainly be ascribed to Hitler and the Nazi Party.

Suggested Responses:

1. *American nativism, anti-Semitism, fear of another Depression, and focus on winning the war inhibited our response to the Holocaust.*

2. *The United States can be held partially responsible for the annihilation of six million Jews. Extreme immigration restrictions based on racist perspectives closed our doors to the victims. We failed to adopt measures to assist them even when no interference with military necessities was involved.*

3. *President Roosevelt was involved in war on several fronts. Until Pearl Harbor, he was occupied with efforts to end the Depression. However, as chief executive, he was responsible for his decision to delegate authority to a State Department that would deliberately fail to mount a rescue program.*

4. *If the War Refugee Board had been formed earlier, it might have been much more successful in its efforts to rescue European Jews.*

6. Point out that the Holocaust experience leads to questions such as these:

   1. To what extent does the United States bear responsibility for helping victims of oppression in other countries?

   2. Under what circumstances does one nation have the right and responsibility to intervene in another's affairs?

   3. What forms of intervention should be used?

   4. What implications does your answer have for U.S. policy in Cambodia, Afghanistan, South Africa, Nicaragua, and other areas?

   5. Would another country have been justified in intervening in our policy of interning Japanese Americans, or in our policy of relocating Native Americans?

On the Eve of War

Sometimes seemingly insignificant incidents have enormous implications for the future. The *St. Louis* incident is such a case. Read the brief explanation and analyze it using the questions that follow.

> In May 1939, only a few months before war began in Europe, a passenger ship called the *St. Louis* left Germany carrying nearly a thousand refugees, most of whom were Jews. Many of these people had already qualified for, but had not yet received, American visas. They arranged for temporary Cuban tourist visas that would enable them to wait outside of Germany for U.S. visas. By the time the *St. Louis* reached Havana, however, the Cuban government had changed its visa regulations. It refused to allow most of the refugees to land.
>
> Forced to leave Cuban waters, the *St. Louis* sailed up the Florida coast. The U.S. Coast Guard followed close behind to prevent any passengers from swimming ashore. The State Department refused to allow the refugees to land without special legislation by Congress or an executive order from the president. Efforts by American Jewish organizations to work out a compromise failed. The desperate passengers aboard the *St. Louis* sent President Roosevelt a telegram pleading their case; he never replied.
>
> Political realities may have influenced Roosevelt's decision to remain silent. Most Americans were anxious to stay out of the approaching European war. Many felt that America's best interest lay in avoiding foreign conflicts. Others were disillusioned by the experience of the U.S. intervention in World War I and wanted to avoid the loss of American lives. These views had strong support in Congress. In addition, President Roosevelt knew that the United States was not yet prepared for war and was reluctant to antagonize the Nazi regime.
>
> Finally, the *St. Louis* returned to Europe and several nations granted asylum to the refugees. But when Hitler's troops marched through Europe, most of the *St. Louis'* ill-fated passengers were eventually caught by the Nazis and sent to concentration camps.
>
> On the eve of World War II, a bill that would have admitted Jewish refugee children above the regular quota limits was introduced in Congress. President Roosevelt took no position on the bill, and it died in committee in the summer of 1939. Polls at the time indicated that two-thirds of Americans opposed taking in Jewish refugee children.[1]

1. What is the question at issue?

2. What facts did President Roosevelt have in making his decision on the *St. Louis* incident?

3. What broad concepts are involved in this issue?

[1] Constitutional Rights Foundation (Spring 1994, Vol. 10, No. 2). *Bill of Rights in Action* (1–3).

4. What factors probably influenced FDR the most when he made his decision on this issue?

5. What assumptions do you surmise he was making at the time?

6. What were the president's primary foreign policy goals at the time?

7. What was the president's solution to the problem in 1939?

8. What were the consequences of his decision for each of the groups below?

   a. The children

   b. U.S. foreign relations

   c. President's political fortunes

   d. President's reputation as a humanitarian

The United States and the Holocaust

Read the selections below and answer the questions which follow. Be prepared to discuss your responses.

The Holocaust

1. Before 1941, Nazis enacted increasingly repressive measures against Jews, who were permitted and sometimes forced to emigrate.

2. In 1941, the Nazi plan for invading Russia included extermination of Jews in conquered territories.

3. Also in 1941, Nazis banned Jewish emigration from German territories.

4. At the Wannsee Conference in January, 1942, the Nazis planned systematic annihilation of European Jews: "The final solution to the Jewish problem."

5. By summer, 1942, Jews were being transported from conquered territories to numerous concentration camps and to six extermination centers.

Climate in United States

6. Anti-Semitism was widespread and sometimes violent during pre-war and war years, especially in Boston and New York City.

7. High United States unemployment rates stimulated anti-immigration attitudes before Pearl Harbor. During the war, many feared a new crisis would occur when servicemen sought postwar civilian employment.

United States Knowledge of "Final Solution"

8. American Jewish press reported early information, obtained from the Jewish Telegraphic Agency, about Nazi persecution of Jews.

9. In August, 1942, American Jewish leaders received the Riegner Report revealing the Nazi extermination plan. The United States State Department requested no publicity pending confirmation of information. Jewish leaders complied with the request.

10. In November, 1942, Under Secretary of State Sumner Welles confirmed the report to Dr. Stephen S. Wise, a prominent American Jewish leader and rabbi. Wise then gave a press conference.

11. United States media placed little emphasis on the Jewish plight in Europe. Throughout the war, newspaper stories were minimized. After August 1943, Hearst publications advocated rescue efforts. Popular magazines and radio generally avoided the subject.

12. Americans tended to be skeptical about "final solution" information, partly because atrocity reports during World War I had proved to be inflated.

American Jews

13. During the 1930s, American Jews supported restriction of immigration.

14. As a group, American Jews were staunchly committed admirers of Roosevelt.

15. Disunity characterized American Jews, with splits between uptown and downtown, reform and orthodox, Zionists and anti-Zionists, Germans and Eastern Europeans.

16. Jewish groups were responsible for numerous rallies and demonstrations in sympathy with European Jews. In particular, Peter Bergson's Emergency Committee to Save the Jewish People, founded in July 1943, sponsored numerous successful projects to shape public opinion. American Zionists and "Bergsonites" were bitterly opposed to one another.

United States Government

17. From July 1, 1940, to June 30, 1941, the United States admitted only 48 percent of the immigrant quota. The next year it dropped to 19 percent, and the following three years the total was under 10 percent of the allowance.

18. Before December 1941, the United States was prone to isolationism; after the Pearl Harbor disaster, the United States was involved in war on several fronts, with victory far from certain.

19. President Roosevelt delegated communications about the Jewish plight in Europe to the State Department. His position was that American victory in Europe was the Jew's only hope.

20. Breckinridge Long was made head of the Special War Problems Division of the State Department in 1940, a position that enabled him to make his anti-immigration position national policy.

21. Early in 1943, the British Foreign Office sent a memo to the State Department including these words: "There is a possibility that the Germans or their satellites may change over from the policy of extermination to one of extrusion, and aim as they did before the war at embarrassing other countries by flooding them with alien immigrants."

22. In April 1943, English and American officials agreed at the Bermuda Conference to recommend "that no approach be made to Hitler for the release of potential refugees."

23. In January 1944, the Treasury Department, under Secretary Henry Morgenthau, produced a "Report to the Secretary on the Acquiescence of This Government in the Murder of the Jews." The report found the State Department "guilty not only of gross procrastination and willful failure to act, but even of willful attempts to prevent action from being taken to rescue Jews from Hitler."

24. From November 1943, to January 1944, Congress discussed a Rescue Resolution which seemed likely to pass.

25. In January 1944, Roosevelt issued an Executive Order creating the War Refugee Board (WRB), which enacted an energetic program aiming to rescue European Jews.

26. During 1944, the United States bombed strategic German targets including areas of Auschwitz, but made no attempt to hit the gas chambers.

Sources:

Henry L. Feingold, *The Politics of Rescue* (New York: Waldon Press, Inc., 1970).

David S. Wyman, *The Abandonment of the Jews: America and the Holocaust, 1941–1945* (New York: Pantheon Books, 1984).

In considering each of the following questions:

a. Identify and discuss specific relevant points of information from the previous list.

b. Formulate a concise statement summarizing your position.

1. Identify and explain cultural, economic, and political factors in U.S. policy toward the Nazi "final solution."

2. To what extent can the United States be held accountable for the Holocaust?

3. To what extent can President Roosevelt be held accountable?

4. What should the United States have done?

Lesson 17
World War II Conferences

Objective
- To form generalizations about Cold War origins

Notes to the Teacher

Contemporary research indicates that the roots of the Cold War can be found during that time of allied cooperation so unique and necessary in winning World War II. Historians agree that surface amity covered the usual East-West mistrust. This lesson examines this suspicion without taking sides. Consequently, when students master the events, their questions and research should lead to a balanced account. Useful specialized studies that verify the controversial origins of the Cold War include:

Gaddos, John Lewis. *The U.S. and Origins of the Cold War, 1942–1947* (New York: Columbia University Press, 1972).

Graebner, Norman A. *Cold War Diplomacy, 1945–1975* (New York: D. Van Nostrand Co., Inc., 1977).

May, Earnest R. *"Lessons" of the Past: The Use and Misuse of History in American Foreign Policy* (New York: Oxford University Press, 1973).

Paterson, Thomas G. *On Every Front: The Making of the Cold War* (New York: Norton, 1979).

Patterson, James T. *Paths to the Present* (Minneapolis: Burgess Publishing Co., 1975).

Students begin by completing a homework assignment on World War II conferences. In class, they discuss broader issues of the wartime alliance, role play concerns of the Allies at the end of the war, and develop a generalization relating the origins of the Cold War and the experiences of the Allies during the war years.

Procedure

1. Introduce the lesson using material in the Notes to the Teacher.

2. Have students complete **Handout 20** for homework. Review their answers and encourage students to ask original questions.

Suggested Responses:

1. *Concentrate first on defeating Hitler, the primary enemy, while merely containing the Japanese. When that task was completed, the Allies would mount a stronger attack against Japan.*

2. *Delay in opening a second front*

3. *Recognition of the Polish government-in-exile*

4. *Unconditional surrender*

5. *The opening of the second front*

6. *Setting up a front government in Dublin (27 July)*

7. *Second Moscow Conference (9–10 October, 1944)*

8. *The Allied promised at Yalta to give Russia the Kurile Islands and the southern half of Sakhalin*

9. *The number of votes the Soviets were allowed and the meaning of the vote in the security council*

10. *Either the temporary zones of occupation or the placement of Berlin*

11. *The countries of present-day Eastern Europe*

12. *The demand for $20 billion in reparations*

List students' further questions on the board; discuss them, or assign them as cooperative research projects.

3. The foregoing exercise should stimulate further discussion on topics such as:

   a. What pledges were made in the Atlantic Charter?

   b. What was the Comintern?

   c. Where was the Curzon Line?

   d. What does Kommondatura mean?

4. Proceed to broader questions, such as:

   e. Why were Soviets so adamant about Poland?

   f. Was the second front issue mishandled?

   g. If there was so much trouble with the Grand Alliance, why did it continue to function?

   h. Why allow the Soviets more votes in the United Nations?

   i. Were United States' interests betrayed at Yalta?

   (**Note:** These questions can lend themselves to research, essay, and speech assignments.)

   Suggested Responses:

   a. *No territorial self-aggrandizement, self-determination for nations, freedom of speech and worship, freedom from want and fear, freedom of the seas, reduction of armaments, abandonment of force, and a permanent system of general security*

   b. *Communist International aimed at spreading communism among nations.*

   c. *Line established to mark a new Polish border that would give about one-third of prewar Poland in the east to the Soviet Union in return for territory on Poland's western and northern border*

   d. *Military government*

   e. *After invasion of their country in two world wars, they wanted a buffer of "friendly" territory on their borders.*

   f. *The Soviet Union insisted that the other Allies had delayed opening a second front in Europe in order to "bleed them white" so that they would not be a threat at the end of the war.*

   g. *It had been necessary to work together to defeat a powerful German threat.*

   h. *The Soviets insisted they had done more than the others to defeat the Germans and that the countries in the British Commonwealth would vote together to dilute their influence.*

   i. *After the war, many people in the United States believed they had given up much at Yalta to gain Soviet help in the war against Japan. At the time of the concessions, the United States did not know that they would have an atomic bomb and that Soviet assistance would be unnecessary.*

5. Divide the class into small groups with each assigned to take the position of either the Soviet Union or the other European Allies. (United States, Britain, and France) at the end of the war. Ask each group to consider the following question: How has the behavior of the other side caused you to be suspicious of their intentions? Cite three examples, and explain the issues from your point of view.

6. After group presentations on the question above, have each student write a one-sentence thesis assessing the extent to which roots of the Cold War may be found in agreement made at wartime conferences of the Allies.

Analyzing the World War II Conferences

Use the description of WWII conferences that follows to help you analyze Allied cooperation during the war.

International Conferences, Declarations, and Agreements, 1941—1945

1941

22 Dec. Prime Minister Winston Churchill arrived in Washington for a series of conferences with President Roosevelt. The fundamental basis of joint strategy was affirmed: to concentrate upon the defeat of the Axis in Europe (which was viewed as the decisive theater of war), and to follow a policy of containment in the Far East until military successes in Europe or mounting Allied resources permitted stronger blows against Japan. The last of this series of conferences was held on 14 Jan. 1942. The Declaration of the United Nations was drafted and the Combined Chiefs of Staff and the Munitions Assignment Board was set up.

1942

1 Jan. United Nations Declaration was signed at Washington. Twenty-six nations, including the U.S., Great Britain, the Soviet Union, and China, affirmed the principles of the Atlantic Charter, pledged the employment of their full military and economic resources against the Axis, and promised not to make a separate armistice or peace with the common enemies.

27 Jan. Anglo-American Combined Raw Materials Board established at Washington.

6 Feb. Joint Anglo-American War Council established at Washington.

29 May. The Soviet Foreign Minister, Vyacheslav M. Molotov, arrived in Washington for conferences with President Roosevelt and other high U.S. officials. Among the results of the meeting was a new Lend-Lease protocol with Russia. The agreement provided that materials or data received from the U.S. would not be transferred to other parties without U.S. consent and that materials still available at the end of the war would be returned to the U.S. The new agreement went into effect on 1 July.

July. The Combined Chiefs of Staff, meeting in London, decided to invade North Africa and to postpone a 2nd front in Europe as well as the Pacific offensive.

12–15 Aug. 1ST MOSCOW CONFERENCE. Principal participants were Soviet Premier Joseph V. Stalin, Prime Minister Churchill, and W. Averell Harriman, who represented President Roosevelt. Churchill, with the support of Harriman, informed Stalin that it was not possible to open a 2nd front in Europe in 1942.

1943

14–24 Jan. CASABLANCA CONFERENCE was held in French Morocco. President Roosevelt and Prime Minister Churchill declared that the war would be fought until the "unconditional surrender" of the enemy had been secured. Agreement in principle was reached on a second front, but not on its location. U.S. officials favored an invasion of the Continent through France. The British urged an assault on the "soft underbelly" of Europe (*i.e.,* Italy and the Balkans). A compromise was reached on the invasion of Sicily and Italy without prejudice to the ultimate invasion of Europe from the west. No agreement was worked out on the conflicting claims for leadership of the Gens. Charles de Gaulle and Henri Giraud, who also attended the conference. Gen. Dwight D. Eisenhower was placed in supreme command of the North African theater.

25 Apr. The Soviet Union broke off its relations with the Polish government-in-exile.

12–25 May. ANGLO-AMERICAN CONFERENCE (TRIDENT) at Washington planned global strategy and the opening of a 2nd front in Europe. President Roosevelt, Prime Minister Churchill, and Combined Chiefs of Staff, and many U.S. and British officials took part. The date (1 May 1944) for the Normandy invasion was definitely set and the seizure of the Azores authorized unless Portugal could be persuaded by negotiation to grant the use of bases on the islands. The conference also agreed to step up the quantity of aviation gasoline being flown over "the hump" from India to China.

22 May. Moscow announced the dissolution 15 May of the 3rd International (Comintern).

11–24 Aug. 1ST QUEBEC CONFERENCE (QUADRANT) attended by President Roosevelt, Prime Minister Churchill, and top-ranking advisers including the Combined Chiefs of State, reaffirmed 1 May 1944 as the target date for the Normandy invasion (OVERLORD), which was to be supplemented by landings in Southern France (ANVIL, later DRAGOON). Agreement was reached on stepping up military operations in the Far East, particularly in Burma, and a Southeast Asia Command was established, with Lord Louis Mountbatten as Supreme Allied Commander. The Chiefs of the Naval Staffs reported that the Battle of the Atlantic against the U-boat had turned in favor of the Allies.

19–30 Oct. MOSCOW CONFERENCE OF FOREIGN MINISTERS was the first Allied 3-power meeting of World War II. It was attended by Secretary of State Cordell Hull, Foreign Minister V.M. Molotov, together with U.S., British, and Soviet military officials. The most controversial point in the discussions involved the status of the Polish government-in-exile at London, which the Soviet Union refused to recognize. The U.S. and Great Britain assured the Russians that preparations for opening a 2nd front in Europe were under way. Stalin made an unconditional promise that after Germany's defeat Russia would enter the war against Japan. The conference established a European Advisory Commission for the purpose of formulating a postwar policy for Germany. The Moscow Declaration issued at the close of the conference recognized "the necessity of establishing at the earliest practicable date a general international organization, based on the principle of sovereign equality of all peace-loving states, and open to membership by all such states, large and small, for the maintenance of international peace and security."

22–26 Nov. 1ST CAIRO CONFERENCE. President Roosevelt and Prime Minister Churchill conferred with Generalissimo and Madame Chiang Kai-shek regarding the war in the Far East. The Declaration of Cairo (1 Dec.) affirmed that the 3 powers would prosecute the war against Japan until her unconditional surrender and that they had no desire for territorial expansion; that Japan should be deprived of all Pacific islands acquired since 1914, whether by capture or League of Nations mandate; that all territories which Japan had taken from the Chinese, such as Manchuria, Formosa, and the Pescadores, should be restored to China; and that the 3 powers were "determined that in due course Korea should become free and independent."

At the **2nd Cairo Conference** (4–6 Dec.) Roosevelt and Churchill held discussions with the president of Turkey, Ismet Inönü. This conference affirmed the alliance between Great Britain and Turkey and noted "the firm friendship existing between the Turkish people," the U.S., and the Soviet Union. As a result of military decisions taken at the 2nd Cairo Conference, the command of the invasion of Western Europe was conferred on Gen. Dwight D. Eisenhower.

28 Nov.–1 Dec. TEHERAN CONFERENCE, held at the capital of Iran, was attended by President Roosevelt, Prime Minister Churchill, and Premier Stalin. It was the 1st 3-power war conference in which Stalin took a personal part. The chief subject of the meeting was the projected Anglo-American invasion of Western Europe, supported by a flanking invasion through Southern France, and the timing of this assault with the Soviet offensive against Germany. Stalin reaffirmed his promise to enter the war against Japan. The conference formulated a plan for an international organization to keep the peace.

1944

27 July. The Polish Committee of National Liberation, organized at Moscow, was recognized by the Soviet government. The committee, which later transferred its headquarters to Lublin, was entrusted with administrative control of Polish areas taken by the Red Army.

21 Aug.–7 Oct. DUMBARTON OAKS CONFERENCE, held near Washington, D.C., was attended by representatives of the U.S., Great Britain, the Soviet Union, and China (with the last 2 meeting separately, since Russia was still at peace with Japan). The conference discussed the draft of a charter for a permanent postwar international organization for maintaining world peace and security. The tentative proposals (known as the Dumbarton Oaks Plan) served as the basis for the Charter of the United Nations. Agreement on the veto issue could not be reached, Russia refusing to agree to bar a member of the Security Council from voting on a question to which it was itself a party.

11–16 Sept. 2ND QUEBEC CONFERENCE, attended by President Roosevelt and Prime Minister Churchill, considered strategic plans for final victory over Germany and Japan. The chief subjects of the conference were the demarcation of the zones of occupation following the conquest of Germany and the policy governing the postwar treatment of that nation. The Morgenthau plan (sponsored by Secretary of the Treasury Henry Morgenthau, Jr.) for reducing Germany to an agrarian economy was tentatively approved at this conference, but was rejected by President Roosevelt a month later.

9–18 Oct. 2ND MOSCOW CONFERENCE, attended by Prime Minster Churchill and Premier Joseph Stalin, divided the Balkans into spheres, Russia to predominate in Rumania, Bulgaria, and Hungary, Great Britain in Greece, with Yugoslavia to be shared. It was generally agreed that the Curzon Line should bound Poland on the east and the Oder River on the west. Roosevelt, who was not a party to these arrangements, let it be known that he would not be bound by them.

1945

Jan. Malta Conference. Combined Chiefs of Staff planned final campaign against Hitler.

4–11 Feb. YALTA CONFERENCE, held in the Crimea, was attended by President Roosevelt, Prime Minister Churchill, and Premier Stalin, together with their top diplomatic and military advisers. Most of the important agreements remained secret until the postwar period. In exchange for her pledge to enter the war in the Far East, Russia was given the Kurile Islands, the southern half of Sakhalin, and an occupation zone in Korea, and was granted privileged rights in Manchuria and in the Chinese cities of Dairen and Port Arthur. In addition, the U.S. and Great Britain agreed to recognize the autonomy of Outer Mongolia, which had severed its connections with China and come under Soviet influence. The U.S. and Great Britain also agreed to award eastern Poland to the Soviet Union. Poland's eastern border was fixed on the Curzon Line; and that nation was to receive territorial compensation in the north and west at the expense of Germany. Agreement was reached for reorganizing the Polish (Lublin) government on a broader democratic basis. The Russian demand of $20 billion in reparation payments from Germany, to be taken out of current production, was referred to a reparations commission. The 3 powers reaffirmed the "unconditional surrender" formula and issued a Declaration of Liberated Europe pledging the Big Three to support postwar governments in the liberated states which would be representative of the popular will through free elections. The conferees announced they had worked out a formula for voting procedure in the Security Council and that a conference to elaborate the United Nations Charter would convene at San Francisco on 25 Apr. It was secretly agreed that the Ukraine and Byelo-Russia would be accorded full and equal membership in the United Nations organization on the footing of independent nations.

5 Apr. The Soviet Union denounced its 5-year nonaggression pact with Japan.

21 Apr. The Soviet Union concluded a 20-year mutual assistance pact with the Polish Provisional Government (the Lublin regime).

25 Apr.–26 June. UNITED NATIONS CONFERENCE ON INTERNATIONAL ORGANIZATION, attended by delegates of 50 nations, assembled at San Francisco to draft the Charter of the United Nations Organization (UNO). The Russians at San Francisco interpreted the Yalta voting formula to mean that a nation could use the veto to forbid the Security Council from even discussing questions which might require force in their settlement. Secretary of State Edward R. Stettinius, Jr., threatened that the U.S. would not participate in the organization unless the Russians yielded. The deadlock was broken when President Truman directed Harry L. Hopkins, then in Moscow, to take the issue to Stalin. The latter agreed that the veto should not be used to prevent discussion. Following the announcement (7 June) of this compromise, a draft Charter was worked out. The Charter of the United Nations provided for six chief organs: (1) a General Assembly of all member nations as the policy-making body, each nation to have a single vote; (2) a Security Council of 11 members in continuous session for deciding diplomatic, political, or military disputes, the Big Five (the U.S., Great Britain, the Soviet Union, France, and China) to have permanent seats, the other 6 to be held for 2-yr. terms; (3) an Economic and Social Council of 18 members elected by the General Assembly for the purpose of dealing with human welfare and fundamental rights and freedoms; (4) an International Court of Justice (sitting at The Hague) for dealing with international legal disputes, its 15 judges to be elected by the General

Assembly and the Security Council; (5) a Trusteeship Council made up of states administering trust territories, the permanent members of the Security Council, and members elected by the General Assembly for a 3-yr. term; and (6) a Secretariat, headed by the Secretary-General, for performing the routine administrative work of the UNO, the staff to be selected from nations holding membership in the UN. The Charter was unanimously approved on 25 June and signed on the following day.

5 June. EUROPEAN ADVISORY COMMISSION established German occupation zones, assigning eastern Germany to Russia, dividing the south between the U.S. and France, and placing Great Britain in charge of the west. Berlin was shared among the occupying powers and placed in the heart of the Soviet zone, leaving all ground approaches dominated by the Russians. The administration of Berlin was entrusted to a military Kommandatura.

17 July–2 Aug. POTSDAM CONFERENCE, held near Berlin, was attended by President Harry S. Truman, Prime Minister Churchill (who after 28 July was replaced by the newly chosen British Prime Minister, Clement R. Attlee, head of the Labour government), and Premier Stalin. Also present, in addition to other top-ranking officials, were Secretary of State James F. Byrnes, Foreign Secretary Anthony Eden (who after 28 July was replaced by Ernest Bevin), and Foreign Secretary V.M. Molotov. The first declaration issued by the conference was the "unconditional surrender" ultimatum (26 July) presented to Japan. The chief questions before the conference were the plan for the occupation and control of Germany and the settlement of various European problems. A Council of Foreign Ministers, its members drawn from the Big Five, was established and entrusted with the preparation of draft treaties with Austria, Hungary, Bulgaria, Rumania, and Finland, and with the proposal of settlements of outstanding territorial questions. The Council was also authorized to negotiate an agreement with a central German government whenever the latter should come into being. The occupation authorities were to conduct programs designed to denazify, decentralize, disarm, and democratize Germany, which was to be treated during the occupation period as a single economic unit. Provision was made for the trial of war criminals (shortly after the conference an International Military Tribunal was set up). Final delimitation of the Polish-German frontier was left to the peace treaty. The Soviet Union abandoned its $20-billion reparations demand in exchange for a reparations schedule based on a percentage of useful capital equipment in the Western zone and materials in the Eastern zone. The conference agreed that Germany should make good for losses suffered at its hands by the United Nations. Provision was made for the mandatory transfer of 6,500,000 Germans from Hungary, Czechoslovakia, and Poland to Germany. Economic agreements were reached concerning German industry, foreign trade, finance, communications, and transportation. At the earliest practicable date the German economy was to be decentralized for the purpose of eliminating excessive centralization of economic power as exemplified by cartels, syndicates, and trusts. Primary emphasis in the German economy was to be given to the development of agriculture and peaceful domestic industries.

14 Aug. The Sino-Soviet treaty signed at Moscow formalized China's consent to the concessions granted to the Soviet at the Yalta Conference.[1]

[1] Richard Morris (ed.), *Encyclopedia of American History* (New York: Harper & Row, 1976), **454–460.**

1. What basic wartime strategy was decided at the December 22, 1941, meeting of Prime Minister Churchill and President Roosevelt?

2. What possible reason could the Soviets give for breaking off relations with the Polish government-in-exile? (25 April 1943)

3. What issue remained unsettled after the Moscow Conference of Foreign Ministers?

4. What decision at the first Cairo Conference apparently caused the Japanese to fight with more zeal?

5. Although Stalin was not primarily interested in defeating Japan, what seemed to convince him to join the Allies in this venture?

6. How did the Soviets plan to settle the Polish question?

7. At what point were the Soviets given primary responsibility for the Balkans?

8. What evidence can you find that the Soviets needed encouragement to join the war against Japan?

9. In spite of the news of the formation of the United Nations, what controversies remained between the West and the Soviet Union?

10. What was the most awkward decision made by the European Advisory Commission on June 5?

11. What countries were not mentioned at the Potsdam Conference?

12. What evidence is there that the West had justification to mistrust the Soviets? As you answer the question, think about further problems or puzzles that remained unanswered. Some subjects include Poland, United Nations, transfer of Germans, etc.

Part 2
The Postwar World— Adjusting to Change

The end of World War II marked a major watershed in history. The year 1945 ushered in the Atomic Age, the Cold War, the United Nations, and the beginning of the end of colonialism in Asia and Africa. To help students see this larger picture of American development, it needs to be made clear to students how the major developments of the next half century stem from World War II experiences. Cold War foreign policy, the Civil Rights Movement, women's liberation, early postwar economic prosperity, the Korean Conflict, and the Vietnam War all have their origins in that great war. Again, in this unit as in Part 1, it may be useful to divide the unit into smaller teaching/testing segments. At the conclusion of the unit, students should be able to answer the following basic questions:

- Why would the Soviet Union view origins of the Cold War differently from the United States?

- To what extent did the Truman Doctrine set a precedent for a sound foreign policy in the future?

- How did McCarthyism affect American thinking?

- Why did President Truman fire General MacArthur?

- How effectively did Presidents Truman and Eisenhower build on prosperity stemming from wartime savings?

- To what extent were the New Frontier and the Great Society the logical successors of the New Deal?

- Why did the United States become involved in the Vietnam War?

- Why did the Civil Rights Movement become more violent in the mid-1960s?

- To what extent has the women's liberation movement changed the role and status of women?

- How might the United States extend the Civil Rights Movement to include justice and fairness for Native Americans?

- Why was President Nixon forced to resign as a result of the Watergate break-in?

- How effective have recent American presidents been in solving key issues of domestic and foreign policy?

- In what ways does contemporary American art mirror the values of American society?

Lesson 18 Cold War Revisited

Lesson 19 The Truman Doctrine

Lesson 20 McCarthyism and the Climate of Fear

Lesson 21 Korean Inquiry

Lesson 22 Economic Recovery after World War II

Lesson 23 The New Frontier and Great Society

Lesson 24 Vietnam—A Reappraisal

Lesson 25 The Black Revolution—Where Do We Go from Here?

Lesson 26 Women's Rights—A Chronicle of Reform

Lesson 27 Native Americans—A Forgotten Minority

Lesson 28 The Crimes of Watergate

Lesson 29 Evaluating Recent Presidents

Lesson 30 Social History and Contemporary Art

Lesson 18
Cold War Revisited

Objective
- To analyze events of the Cold War from different perspectives

Notes to the Teacher
A continuation of the previous lesson, this lesson seeks to order the controversial Cold War events of the period from 1946–1963. In this lesson, students work in groups to complete a homework assignment viewing the Cold War from different perspectives. After the group reports, they read the Atlantic Charter and consider to what extent U.S. foreign policy during the Cold War matched the ideals of the document and why the Soviet Union viewed U.S. adherence to these principles as threatening. In this broad-ranging assignment, you will want to ensure that atomic diplomacy, containment, self-determination for Europe, the challenge from Korea and China, Vietnam, and the Cuban Missile Crisis are discussed under the framework of the Cold War. Later lessons deal with issues such as these in greater detail.

Procedure
1. Distribute part A of **Handout 21**. Divide the class into small groups and have the groups complete the assignment as directed.

2. Have each group present its findings. Results can be placed on the board or formal time lines can be displayed around the classroom, and similarities and differences discussed.

3. Distribute part B of **Handout 21**. Have students review the provisions of the Atlantic Charter.

Suggested Responses:

a. *Affirmation of the right of self-government for all*

b. *Economic security*

c. *Free access to trade*

d. *Reaffirmation of Wilson's vision of freedom of the seas, freedom from fear of aggression*

e. *Establishment of a permanent system of general security*

4. To complete the lesson, have students consider the following issues:

a. To what extent did our Cold War foreign policy conform to the ideals in the Atlantic Charter? (In responding to this question, an excellent essay topic, students should include evidence such as the Truman Doctrine, Marshall Plan, Berlin Airlift, Point IV, Korea, Vietnam, and the Cuban Missile Crisis.)

b. Why would a U.S. foreign policy based on the Atlantic Charter seem threatening to the Soviet Union? (After repeated invasions of their territory, the USSR felt compelled to seek protective buffers on their borders. Any policy by the United States that frustrated that effort was viewed as threatening to Soviet security and led to conflict.)

Use students' responses as a springboard for a concluding discussion.

Toward Understanding the Cold War

Part A.

For homework, take the view assigned to your group. Use that perspective in researching the responses required for your group. Use the years 1946 to 1963 in compiling your information.

Group A

Man's understanding of history is always shaped by influences arising in the present. There is no such thing as absolute historical objectivity, only the necessity to seek it. But in no realm of historical discussion is that search more difficult than in contemporary diplomatic history.[1]

Find articles, cartoons, or personal statements showing how interpretations of current events of 1946–1963 colored the thinking of one side in the Cold War toward the actions of the other. Try to find examples from both the United States and the Soviet Union.

Group B

Truman's diplomatic problems in 1945 were threefold. First, since the prewar collective security system in Europe had been shattered, the reconstruction of American alliances in Europe to preserve a new balance of power there was imperative for American security. Germany was crushed, England and France were exhausted, and in this power vacuum Soviet hegemony seemed virtually unchallenged. Second, the organization of the United Nations required immediate attention. The United States was expected to play a leading role in putting it in operation. A third immediate problem was the rebuilding of many war-ravaged areas in Europe, a task that could be accomplished only if the United States assumed major responsibility.[2]

Following World War II, some people contended that the United States had a primary responsibility for world peace. Research diverse views of the Truman administration including memoirs. Evaluate the previously-stated contention in light of its time.

---

[1] Gaddis Smith as found in Richard L. Watson and William A. Cartwright eds., *The Reinterpretation of American History and Culture* (Washington, D.C.: The National Council for the Social Studies, 1973), 543.

[2] Gerald D. Nash, *The Great Transition* (Boston: Allyn and Bacon, Inc., 1971), 411.

Group C

Initially the Cold War resulted from a myriad of major and minor disagreements which flowed from the determination of the victorious allies of 1945 to restore war-torn Europe to a condition which conformed to their perceptions of an ideal world. For the United States and Britain that best of all worlds conformed overwhelmingly to that fashioned at Versailles; for the Soviets the postwar era required, if it would satisfy historic Russian purposes at all, the elimination of the Versailles Treaty's essential provisions, especially its Eastern European settlements and its reaffirmation of Western predominance in Europe. This massive divergence in purpose, rendered inflexible by a profound conflict over the ultimate intentions implied by competing ideological imperatives, gradually disintegrated into a Cold War.[3]

Review provisions of the Treaty of Versailles, particularly those dealing with Eastern European settlements and those designed to preserve Western dominance. Explain why the peace of Versailles would have been so beneficial to Britain and the United States and why the same provisions were totally unacceptable to the Soviet Union.

Group D

The primary objective of United States policy toward the Soviet Union is to convince Soviet leaders that it is in their interest to participate in a system of world cooperation, that there are no fundamental causes for war between our two nations, and that the security and prosperity of the Soviet Union, and that of the rest of the world as well, is being jeopardized by the aggressive militaristic imperialism such as that in which the Soviet Union is now engaged.[4]

Memorandum from Clark Clifford to President Truman, September 24, 1946

List and explain actions taken by the Soviet Union between 1946 and 1963 that the United States considered aggressive. How did the Soviet Union explain their actions in these instances?

Group E

The Russian leaders are keen judges of human psychology, and as such they are highly conscious that loss of temper and of self-control is never a source of strength in political affairs. They are quick to exploit such evidences of weakness. For these reasons, it is a *sine qua non* of successful dealing with Russia that the foreign government in question should remain at all times cool and collected and that its demands on Russian policy should be put forward in such a manner as to leave the way open for a compliance not too detrimental to Russian prestige.[5]

George Kennan in *Foreign Affairs*, July, 1947

During the period 1946–1963, what U.S. actions most threatened the Soviet Union, and why? In which instances did the United States allow the USSR to back down while saving their prestige? Explain your answer.

---

[3] Norman A. Graebner, *Cold War Diplomacy: American Foreign Policy 1945–1975* (New York: D. Von Nostrand Company, Inc., 1977), III.

[4] William H Chafe and Harvard Sithoff, *A History of Our Time* (New York: Oxford University Press, 1983), 39.

[5] Walter LaFeber (comp.), *America in the Cold War: Twenty Years of Revolution and Response 1947–1967* (New York: Wiley, 1969), 44.

Part B.

Read the Atlantic Charter below and compile a list of principles on which the United States and United Kingdom sought to base their foreign policy.

The Atlantic Charter, August 14, 1941

Declaration of Principles, Known as the Atlantic Charter, by the President of the United States of America and the Prime Minister of the United Kingdom, August 14, 1941

Joint declaration of the President of the United States of America and the Prime Minister, Mr. Churchill, representing His Majesty's Government in the United Kingdom, being met together, deem it right to make known certain common principles in the national policies of their respective countries on which they base their hopes for a better future for the world.

First, their countries seek no aggrandizement, territorial or other;

Second, they desire to see no territorial changes that do not accord with the freely expressed wishes of the peoples concerned;

Third, they respect the right of all peoples to choose the form of government under which they will live; and they wish to see sovereign rights and self-government restored to those who have been forcibly deprived of them;

Fourth, they will endeavor, with due respect for their existing obligations, to further the enjoyment by all States, great or small, victor or vanquished, of access, on equal terms, to the trade and to the raw materials of the world which are needed for their economic prosperity;

Fifth, they desire to bring about the fullest collaboration between all nations in the economic field with the object of securing, for all, improved labor standards, economic advancement and social security;

Sixth, after the final destruction of the Nazi tyranny, they hope to see established a peace which will afford to all nations the means of dwelling in safety within their own boundaries, and which will afford assurance that all the men in all the lands may live out their lives in freedom from fear and want;

Seventh, such a peace should enable all men to traverse the high seas and oceans without hindrance;

Eighth, they believe that all of the nations of the world, for realistic as well as spiritual reasons must come to the abandonment of the use of force. Since no future peace can be maintained if land, sea, or air armaments continue to be employed by nations which threaten, or may threaten, aggression outside of their frontiers, they believe, pending the establishment of a wider and permanent system of general security, that the disarmament of such nations is essential. They will likewise aid and encourage all other practicable measures which will lighten for peace-loving peoples the crushing burden of armaments.[6]

[6] Source: U.S. Department of State, Office of Public Affairs, *In Quest of Peace and Security: Selecting Documents on American Foreign Policy 1941–1951* (Washington: Government Printing Office, 1951), 1–2.

Lesson 19
The Truman Doctrine

Objective
• To evaluate the wisdom of the Truman Doctrine

Notes to the Teacher
Truman's historic announcement in 1947 has provoked increasing controversy among diplomatic historians. Early interpretations praised the Truman Doctrine as courageous and prophetic. Some claim that the record of the Truman Administration hinges on this unique turn in foreign policy. Revisionists and others criticize the Truman Doctrine as too restrictive and simplistic.

Students read President Truman's speech to Congress and discuss the issue, facts of the situation, assumptions, and consequences of the fateful change in American foreign policy. With this background, students attempt to evaluate the wisdom of the policy. To conclude the lesson, students assume the role of a State Department official charged with advising incoming President Eisenhower on an appropriate direction for U.S. foreign policy.

Procedure
1. For homework, assign students to read the Truman Doctrine, found in part A of **Handout 22**.

2. In class, discuss the following points:

    a. Why was the Truman Doctrine a historic change in American foreign policy? (*It was the first application of the policy of containment and the first time the United States had strayed from President Washington's Farewell Address advice on maintaining peacetime isolation.*)

    b. Review events leading up to the Truman Doctrine including the following:

    • George Kennan's analysis of Soviet behavior

    • Soviet reluctance to leave Iran

    • Difficulty in implementing the Potsdam agreements

    • Inability to reach an accord to control atomic energy (Bernard Baruch Plan)

    • Winston Churchill's Iron Curtain Speech in Fulton, Missouri

    • Both Houses return a Republican majority in 1946

    • England announces that she can no longer provide aid to Greece and Turkey, February 21, 1947

    c. Explain the problem that led to announcement of the Truman Doctrine.

    • The democratic government of Greece was threatened by border countries led by Communists.

    • Turkey needed help as well, although the reasons given were superficial.

    d. What was the U.S. response?

    • Our support for the United Nations led us to aid those countries threatened by totalitarian regimes.

    • Such a threat undermined our security.

    e. What did our policy promise?

    • To support those who risked subjugation

    f. Ask students to brainstorm the assumptions the Truman administration made at the time. One mark of critical thinkers is the ability to recognize assumptions. The Truman Doctrine is literally filled with assumptions about Greece and Turkey; Soviet intentions; England; and U.S. resources, responsibilities, best interests, and chances for success. The possibilities here are almost endless. Do not be satisfied with a short list. It may help if students reread the document line by line to do this activity carefully.

3. Have students complete the chart in part B of **Handout 22**. Discuss their responses.

Suggested Responses:

Czechoslovakia— *Americans reacted violently but could only protest.*

They soon helped organize NATO to protect the United States and its Western European allies.

Berlin Blockade—*The Berlin Airlift (successful by February 1949)*

China—*United States publishes White Paper in August 1949, explaining why we could do nothing about the takeover.*

Korea—*Active military intervention after a successful United Nations resolution*

4. To conclude the lesson, discuss part C of **Handout 22** as a class activity. Use the questions at the end of the scorecard as a basis for discussion and debate. Be sure to ask students to support their positions on questions.

Suggested Assignment

Have students compare George Kennan's original advice to the Truman administration with his second thoughts written twenty years later. Such a comparison reveals the idealism in our foreign policy.

Suggested Source

"X," The Sources of Soviet Conduct." *Foreign Affairs*, Vol XXV, July 1947, 566–582.

Kennan, George F. *Memoirs, 1925–1950.* Boston: Little, Brown, and Co., 1967, 364–367.

Note: Both articles can be found in Walter LaFeber, *America in the Cold War: Twenty Years of Revolution and Response 1947–1967.* New York: Wiley, 1969.

Helpful teacher sources include

Charles S. Maier, "Revisionism and the Interpretation of Cold War Origins," *Perspectives in American History IV*, 1970 Donald Fleming and Bernard Baily, eds. Cambridge, Mass.: Charles Warren Center for Studies in American History, Harvard University, 313–350.

Ernest R. May, *Lessons of the Past.* New York: Oxford University Press, 1973.

The Truman Doctrine

Part A.

Read the following document in preparation for a class discussion on this historic shift in U.S. foreign policy.

President Truman delivered this message to Congress on March 12, 1947.

The gravity of the situation which confronts the world today necessitates my appearance before a joint session of the Congress. The foreign policy and the national security of this country are involved.

One aspect of the present situation, which I wish to present to you at this time for your consideration and decision, concerns Greece and Turkey.

The United States has received from the Greek Government an urgent appeal for financial and economic assistance. Preliminary reports from the American Economic Mission now in Greece corroborate the statement of the Greek Government that assistance is imperative if Greece is to survive as a free nation.

I do not believe that the American people and the Congress wish to turn a deaf ear to the appeal of the Greek Government.

Greece is not a rich country. Lack of sufficient natural resources has always forced the Greek people to work hard to make both ends meet. Since 1940, this industrious, peace loving country has suffered invasion, four years of cruel enemy occupation, and bitter internal strife.

The very existence of the Greek state is today threatened by the terrorist activities of several thousand armed men, led by Communists, who defy the Government's authority at a number of points, particularly along the northern boundaries. A commission appointed by the United Nations Security Council is at present investigating disturbed conditions in Northern Greece and alleged border violations along the frontiers between Greece on the one hand and Albania, Bulgaria, and Yugoslavia on the other.

Meanwhile, the Greek Government is unable to cope with the situation. The Greek Army is small and poorly equipped. It needs supplies and equipment if it is to restore the authority to the Government throughout Greek territory.

Greece must have assistance if it is to become a self-supporting and self-respecting democracy. The United States must supply that assistance. We have already extended to Greece certain types of relief and economic aid but these are inadequate. There is no other country to which democratic Greece can turn. No other nation is willing and able to provide the necessary support for a democratic Greek Government.

The British Government, which has been helping Greece, can give no further financial or economic aid after March 31. Great Britain finds itself under the necessity of reducing or liquidating its commitments in several parts of the world, including Greece.

We have considered how the United Nations might assist in this crisis. But the situation is an urgent one requiring immediate action, and the United Nations and its related organizations are not in a position to extend help of the kind that is required.

It is important to note that the Greek Government has asked for our aid in utilizing effectively the financial and other assistance we may give to Greece, and in improving its public administration. It is of the utmost importance that we supervise the use of any funds made available to

Greece, in such a manner that each dollar spent will count toward making Greece self-supporting, and will help to build an economy in which a healthy democracy can flourish.

No government is perfect. One of the chief virtues of a democracy, however, is that its defects are always visible and under democratic processes can be pointed out and corrected. The Government of Greece is not perfect. Nevertheless, it represents 85 percent of the members of the Greek Parliament who were chosen in an election last year. Foreign observers, including 692 Americans, considered this election to be a fair expression of the views of the Greek people.

The Greek Government has been operating in an atmosphere of chaos and extremism. It has made mistakes. The extension of aid by this country does not mean that the United States condones everything that the Greek Government has done or will do. We have condemned in the past, and we condemn now, extremist measures of the right or left. We have in the past advised tolerance, and we advise tolerance now.

Greece's neighbor, Turkey, also deserves our attention. The future of Turkey as an independent and economically sound state is clearly no less important to the freedom-loving peoples of the world than the future of Greece. The circumstances in which Turkey finds itself today are considerably different from those of Greece. And during the war, the United States and Great Britain furnished Turkey with material aid. Nevertheless, Turkey now needs our support.

Since the war Turkey has sought financial assistance from Great Britain and the United States for the purpose of effecting that modernization necessary for the maintenance of its national integrity. That integrity is essential to the preservation of order in the Middle East.

The British Government has informed us that, owing to its own difficulties, it can no longer extend financial or economic aid to Turkey. As in the case of Greece, if Turkey is to have the assistance it needs, the United States must supply it. We are the only country able to provide that help.

I am fully aware of the broad implications involved if the United States extends assistance to Greece and Turkey, and I shall discuss these implications with you at this time.

One of the primary objectives of the foreign policy of the United States is the creation of conditions in which we and other nations will be able to work out a way of life free from coercion. This was a fundamental issue in the war with Germany and Japan. Our victory was won over countries which sought to impose their will, and their way of life, upon other nations.

To ensure the peaceful development of nations, free from coercion, the United States has taken a leading part in establishing the United Nations. The United Nations is designed to make possible lasting freedom and independence for all its members. We shall not realize our objectives, however, unless we are willing to help free people to maintain their free institutions and their national integrity against aggressive movements that seek to impose upon them totalitarian regimes. This is no more than a frank recognition that totalitarian regimes imposed on free peoples, by direct or indirect aggression, undermine the foundations of international peace and hence the security of the United States.

The peoples of a number of countries of the world have recently had totalitarian regimes forced upon them against their will. The Government of the United States has made frequent protests against coercion and intimidation, in violation of the Yalta Agreement, in Poland, Rumania and Bulgaria. I must also state that in a number of other countries there have been similar developments.

At the present moment in world history nearly every nation must choose between alternative ways of life. The choice is too often not a free one.

One way of life is based upon the will of the majority, and is distinguished by free institutions, representative government, free elections, guarantees of individual liberty, freedom of speech and religion, and freedom from political oppression.

The second way of life is based upon the will of a minority forcibly imposed upon the majority. It relies upon terror and oppression, a controlled press and radio, fixed elections, and the suppression of personal freedoms.

I believe that it must be the policy of the United States to support free peoples who are resisting attempted subjugation by armed minorities or by outside pressures.

I believe that we must assist free peoples to work out their own destinies in their own way.

I believe that our help should be primarily through economic and financial aid which is essential to economic stability and orderly political processes.

The world is not static, and the status quo is not sacred. But we cannot allow changes in the status quo in violation of the Charter of the United Nations by such methods as coercion, or by such subterfuges as political infiltration. In helping free and independent nations to maintain their freedom, the United States will be giving effect to the principles of the Charter of the United Nations.

It is necessary only to glance at a map to realize that the survival and integrity of the Greek nation are of grave importance in a much wider situation. If Greece should fall under the control of an armed minority, the effect upon its neighbor, Turkey, would be immediate and serious. Confusion and disorder might well spread throughout the entire Middle East.

Moreover, the disappearance of Greece as an independent state would have profound effect upon those countries in Europe whose peoples are struggling against great difficulties to maintain their freedoms and their independence while they repair the damages of war.

It would be an unspeakable tragedy if these countries, which have struggled so long against overwhelming odds, should lose that victory for which they sacrificed so much. Collapse of free institutions and loss of independence would be disastrous not only for them but for the world. Discouragement and possibly failure would quickly be the lot of neighboring peoples striving to maintain their freedom and independence.

Should we fail to aid Greece and Turkey in this fateful hour, the effect will be far reaching to the West as well as to the East. We must take immediate and resolute action.

I therefore ask the Congress to provide authority for assistance to Greece and Turkey in the amount of $400,000,000 for the period ending June 30, 1948. In requesting these funds, I have taken into consideration the maximum amount of relief assistance which would be furnished to Greece out of the $350,000,000 which I recently requested that the Congress authorize for the prevention of starvation and suffering in countries devastated by the war.

In addition to funds, I ask the Congress to authorize the detail of American civilian and military personnel to Greece and Turkey, at the request of those countries, to assist in the tasks of reconstruction, and for the purpose of supervising the use of such financial and material assistance as may be furnished. I recommend that authority also be provided for the instruction and training of selected Greek and Turkish personnel.

Finally, I ask that the Congress provide authority which will permit the speediest and most effective use, in terms of needed commodities, supplies, and equipment, of such funds as may be authorized.

If further funds, or further authority, should be needed for purposes indicated in this message, I shall not hesitate to bring the situation before the Congress. On this subject the Executive and Legislative branches of the Government must work together.

This is a serious course upon which we embark. I would not recommend it except that the alternative is much more serious.

The United States contributed $341,000,000,000 toward winning World War II. This is an investment in world freedom and world peace.

The assistance that I am recommending for Greece and Turkey amounts to little more than 1 tenth of 1 percent of this investment. It is only common sense that we should safeguard this investment and make sure that it was not in vain.

The seeds of totalitarian regimes are nurtured by misery and want. They spread and grow in the evil soil of poverty and strife. They reach their full growth when the hope of a people for a better life has died. We must keep that hope alive. The free peoples of the world look to us for support in maintaining their freedoms.

If we falter in our leadership, we may endanger the peace of the world—and we shall surely endanger the welfare of our own Nation.

Great responsibilities have been placed upon us by the swift movement of events. I am confident that the Congress will face these responsibilities squarely.[1]

[1] Harry S. Truman, as quoted in *The Record of American Diplomacy: Documents and Readings in the History of American Foreign Relations* (New York: Alfred A. Knopf, 1959), 723–727.

Part B.

Complete the following chart on subsequent U.S. foreign policy moves.

Event or circumstance	Appropriate U.S. action, according to the Truman Doctrine	Action taken
Communist Coup d'etat in Czechoslovakia, February 1948		
Soviet Blockade of West Berlin, June 1948		
China's fall to the Communists, late 1949		
North Korea's invasion across the 38th parallel, June 1950		

Part C.

To conclude the lesson, answer these questions.

1. What did the Truman administration set as its foreign policy goals?

2. To what extent were we able to carry out our foreign policy aims?

3. How often did we resort to the military solution as an expedient?

4. Was the Truman Doctrine too idealistic? Explain.

5. Some critics claim the Truman Doctrine put the United States on a path toward overestimating its ability to control foreign affairs and overcommitting its resources. To what extent do you agree with this assessment?

6. Would you have supported the Truman Doctrine in 1947?

7. To what extent do recent events in the former Soviet Union suggest that the United States may have operated under false assumptions in the years immediately after World War II?

Lesson 20
McCarthyism and the Climate of Fear

Objective
- To recognize long-term effects of McCarthyism and the Red Scare

Notes to the Teacher
The early years after World War II had been a unique time in American history. For four years the United States, with its sole possession of atomic power, dominated the world. Soviet testing of an atomic bomb in 1949 and a much more powerful hydrogen bomb in 1953 shattered Americans' sense of security and spurred an almost irrational fear of communism. The fall of China in 1949 heightened fear that something was drastically amiss in America. Perhaps there really were communists in high offices in America. Senator Joseph McCarthy achieved momentary power by exploiting this fear and riding its crest of popularity.

This lesson explores the climate that enabled a man like McCarthy to attain great power and notoriety. Prior to the lesson, students should review material in their textbook concerning the McCarthy Era and complete **Handout 23**. With this factual background, they are prepared for a group discussion on the best ways of promoting loyalty in America.

Procedure
1. Introduce the lesson using material in the Notes to the Teacher.

2. Have students complete **Handout 23** as a homework assignment.

3. Review their responses. Allow time for sharing and discussion.

    Suggested Responses:

    1. *He needed an issue for his reelection campaign.*

    2. *Klaus Fuchs, the Rosenbergs, and other convicted spies helped lend credence to the belief that our government was full of communists.*

3. *In times of uncertainty, we tend to believe the person who yells the loudest. McCarthy was in the right place at the right time, and people wanted to believe him.*

4. *It jeopardized personal rights by invading privacy and interfering with free expression of ideas.*

5. a. *26 May, 1938—House established Commission on Un-American activities to investigate anti-American organizations.*

    b. *28 June, 1940—Smith Act required all aliens in United States to register and made it illegal to advocate the overthrow of government by force.*

    c. *21 March, 1947—Executive Order 9835 established loyalty program and instituted procedures requiring investigation of people seeking government jobs.*

    d. *23 September, 1950—McCarran-Nixon Internal Security Act required communists to register with the government and established a subversive activities control board.*

7. *It reflects their constant belief in a communist threat.*

8. *The Senate investigated the army's charges that McCarthy had overstepped his bounds when he began to investigate army security and top-level army leaders after the army refused to give preferential treatment to one of McCarthy's assistants.*

9. *The televised Army-McCarthy hearings presented a clear contrast between the eloquent and persuasive reasoning of Joseph Welch, the army's attorney, and the irresponsible and savage charges of Joseph McCarthy. Senate censure soon followed.*

10. *Students' responses should recognize the impact of the breakup of the Soviet Empire.*

4. Divide the students into five groups, and assign one of the following questions to each group:

   a. What possible good resulted from the Red Scare?

   b. What lessons should we learn from the McCarthy experience?

   c. What if McCarthy had died during World War II?

   d. Was McCarthy a patriot?

   e. Were the Russians a real or an imaginary enemy in the early 1950s?

5. Select one member from each group to participate in a panel discussion of the following questions: What does it mean to be loyal in America? What are the best ways to promote loyalty?

McCarthyism

Complete the following questions in preparation for class activities on the McCarthy Era and the Red Scare.

1. What originally prompted Senator McCarthy to make his infamous speech claiming he held in his hand names of 205 known communists in the State Department?

2. We were sure that the Russians were not intelligent enough to build their own atomic bomb. We felt vindicated when Klaus Fuchs, the Rosenbergs and several others were convicted as spies. How did these events help/hurt the Red Scare mood?

3. After we found out that the Soviets had the atomic bomb, we became increasingly sensitive about threats to internal security. How did this feeling pave the way for McCarthy's Red Scare?

4. Did the Red Scare violate constitutional rights of American citizens? Explain your answer.

5. List and explain the four major pieces of anti-communist legislation.

6. To what extent were these laws effective in accomplishing their objectives?

7. Explain the American public's initial faith in McCarthy.

8. Why did the Senate hold the Army-McCarthy hearings in 1954?

9. How did the hearings lead to Senator McCarthy's downfall?

10. How does the media portray communism today?

Lesson 21
Korean Inquiry

Objective
- To analyze U.S. involvement in the Korean Conflict through a court of inquiry

Notes to the Teacher

The Korean Conflict is one of the least publicized and discussed wars in American history, save for the television series "M.A.S.H." Yet it was a direct expression of the Cold War and American policy towards the communistic Soviet Union and China.

At the conclusion of World War II, Korea, a former colony of Japan, was divided at the 38th parallel with North Korea controlled by the USSR and South Korea instituting an independent anti-communist government following UN-supervised elections. In June 1950, North Korea invaded South Korea. With the Soviet Union still boycotting the United Nations Security Council after its refusal to seat communist China, the Security Council was able to agree that the United Nations should send South Korea military support. The United Nations contingent, largely composed of American and South Korean forces, was headed by General Douglas MacArthur. After heavy initial losses, the UN counterattack drove the North Koreans back and pursued them considerably beyond the 38th parallel. The communist Chinese entry into the war at that point set the stage for the drama that soon unfolded between President Truman and General MacArthur.

Students role-play a board of inquiry to investigate the Truman-MacArthur conflict. After the class presentations, students conclude the lesson by evaluating the actions of both Truman and MacArthur.

Procedure

1. Introduce the lesson using material in the Notes to the Teacher.

2. On the day prior to discussion of the lesson, introduce the lesson, divide the class into their respective groups, and direct them to complete part A of **Handout 24** for homework in preparation for the board of inquiry in class on the following day. Seat students in their respective groups.

3. Explain the procedure.

   A board of inquiry is operated by military procedure involving a prosecutor, a legal officer, and panel of judges (all officers). Unlike civil courts, the defendant is presumed guilty until proven innocent.

4. Select one prosecutor, one president, one general, a timer, and five officers of the court. Allow five to ten minutes for immediate preparation.

5. Have students role-play the Court of Inquiry investigating MacArthur's role. Include the judges' verdict.

6. Repeat procedure 4, having a new group role-play an investigation of Truman's role.

7. Conclude by having students evaluate the actions of the United Nations, President Truman, and General MacArthur by completing part B of **Handout 24**. Be sure to debrief this writing activity to be sure that students recognize that the UN's mission was necessarily a limited one and that in this country the president has a constitutional role as Commander-in-Chief.

Investigating the Truman-MacArthur Conflict

Part A.

Use your text and other sources to research the following questions. Specialize in those relevant to your assigned role as President, General, or prosecutor.

President Truman

1. What is your policy toward Russia and China?

2. Why did you involve the United Nations in the Korean conflict?

3. Were you pleased with General MacArthur's action in Korea? Why or why not?

4. Why were you so cautious about an all-out war with China?

5. Why did you choose to fire MacArthur? Did you have any other options?

6. Why were you concerned about Formosa?

7. Why did you insist that the war be limited?

General MacArthur

1. What were your duties as Supreme Commander in Korea?

2. When you found yourself in trouble at Pusan, what did you do?

3. Why were you so sure the Chinese would not cross the Yalu River?

4. Who do you think should have ultimate control of war strategy, the military or politicians? Why?

5. What was your policy toward Asia?

6. How was your attitude concerning Asian policy received by our Allies?

7. What led you to believe you knew more than the president about affairs in Asia?

Part B.

To conclude the lesson, draw conclusions about the actions of President Truman, General MacArthur, and the United Nations by responding to the following questions. *In each case, be sure to explain your reasoning.*

1. What was the role of the United Nations in Korea?

2. Was the United Nations justified in attacking North Korea?

3. Was Truman right in firing MacArthur?

4. Was MacArthur a patriot or a rebel?

5. Did he try to usurp presidential prerogative?

6. Whose strategy was better, the president's or the general's?

7. Should the United Nations chalk up the experience in Korea as a victory?

Lesson 22
Economic Recovery after World War II

Objectives

- To analyze President Truman's postwar wage-price policy

- To use statistics as a basis for hypotheses about the U.S. economy through the Truman and Eisenhower administrations

Notes to the Teacher

With the conclusion of World War II, economists expected the United States to experience another depression. The Truman administration struggled to achieve a balance of federal control with free collective bargaining. The policies were inadequate, and massive labor strikes ensued. Yet the result was not a depression, but unprecedented economic development.

President Eisenhower's "Modern Republicanism" attempted to reduce the growth of the federal government and promote new and stronger forms of government-business cooperation. Recognizing the popularity of Social Security, the minimum wage, unemployment insurance, and labor and farm programs, Eisenhower made no attempt to undo those programs, but he did try to lower taxes for industries and capital, and he lifted Korean War wage and price controls. The theme of Eisenhower's approach might be best characterized by the comment of his defense secretary, Charles Wilson, during his confirmation hearings: "What is good for our country is good for General Motors, and vice versa."

In this lesson, students integrate several basic economic concepts into their study of history. The lesson's activities require students to use both readings and statistics to evaluate the successes and failures of early postwar economic policies.

Procedure

1. Introduce the lesson using information in the Notes to the Teacher.

2. Have students complete part A of **Handout 25**. Conduct a discussion based on students' responses.

Suggested Responses, Part A:

1. *Dangers of inflation, deflation, depression, commodity shortages, widespread labor strikes*

2. *Continuation of New Deal approach; reliance on cooperation of labor and management; necessity of compromise with demands of labor and management*

3. *Ambiguous; acceptance of fact that controls were not furthering stabilization; reliance on the people to resist inflation; leaving collective bargaining in the hands of labor and management; perhaps Truman simply did not know what to do with the economic situation; no evidence of certainty of economic success*

3. Emphasize that, at the close of 1946, it was not clear whether or not the United States could convert to peacetime economy without either extreme inflation or deflation, either of which would almost certainly lead to depression.

4. Have students complete part B of **Handout 25**. (Be sure to review the terms GNP, GNP per capita, and unemployment rate.)

5. Conduct a discussion based on the handout questions.

Suggested Responses, Part B:

1. *Statistics suggest increasing prosperity but also increased cost of living.*

2. *Compared to prewar circumstances, America was affluent. Note rising salaries, GNP, and automobile ownership, as well as low unemployment rate.*

3. *Parallel rising cost of living suggests continuous inflation, limiting real value of increased income.*

6. Have students read sections in their textbooks describing the U.S. economy from 1945 to 1960. Conduct a brief discussion comparing and contrasting students' evaluations based on **Handout 25** with the text's generalizations.

125

Postwar Wage-Price Policy

Part A.

Read the following postwar wage-price policy statements and answer the questions.

In August 1945, President Truman began his plan for reconversion from wartime economy with the Stabilization Act:

> Our national welfare requires that during the reconversion period production of civilian goods and services go forward without interruption, and that labor and industry cooperate to keep strikes and lockouts at a minimum.
>
> 1. In the near future I shall call a conference of representatives of organized labor and industry, for the purpose of working out by agreement means to minimize the interruption of production by labor disputes in the reconversion period.
>
> 2. Pending the completion of the conference and until some new plan is worked out and made effective, disputes which cannot be settled by collective bargaining and conciliation, including disputes which threaten a substantial interference with the transition to a peacetime economy, should be handled by the War Labor Board under existing procedures. For that interim period I call upon representatives of organized labor and industry to renew their no-strike and no-lockout pledges. . . .
>
> 3. . . . wage adjustments which might affect prices must continue to be subject to stabilization controls. With the ending of war production, however, there is no longer any threat of an inflationary bidding up of wage rates by competition in a short labor market. I am therefore authorizing the War Labor Board to release proposed voluntary wage increases from the necessity of approval upon condition that they will not be used in whole or in part as the basis for seeking an increase in price ceilings. Proposed wage increases requiring price relief must continue to be passed upon by the Board.[1]

Early in October, Secretary of the Treasury, Fred M. Vinson, warned:

> During the coming year we shall find ourselves in a somewhat paradoxical situation. The rate of government expenditures—and particularly those expenditures which find their way currently into the pockets of consumers—will be declining rapidly. Millions of workers will be laid off and forced to seek new jobs. As the labor market loosens, the workers' total income will decline. Overtime pay will rapidly diminish. Many workers who have been promoted to well-paid classifications will find themselves reclassified into less remunerative jobs. Workers, in many instances, will have to move long distances in search of new jobs. In many States, unemployment compensation, under existing legislation, will not prove adequate to sustain mass purchasing power.[2]

He went on to note the imperative of avoiding both inflation and deflation.

---

[1] Harry S Truman, as quoted in *The Truman Administration: A Documentary History*, ed. Barton J. Bernstein and Allen J. Matusow (New York: Harper & Row, 1966), 48–49.

[2] Fred M. Vinson, as quoted in *The Truman Administration: A Documentary History*, 49.

At the end of October, under pressure from labor conflicts, President Truman modified his wage-price program. He stated:

> Like most of you, I have been disturbed by the labor difficulties of recent weeks. These difficulties stand in the way of reconversion; they postpone the day when our veterans and displaced war workers can get back into good peacetime jobs. We need more of the good sense, the reasonableness, the consideration for the position of the other fellow, the teamwork which we had during the war. . . .
>
> I am convinced that we must get away as quickly as possible from Government controls, and that we must get back to the free operation of our competitive system. Where wages are concerned, this means that we must get back to free and fair collective bargaining.
>
> As a free people, we must have the good sense to bargain peaceably and sincerely. We must be determined to reach decisions based upon our long-range interest . . .
>
> If management does grant a wage increase, it is not prevented from coming in thereafter and requesting Government approval to have the wage increase considered for purposes of increasing prices. Whether such approval is sought before or after the wage increase is given, it receives the same consideration. . . .
>
> The second point is new and is very important. It is something which I am sure will help industry get over this very difficult period of readjustment. In cases where no approval of the wage increase has been requested by management, or even where a request has been made and denied by the Government, industry will not be asked by the Government to take an unreasonable chance in absorbing such wage increases. After a reasonable test period which, save in exceptional cases, will be six months, if the industry has been unable to produce at a fair profit, the entire wage increase will be taken into account in passing upon applications for price ceiling increases.
>
> The Office of Price Administration will have to give its prompt consideration to all applications for price increases.
>
> This is your Government's wage-price policy. For the time being, the machinery that administers it will remain the same as during the war.
>
> But, as you know, I have called a conference here in Washington of the representatives of management and labor. It will start next week.[3]

During January, 1946, the labor situation worsened. Three-quarters of a million steelworkers went on strike. Also striking were meat packers, electrical workers, and employees of General Motors. On February 14, President Truman again altered his stabilization program:

> I am now modifying our wage-price policy to permit wage increases within certain limits and to permit any industry placed in a hardship position by an approved increase to seek price adjustments without waiting until the end of a six months' test period, as previously required. . . .
>
> I am authorizing the National Wage Stabilization Board to approve any wage or salary increase, or part thereof, which is found to be consistent with the general pattern of wage or salary adjustments established in the industry or local labor market area . . . provision is made for the approval of increases found necessary to eliminate gross inequities as between related industries, plants, or job classifications, or to correct substandards of living, or to correct disparities between the increase in wage or salary rates. . . .[4]

[3] Harry S Truman, as quoted in *The Truman Administration: A Documentary History*, 53, 55–56.

[4] *The Truman Administration: A Documentary History*, 66–67.

Finally, shortly after the 1946 elections, Truman announced:

> There is no virtue in control for control's sake. When it becomes apparent that controls are not furthering the purposes of the stabilization laws but would, on the contrary, tend to defeat these purposes, it becomes the duty of the Government to drop the controls. . . .
>
> . . . some shortages remain and some prices will advance sharply when controls are removed. We have, however, already seen what consumer resistance can do to excessive prices. The consumers of America know that if they refuse to pay exorbitant prices, prices will come down. . . .
>
> Today's action places squarely upon management and labor the responsibility for working out agreements for the adjustment of their differences without interruption of production.[5]

Answer the following questions:

1. What economic dangers did the United States face at the conclusion of World War II?

2. How would you characterize Truman's wage-price policies?

3. Do Truman's comments in November 1946, reflect optimism or pessimism? Explain your position.

[5] *The Truman Administration: A Documentary History*, 84–85.

Part B

Examine the following statistics and reading as indicators of the American experience through the Truman and Eisenhower administrations and then answer the questions.

	1940	1947	1949	1951	1953	1955	1957	1959
Life expectancy at birth	62.9	66.8	68.0	68.4	68.8	69.6	69.5	69.6
GNP	43.9	74.6	79.1	85.6	88.3	90.9	97.5	101.6
GNP per capita	754	1,605	1,719	2,129	2,286	2,408	2,576	2,731
Average annual income of a full-time employee	1,299	2,589	2,844	3,217	3,581	3,851	4,230	4,594
Average annual income of a full-time railroad worker	1,906	3,211	3,703	4,161	4,415	4,697	5,416	6,054
Average annual income of a full-time employee in health services	927	1,821	1,912	2,099	2,335	2,497	2,660	2,907
Average annual income of a nonsalaried dentist	3,281 (for 1941)	6,610	7,146	7,820	10,873 (for 1952)	12,480	14,311	—
Retail price of one pound of bread	0.08	0.12	0.14	0.16	0.16	0.18	0.19	0.20
Retail price of one pound of round steak	0.36	0.76	0.85	1.09	0.92	0.90	0.94	1.07
Percentage of families owning at least one car	—	—	56%	60%	61%	70%	75%	74%
Unemployment rate	14.6	3.9	5.9	3.3	2.9	4.4	4.3	5.5

Table 22.1. *Historical Statistics of the United States: Colonial Times to 1970.* U.S. Department of Commerce, Bureau of the Census, 1975.

> The Bureau of Labor Statistics in 1950 calculated that a family income of $3,717 was necessary to maintain a family of four on a "modest but adequate" budget.
>
> In 1935–36 this poorest one-fifth of the families had received just 4.1 per cent of the total family income, and the richest one-fifth had received 51.7 per cent. In 1950 the percentages stood at 4.8 and 45.7, respectively, and by 1958 they were 4.7 and 45.5. The distribution of personal income had actually changed very little. The improvement in the living standard of the poorest one-fifth came about because total income increased tremendously rather than because they got a significantly larger share of this total.
>
> Furthermore, personal income was not regionally well distributed. In 1959 the per capita personal income of the entire United States (total of personal income divided by population) was $2,166. In other words, the mythical average American family received that amount for each family member. State figures showed a great diversity: Connecticut, $2,817; California, $2,661; New York, $2,736; South Dakota, $1,476; Mississippi, $1,162.[6]

1. How would you describe the U.S. economy between World War II and 1960? Cite specific evidence to support your conclusions.

2. In 1958, John Kenneth Galbraith's *The Affluent Society* was published. Was he correct in describing the United States of that period as "affluent"? Support your answer.

3. Pinpoint economic and social dangers suggested by the statistics.

4. How would you rate the overall effectiveness of President Truman's economic policies? Of President Eisenhower's economic programs?

5. What advice would President Truman and President Eisenhower have given to President Kennedy regarding the economy as he entered the presidency?

[6] David A. Shannon, *20th Century America: World War II and Since,* 3rd ed. (Chicago: Rand McNally College Publishing Company, 1974), 143.

Lesson 23
The New Frontier and Great Society

Objective
* To identify and analyze New Frontier and Great Society programs as logical successors to the New Deal

Notes to the Teacher
In the presidential campaign of 1960, John F. Kennedy challenged Americans to commit themselves to a new, active participation in their country. Kennedy, in his skillful presentation of facts and figures, proposed a "New Frontier" characterized by vigor, direction, and adventure. The effectiveness of his administration was limited by his assassination in 1963.

Lyndon Johnson, determined to use to advantage the public's grief over the assassination, pushed hard to secure passage of programs for which Kennedy had fought. His skills as a politician brought early successes, including passage of the Civil Rights Act, the Voting Rights Act, and Medicare. Johnson's own vision of a Great Society began to emerge, but, unfortunately, the war in Vietnam began to consume most of the public's attention and resources in the later years of his administration.

Students complete a homework assignment outlining domestic accomplishments of the Kennedy and Johnson administrations. In class, small groups analyze those administrations and write a concluding paragraph to an essay they might have written linking Kennedy's New Frontier and Johnson's Great Society to the New Deal of Franklin Roosevelt.

Procedure
1. Introduce the topic using material in the Notes to the Teacher.

2. Assign part A of **Handout 26** for homework. Suggested answers may be found on the chart at the end of this section on procedure.

3. In class, assign students to small groups to consider the issues in part B of **Handout 26** and to write the concluding paragraph indicated in part C. Even though students have not written the essay, they will need to have a clear idea of the thesis and supporting evidence they would have chosen in order to write a perceptive and interpretive conclusion.

4. Have small groups share the finished conclusions. Ask the class to evaluate the conclusions both for their interpretations of the two presidencies and for their effectiveness as essay conclusions. Conclusions should go beyond mere summary to a statement of the significance of the topic and/or its historical impact.

Suggested Responses, Part B:
1. *Students' responses should recognize the commitment of all to "promote the general welfare."*

2. a. *Roosevelt's concept of "promoting the general welfare" meant, in large part, helping the unfortunate deal with the Depression.*

   b. *Kennedy would have accepted that responsibility but also saw a need to help the victims of discrimination.*

   c. *Johnson saw still more subtle discrimination of other groups, e.g. the elderly, recent immigrants, and those unable to secure quality education.*

3. *One (of many) assumptions was that "general welfare" required more than monetary support.*

4. *Televised broadcasts of peaceful protests of African-Americans, books such as* The Other America *by Michael Harrington and* A Nation of Immigrants *by John F. Kennedy, television specials on the needs of particular groups, and the example of foreign countries all helped to suggest needed reforms.*

5. *They all attempt to deal with the concerns of less affluent Americans.*

6. *Kennedy and Johnson recognized that money alone would not bring peace, justice, and security for all Americans.*

7. In Roosevelt's case, the Depression and increasing concerns about the war in Europe were limiting factors. Kennedy's assassination and the war in Vietnam hurt the later administrations.

8. Coherence may be less obvious than in the New Deal, but Kennedy and Johnson tried to bring justice to victims of discrimination and "hidden poverty" while trying, at the same time, to guarantee security and education for all.

10. Answers should reflect that the civil rights legislation, Medicare, Immigration Act, and federal aid to education have become permanent features of America's concept of justice.

Sample Chart, Handout 26, Part A:

New Frontier

Program	Provisions	Impact
Manpower Development and Training Act (1962)	Retrained farmers and chronically unemployed farmers	Provided opportunities for the very poor to become self-sustaining
Nuclear Test Ban Treaty (1963)	United States and Soviet Union banned nuclear tests in the atmosphere	Helped to increase security for all Americans
Space Program	In 1961, Kennedy committed United States to putting man on moon by 1970.	Allowed United States to take the lead from Russia in space program
Medical Retardation and Health Centers Act (1963)	Provided funds for research and treatment	Gave needed support for a group unable to speak for themselves

Sample Chart, Handout 26, Part A:

Great Society

Program	Provisions	Impact
Civil Rights Act (1964)	Banned discrimination in jobs, public hotels and restaurants, and voting	Marked the first legislative success of the Civil Rights Movement
Economic Opportunities Act (1964)	Funded a variety of "war on poverty" programs, including the Job Corps, VISTA, HeadStart, Upward Bound, Neighborhood Youth Corps, and College Work Study	Solved few problems because the war in Vietnam required an increasingly large share of national budget
Voting Rights Act (1965)	Allowed for federal registering of voters and federal monitoring of elections and outlawed literacy tests	Strengthened earlier voting laws designed to guarantee voting rights for African-Americans
"Medicare" Act (1965)	Provided federal funding for medical care for the elderly under Social Security	Removed a major inequity in health care
Elementary and Secondary Education Act (1965)	Federal funds given to public schools and funds for instructional materials supplied to public, private, and parochial schools	Helped to increase educational opportunity, particularly for poorer areas
Higher Education Act (1965)	Provided federal funding for student loans and college construction	Helped to make college education affordable for less affluent students
Appalachian Development Act (1965)	Supplied federal funds for a particularly depressed area	New roads, land improvement, and new health centers in the area
Immigration Act (1965)	Gave priority to keeping families together and promoting national needs	Eliminated discrimination based on national origin
Demonstration Cities Act (1966)	Provided funds for rebuilding deteriorated urban areas	Aimed to inspire creativity in solving tough urban problems
Civil Rights Act (1968)	Banned racial discrimination in the sale and rental of housing	Helped to integrate some neighborhoods

The New Frontier and Great Society

Part A.

For homework, complete the following chart on domestic aspects of the New Frontier and Great Society. You will use your completed chart as a resource for an in-class activity.

New Frontier

Program	Provisions	Impact
Manpower Development and Training Act (1962)		
Nuclear Test Ban Treaty (1963)		
Space Program		
Medical Retardation and Health Centers Act (1963)		

Note: Kennedy proposals not enacted before his assassination but enacted later:

- Federal aid to elementary and secondary education
- Medicare
- Voting rights and equal treatment for African-Americans in public accommodations

Great Society

Program	Provisions	Impact
Civil Rights Act (1964)		
Economic Opportunities Act (1964)		
Voting Rights Act (1965)		
"Medicare" Act (1965)		
Elementary and Secondary Education Act (1965)		
Higher Education Act (1965)		
Appalachian Development Act (1965)		
Immigration Act (1965)		
Demonstration Cities Act (1966)		
Civil Rights Act (1968)		

Part B.

In your groups, discuss the following issues related to the New Frontier and Great Society. Perhaps looking ahead to the concluding activity will help you to focus your thinking as you answer the questions below.

1. Is it reasonable to draw parallels between the programs of Franklin Roosevelt, John F. Kennedy, and Lyndon Johnson? Why, or why not?

2. State as succinctly as you can the political philosophy of each president:

   a. Franklin Roosevelt

   b. John F. Kennedy

   c. Lyndon Johnson

3. What new assumptions did Kennedy and Johnson make about the proper role of government?

4. What evidence existed that government needed to assume new responsibilities?

5. How are the programs of the three men similar?

6. How do the visions of Kennedy and Johnson differ from the vision of Roosevelt?

7. What factors limited the possibilities for success for each man?

8. What evidence is there of coherence in the New Frontier and Great Society?

9. What strengths do you see in the programs of Kennedy and Johnson?

10. What has been the impact of the New Frontier and Great Society?

Part C.

To conclude the lesson, assume you have written a journal article exploring links between the New Deal, New Frontier, and Great Society. Write the concluding paragraph of that article.

Lesson 24
Vietnam—A Reappraisal

Objective
- To gain background in the history of U.S. involvement in Vietnam

Notes to the Teacher
Vietnamese struggles for freedom from foreign domination date back nearly two thousand years to the earliest Chinese domination. The French annexed Indochina in the nineteenth century and held it until it was overrun by the Japanese in World War II. A Moscow-trained communist, Ho Chi Minh, created an independence movement, the Viet Minh, to fight against Japan. He soon controlled large areas in the northern part of the country. When the French returned to Indochina following the war, they found northern Vietnam ruled by an elected coalition under a military government.

In 1946, France began an eight-year struggle to reestablish control over all of Indochina. Military superiority enabled the French to gain control of cities and major roads, but the Vietnamese maintained control of villages and hamlets. Three years into the war, the introduction of communist Chinese aid threatened to turn the struggle from a war to preserve French colonialism to a fight against Chinese communism.

Fears of the potential domino effect prompted the United States to support the French. Despite U.S. contributions of nearly one billion dollars in military aid, the French suffered a humiliating defeat at Dienbienphu in 1954. Even increasing military and economic support to South Vietnam did not help. By 1968, after the assistance of 500,000 American troops and a thirty billion dollar military commitment, the South Vietnamese were no nearer victory over the communist Vietcong.

In this lesson, which is intended as an introduction to the war, students create a connection map to help them understand relationships among key personalities and events of this increasingly distant chapter in American history. The connection map helps students to ask perceptive questions and make generalizations about American involvement in the war.

Procedure
1. Introduce the topic using material in the Notes to the Teacher.
2. Distribute **Handout 27** and have students work in small groups to create connection maps. Taking time to review the maps in class helps students realize that there is no single "right" way to view the connections and that creative structures lead to different questions.

Suggested Responses:

1. *Escalation refers to the increasing U.S. military and economic support for the South Vietnamese.*

2. *Ho Chi Minh was the communist North Vietnamese leader.*

3. *Dienbienphu was the disastrous rout of the French by the Vietnamese in 1954.*

4. *Geneva Agreements (1954), which neither the United States nor South Vietnam signed, provided for division of Indochina into four states: neutral Laos and Cambodia; communist North Vietnam; and French-sponsored anti-communist South Vietnam. The 17th parallel would be the dividing line between the two Vietnams, and a vote for a single Vietnamese government was to be held by 1956.*

5. *The Gulf of Tonkin Resolution gave almost unanimous support to President Johnson to make an air strike against North Vietnam after they torpedoed American destroyers patrolling international waters in the Gulf.*

6. *Viet Cong were Vietnamese communists.*

7. *Vietnamization refers to President Nixon's policy of trying to shift the burden of carrying on the war to the South Vietnamese.*

8. *Tet Offensive refers to the major offensive the North Vietnamese mounted at the time of the Vietnamese New Year in 1968. This came as a shock to Americans who had just been told by the American general in command that we were finally winning the war.*

9. Domino theory refers to the assumption that the fall of one country in an area to communism would lead to the fall of nearby countries as well.

10. Draft evaders were those Americans opposed to the war who fled to other countries rather than fight what they believed to be an immoral war.

11. The Laotian and Cambodian incursions were made by the South Vietnamese with American support in 1970 to disrupt supply lines and destroy North Vietnamese bases in those "neutral" countries.

12. Hawks were Americans who supported the war.

13. Doves opposed American involvement.

14. Anti-war protesters staged a variety of demonstrations as it became increasingly clear that the United States would not win the war and that the government had lied to the public about our involvement.

15. Daniel Ellsberg's release of the secret Pentagon Papers to the New York Times revealed to the public that the war had been based on faulty assumptions and that the government had lied about our involvement in the war.

16. Nixon Doctrine was the president's assertion that in the future this country would honor treaty commitments to Asian countries, including military and economic aid, but could not be expected to supply troops for their wars.

17. After a North Vietnamese invasion of South Vietnam, President Nixon responded by ordering the most potent air strike in history on points throughout the country, including Hanoi, the capital, and the port of Haiphong.

18. Secretary of State Henry Kissinger acted as negotiator for the United States in peace talks. He later shared a Nobel Peace Prize with the North Vietnamese negotiator for his role in bringing the war to a close.

19. POWs, or prisoners of war, were a major reason the United States continued to fight long after it became clear that we would not win.

20. Revelations of the U.S. massacre of 300 persons, mostly women and children, in the little South Vietnamese village of My Lai, which had been reported to harbor Viet Cong, did much to fuel anti-war protest in this country.

21. Saigon was the South Vietnamese capital.

22. Paris Peace Agreement provided for a cease-fire, return of American POWs and full accounting for the missing in action, withdrawal of U.S. forces, withdrawal of troops from Laos and Cambodia, and reunification of Vietnam only by peaceful means.

23. Reunification came by consolidation of North Vietnamese control over the entire country.

24. Hanoi was the North Vietnamese capital during the war and is now the capital of the reunited Vietnam.

25. Nguyen Van Thieu was military dictator and, the Viet Cong said, the American government's puppet leader of South Vietnam from 1967 to 1975.

Students' completion of the connection map will, of course, vary. They may categorize in many ways. One possibility might include causes of the war, escalation of the war, persons with conflicting viewpoints on the war, gradual withdrawal of this country from the war, and effects of the war. Students' questions will depend on their categorization, but they might ask questions about why it took so long for the withdrawal, how anti-war protests led to divisiveness, why several administrations managed to mislead the public for so long, or how the peace agreement changed American thinking about U.S. foreign policy.

3. Conclude by asking students to make generalizations about our involvement in the longest war in American history and our subsequent defeat.

Vietnam—A Reappraisal

It is easy to get lost in a maze of facts when studying complex issues. One way to avoid this is to undertake the challenging task of creating a connection map. Listed below are key terms often used in a discussion of America's role in the Vietnam War. Undoubtedly, you have heard many of them discussed in various contexts in the news. Your first task is to make sure that you know the meaning of each one.

The next task is to complete the visual that follows to help you see key relationships. The connection map has a central box for the topic, the Vietnam War. Around it are six boxes for categorizing key ideas related to the central theme. After you have categorized in one box, write 3–7 words along the arrow of your map. These words should make a meaningful sentence, starting with the topic, and ending with the terms in the outer box. Now ask a question beginning *Why?* or *How?* above your statement. Follow the same procedure for categorizing other terms and writing perceptive questions. Where would you find answers to your questions?

Terms

1. escalation
2. Ho Chi Minh
3. Dienbienphu
4. Geneva Agreements (1954)
5. Gulf of Tonkin Resolution
6. Viet Cong
7. Vietnamization
8. Tet Offensive
9. Domino theory
10. draft evaders
11. Cambodian and Laotian incursions
12. hawks
13. doves
14. anti-war protesters
15. Pentagon Papers
16. Nixon Doctrine
17. bombing of Hanoi and Haiphong
18. Henry Kissinger
19. POWs
20. My Lai Massacre
21. Saigon
22. Paris Peace Agreement
23. Reunification
24. Hanoi
25. Nguyen Van Thieu

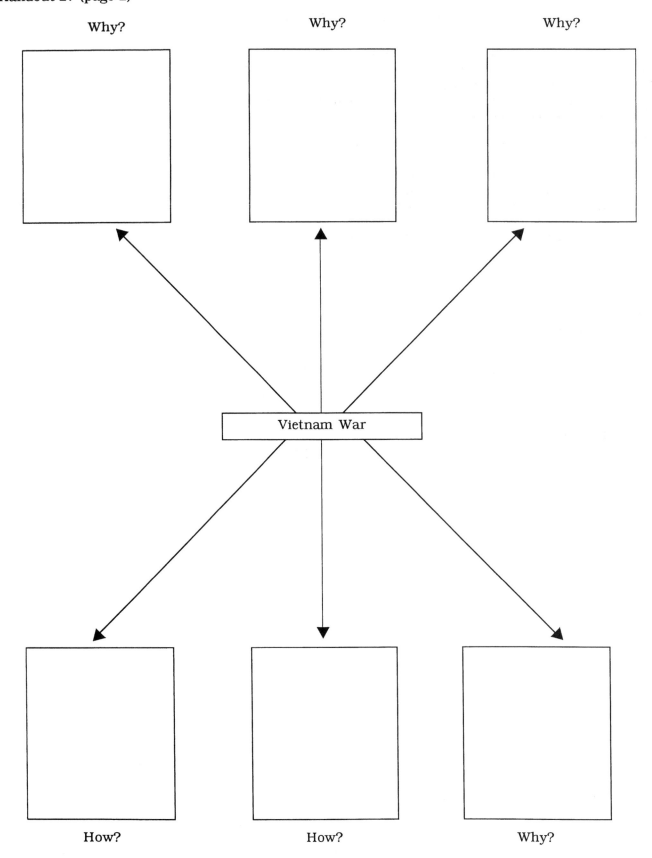

Why?

Why?

Why?

Vietnam War

How?

How?

Why?

Lesson 25
The Black Revolution—
Where Do We Go from Here?

Objectives
- To identify significant individuals and their accomplishments in the Civil Rights Movement

- To analyze forces responsible for advances in the liberation of African Americans

Notes to the Teacher

The tumultuous decades of the 1950s and 1960s literally revolutionized American society, as black and white leaders joined forces to confront institutionalized racism. The Supreme Court decision in *Brown v. Board of Education of Topeka* paved the way for desegregation of public schools, first in the South and then in the North as well. With this significant step toward equality, the Civil Rights Movement quickly gained momentum. Direct action, in the form of boycotts, sit-ins, and marches, helped bring major advances, including the Civil Rights Act of 1964 and the Voting Rights Act of 1965. At that point the Civil Rights Movement reached a critical juncture where unity on the best approach for the future quickly dissolved. Some favored continuation of the peaceful approaches that had brought gains in the past; others argued that only a new militancy would address the frustration of young urban blacks.

In this lesson, individual students adopt the perspective of one of twelve African-American leaders as they debate the future of the Civil Rights Movement in the critical year, 1966. For homework, they research the position of that individual, participate in a round table discussion on the future direction of the Movement, and conclude by writing their own analysis of the most effective steps the movement might have taken in 1966.

Procedure
1. Assign each student one of the twelve roles indicated on **Handout 28**, and have students complete the required research for homework.

2. Begin by reviewing the following key events in the progress for civil rights for African Americans:

   Plessy v. Ferguson, 1896—("Separate but equal" is constitutional.)

   Brown v. Board of Education of Topeka, 1954—("Separate but equal" is inherently unequal and, therefore, unconstitutional.)

   Civil Rights Act of 1957—(*It established a Commission on Civil Rights to investigate and report on situations involving unconstitutional treatment, especially deprivation of the right to vote.*)

   Civil Rights Act of 1964—(*It required equal access in public facilities, school desegregation, and equal employment opportunities.*)

   Voting Rights Act of 1965—(*This act permitted the Attorney General to register voters in areas where discriminatory practices, such as literacy tests and poll taxes, had been used to keep African Americans from voting. It also permitted him to file suits challenging the constitutionality of state poll taxes.*)

3. Allow each student to make his or her prepared remarks to the round table group. (If more than one student has been assigned the same individual, allow pairs to make the presentation together.) Students should take notes during the presentations. At the conclusion of the reports, allow students two or three minutes to prepare two perceptive questions they would like to ask others represented at the round table discussion. Reconvene the round table for this discussion.

Suggested Responses:

1. James Baldwin was an influential African-American writer not attached to a specific organization.

2. *Eldridge Cleaver was an officer in the Black Panther Party and author of* Soul on Ice.

3. *Rosa Parks, who refused to give up her seat to a white man, sparked the successful 1955 Montgomery bus boycott.*

4. *Martin Luther King, Jr., head of the Southern Christian Leadership Conference, won a Nobel Peace Prize for his advocacy of nonviolent protest in behalf of civil rights.*

5. *Roy Wilkins, leader of the N.A.A.C.P., opposed violence and separation. His organization works primarily through the courts.*

6. *James Farmer headed the Congress of Racial Equality and organized the freedom rides.*

7. *Stokely Carmichael was an advocate of Black Power. In 1966, he headed the Student Nonviolent Coordinating Committee, but he later rejected nonviolence.*

8. *Whitney Young, Executive Director of the National Urban League, opposed both violence and separation.*

9. *James Forman wrote the* Black Manifesto *and declared a willingness to fight against whites. He demanded financial reparations to African Americans.*

10. *Huey Newton, a revolutionary in the Black Panther Party, proposed socialism.*

11. *Elijah Muhammad was a Black Muslim leader who advocated a separate black territory in the United States and associated whites with the devil.*

12. *Floyd McKissack, leader of the Congress of Racial Equality, advocated Black Power.*

4. At the conclusion of the round table discussion, ask each student to respond in writing to this question: What would have been the best strategy for African-American leaders to have adopted in 1966 to continue progress toward equality? Explain your rationale for this approach.

5. Have students share their responses, and have the class critique their suggested approaches.

The Black Revolution—Where Do We Go From Here?

The year 1966 marked a critical turning point in the Civil Rights Movement. In that year Stokely Carmichael made the following remark in a publication of the Student Non-Violent Coordinating Committee:

> One of the tragedies of the struggle against racism is that up to now there has been no national organization which could speak to the growing militancy of young black people in the urban ghetto. There has been only a civil rights movement, whose tone of voice was adapted to an audience of liberal whites. It served as a sort of buffer zone between them and angry young blacks. None of its so-called leaders could go into a rioting community and be listened to. In a sense, I blame ourselves—together with the mass media—for what has happened in Watts, Harlem, Chicago, Cleveland, Omaha. Each time the people in those cities saw Martin Luther King get slapped, they became angry; when they saw four little black girls bombed to death, they were angrier; and when nothing happened, they were steaming. We had nothing to offer that they could see, except to go out and be beaten again. We helped to build their frustration.
>
> For too many years, black Americans marched and had their heads broken and got shot. They were saying to the country, "Look, you guys are supposed to be nice guys and we are only going to do what we are supposed to do—why do you beat us up, why don't you give us what we ask, why don't you straighten yourselves out?" After years of this, we are at almost the same point—because we demonstrated from a position of weakness. We cannot be expected any longer to march and have our heads broken in order to say to whites: come on, you're nice guys. For you are not nice guys. We have found you out.[1]

Research your assigned civil rights leader from the list below in preparation for a round table discussion of the best direction for the Civil Rights Movement to take. You will assume the perspective of that person in the class discussion. Be prepared to address the seven points listed in your opening remarks to the group. After those presentations you will have a chance to write two questions to ask individual panelists during the discussion of strategies for the future.

Panelists

1. James Baldwin
2. Eldridge Cleaver
3. Rosa Parks
4. Martin Luther King, Jr.
5. Roy Wilkins
6. James Farmer
7. Stokely Carmichael
8. Whitney Young
9. James Forman
10. Huey Newton
11. Elijah Muhammad
12. Floyd McKissack

[1] Stokely Carmichael, as quoted in Leon Friedman, ed., *The Civil Rights Reader: Basic Documents of the Civil Rights Movement* (New York: Walker and Company, 1967), 139.

Questions

1. Identify your position in the Civil Rights Movement and state what you see as the biggest accomplishment of the Civil Rights Movement to date.

2. What role did you (or your organization) play in achieving that breakthrough?

3. What is your first priority for the Movement at this point?

4. What strategy will be most likely to effect that change?

5. Is violence justified at this point? Explain your reasoning.

6. What is your position on segregation as opposed to integration? Explain your rationale.

7. How important is it to you (and your organization) to work with white leaders to bring equality for African Americans?

Lesson 26
Women's Rights—
A Chronicle of Reform

Objective
- To evaluate and account for progress in the women's rights movement since World War II

Notes to the Teacher
Women's perspectives on their proper role changed forever as a result of their World War II experiences. Wartime necessities brought five million additional women into the work force. Another 350,000 served in the armed forces in the first war where women had regular military status. Although women received less pay than men and suffered various forms of discrimination, they gained a new sense of independence that they could not forget at the end of the war.

At the conclusion of World War II, both the government and private employers encouraged women to return to their kitchens. The postwar baby boom, a comfortable life in the suburbs, and women's clubs did not give women the satisfaction of an income of their own. In the 1950s, older women began returning to work in record numbers. A decade later, a women's rights movement emerged as an outgrowth of the Civil Rights Movement. The effort to pass the Equal Rights Amendment and the controversy over the Supreme Court decision in *Roe v. Wade* highlighted the early years of the movement.

Students create a notebook from an activist grandmother in the women's rights movement to her granddaughter as a graduation gift from college in the seventy-fifth anniversary of the Nineteenth Amendment. Students conclude the project by writing the young woman a letter on the successes and failures in the postwar women's rights movement, the reasons for those successes and failures, where the movement should be headed, and how the young woman can best carry on the family tradition of activism.

Young women in the class are frequently asked to assume the role of males to understand historical issues. It is not inappropriate in this instance to ask young men in the class to complete this project. Contrasts between male and female approaches could provide interesting material for discussion at the conclusion of the project.

Procedure
1. Begin by asking how many of the students feel they have been discriminated against because of their gender. Briefly discuss incidents shared by students.

2. Assign **Handout 29**. Consider having students work in pairs or small groups to complete the project.

Suggested Responses:

3. *National Organization for Women was established by Betty Friedan in 1966 to pressure the government to enforce Title VII. Most members were middle-class women. The organization's goal was "to bring women into full participation in the mainstream of American society now." The organization worked for equal opportunity in employment and encouraged other protests on behalf of equality for women. In its first ten years its membership rose to over 50,000. One success of the organization was securing passage of a law to ban gender references in "help wanted" ads.*

4. *Students might mention passage of the Civil Rights Act of 1964, the Supreme Court decision in* Roe v. Wade *(1973), and Congressional passage of the Equal Rights Amendment (although the ERA failed by three votes to secure ratification by the required 38 states by the deadline in 1982).*

5. *Students might mention Phyllis Schlafly or Marabel Morgan as opponents of the movement. They argued that the ERA was unnecessary since legislation already protected women's rights and they believed the amendment would challenge traditional gender roles, lead to women being drafted, end alimony payments to divorced women, and lead to unisex public restrooms. They helped defeat the ERA.*

8. *Students might mention day care for children; time to fit in work, family, and housework; more single-parent families; competing for jobs traditionally held by men; equal pay for equal work, among others.*

3. Be sure to reserve time in class for students to share their projects, especially their choices of books, quotations, famous firsts, new problems, and the content of the letters to the granddaughter.

Extension Assignment

1. Research and write a one-page biography of one of the leaders of the women's rights movement in the United States since World War II. Possible biography selections include people such as Gloria Steinem or Betty Friedan. Share your findings with classmates.

2. Research and write a one-page biography of one of the leaders of the women's rights movement in the United States in the nineteenth or early twentieth century. Possible biography selections include people such as Elizabeth Cady Stanton and Susan B. Anthony. Share your findings with classmates.

Women's Rights—A Chronicle of Reform

Kay Jacobs was twenty-one years old and recently married when her young husband enlisted in the Army after the Japanese attack on Pearl Harbor. As a present for her twenty-first birthday, her grandmother had given her what Kay considered a priceless gift. Her grandmother had been a suffragist in the campaign to win ratification of the Nineteenth Amendment. She had compiled her own chronicle of the movement and her role in the campaign. Kay was so thrilled with this gift that she vowed to create a similar record of her own work in World War II while her husband was at war and the progress of women in the years thereafter in the hope that she would have a gift of interest to give to her own granddaughter at some future date. That time finally came in 1995, when her granddaughter, Carol Scofield, graduated from college and took her first job in a large engineering firm in Philadelphia.

Your task is to create that record of women's achievements between 1945 and 1995, the seventy-fifth anniversary of the ratification of the Nineteenth Amendment. Your record should include the following:

1. An annotated listing of five books on the women's movement since 1945 that you recommend that your granddaughter read (At least one should present the position of women favoring traditional roles for women.)

2. At least three recent news clippings involving changing conditions in the work force for women

3. A good description paragraph on the organization, goals, strategies, work, and successes of the National Organization for Women (NOW)

4. A description of at least three key legislative or Supreme Court successes for the women's movement in the half century after World War II

5. One or more paragraphs on the leaders, arguments, and accomplishments of groups opposed to the women's liberation movement.

6. Five quotations or cartoons stating key viewpoints you believe your granddaughter should consider regarding the role of women in American society today

7. A list of the ten biggest "firsts" for women in the period 1945–1995 and a brief statement of your rationale for choosing each one

8. A list and explanation of five new problems facing women in American society that were not significant concerns of women fifty years ago

9. A personal letter to your granddaughter, including your assessment of how successful the women's movement has been in the 1945–1995 period, how you account for the successes and failures, what remains to be done, and your advice to your granddaughter regarding the role you would like to see her play in the movement

Lesson 27
Native Americans—A Forgotten Minority

Objective
- To recognize the depth of the problem facing Native Americans in today's society

Notes to the Teacher

Native Americans are the forgotten minority. The Native American world consists of heterogeneous tribes, grouped by a non-Indian world insensitive to their cultural differences. Indians as a people have few political action committees and organizations. Since they comprise only .05 percent of the total United States population, they wield little political leverage. The history of the Native American since the arrival of the non-Indian on the continent and specifically since the establishment of the United States Government, is a history of broken promises, documents obtained by coercion or with less than informed consent, and by physical and cultural displacement.

In this two-day lesson, students begin by reading an article entitled "Bureau of Caucasian Affairs" and finding as many examples of satire as possible. In class they read and discuss two articles on the situation of Native Americans today. To conclude the lesson, have students imagine that a new president has taken office and is intent on making the ideal of equality a reality for Native Americans. The students are the presidential advisers assigned to outline a ten-year program, including implementation steps for making it happen. Remind students that they must be able to explain/defend their plan and implementation procedures.

It might be helpful to begin this lesson with a general discussion on Native Americans. A few brief notes concerning some historical data and facts on BIA (Bureau of Indian Affairs) policy are included for your benefit.

- Indians were first removed from their lands and put on a reservation in 1758 in New Jersey.

- The Indian Removal Act was passed in 1883, and about 100,000 Indians were removed from ancestral lands to reservations established in Oklahoma.

- By the 1880s nearly all Native Americans were living on reservations.

- The attitude of U.S. officials toward the "forced reservation" system was expressed by Francis Walker, Commissioner of Indian Affairs from 1871–73:

  The Indians should be made as comfortable on, and uncomfortable off, their reservations as it was within the power of the government to make them; that such of them as went right should be protected and fed, and such as went wrong should be harassed and scourged without intermission.[1]

- Indians on reservations were discouraged from practicing their own religion and encouraged to practice Christianity.

- Indians were told that they were wards of the U.S. government and not free people.

- Reservations were usually placed in desolate remote lands.

- Unemployment on many reservations averages 65 percent.

- BIA policy was to send all children at age six to a boarding school.

- BIA policy encourages the Indian to remain on the reservation until death, which usually comes at an early age.

- Indians on reservations were required to speak English to get needed supplies.

- The Indian could not vote and was not recognized as a citizen until 1924.

- In 1953, over one hundred small bands and twelve tribes were terminated from the federal registry, removing their status as legal tribes.

[1] *American Indians* (Washington DC: BIA Printing Office, 1984), 2.

Procedure

1. Introduce the topic using material in the Notes to the Teacher.

2. Assign part A of **Handout 30** for homework.

3. Review responses in class.

   Suggested Examples of Satire:

   U.N.A. Action

   1. *Bought California from Whites; opening it to settlement*

   2. *Three derelicts were established to be spokesmen for Whites.*

   Federal Government or B.I.A. Action:

   1. *Bought California from Indians; opened it to settlement*

   2. *Any Indian found to be in right place at right time was given tribal responsibility. Tribal chiefs were ignored; their authority was challenged.*

4. Distribute part B of **Handout 30** and have students complete it.

Suggested Responses:

1. *Underdeveloped desert*

2. *Just restitution? Government handout?*

3. *Little industrial or agricultural development*

4. *Opportunity; urban poverty*

5. *Japanese internment lasted less than two years. Both, however, reflect adamant racism.*

6. *They represent smallest minority group in cities.*

7. *Tribal stoicism*

8. *Inability to compete; pattern of having been "cared for"*

9. *It is symptomatic and rampant.*

5. As a class, brainstorm a list of problems facing Native Americans today and discuss possible solutions. Problems include poor education, lack of adequate health care, discrimination, lack of good jobs, alcoholism, child abuse, poor housing, poverty, isolation, reservations on the poorest land, and lack of water, among others.

6. To conclude the lesson, have students, working in small groups, complete part C of the handout. Reserve time for students to critique group plans.

Bureau of Caucasian Affairs

Part A.

This article appeared in a Native American activist newsletter. Read it, listing on your own paper examples of satire.

"United Native Americans are proud to announce that it has bought the state of California from the whites and is throwing it open to Indian settlement—U.N.A. bought California from three winos found wandering in San Francisco. U.N.A. decided the winos were spokesmen for the white people of California. These winos promptly signed the treaty, which was written in Sioux, and sold California for three bottles of wine, one bottle of gin, and four cases of beer.

Lehman L. Brightman, the Commissioner of Caucasian Affairs, has announced the following new policies: The Indians hereby give the whites four large reservations of ten acres each at the following locations: Death Valley, the Utah Salt Flats, the Badlands of South Dakota, and the Yukon in Alaska. These reservations shall belong to the whites 'for as long as the sun shines or the grass grows,' (or until the Indians want it back).

All land on the reservation, of course, will be held in trust for the whites by the Bureau of Caucasian Affairs, and any white who wants to use his land in any way must secure the permission of commissioner Brightman.

Of course, whites will be allowed to sell trades and handicrafts at stands by the highway. Each white will be provided annually with one blanket, and one pair of tennis shoes, and a supply of Spam, a copy of 'The Life of Crazy Horse.'

If you are competent enough, you will be able to be a BCA reservation super-intendent. Applicants must have less than one year of education, must not speak English, must have an authoritarian personality, proof of dishonesty, and a certificate of incompetence. No whites need apply. Commissioner Brightman also announced the founding of four boarding schools, to which white young-sters will be sent at the age of six (6). 'We want to take those kinds far away from the backward culture of their parents,' he said. The school will be located on Alcatraz Island; the Florida everglades; Point Barrow, Alaska and Hong Kong.

All courses will be taught in Indian languages, and there will be demerits for anyone caught speaking English. . . . All students arriving at the school will immediately be given IQ tests to determine their understanding of Indian language and hunting skills.

Hospitals will be established for the reservations as follows: Whites at Death Valley may go to the Bangor, Maine Hospital; those at the Utah Salt Flats may go to the Juneau, Alaska Hospital; those at the Yukon, may go to the Miami Beach Hospital, and those at the Badlands, may go to the hospital in Honolulu, Hawaii. Each hospital will have a staff of two part-time doctors, a part-time chiropractor who have all passed a first-aid test, and each hospital will be equipped with a scalpel, a jack knife, a saw, modern tourniquet, and a large bottle of aspirin.

In honor of the whites, many cities, street cars and products will be given traditional white names.

. . . One famous Indian movie director has even announced that in his upcoming film, 'Custer's Last Stand,' he will use many actual whites to play the parts of soldiers, speaking real English, although, of course, the part of Custer will be played by noted Indian actor, Jay Silverheels. Certain barbaric white cus-toms will, of course, not be allowed. Whites will not be allowed to practice their heathen religions, and will be required to attend Indian ceremonies. Mission-aries will be sent from each tribe to convert the whites on the reservations. White churches will either be made into amusement parks or museums, or will be torn down and the bricks and ornaments sold as souvenirs and curiosities."

Author Unknown

Native Americans—"Beggars in Our Own Land"

Part B.

Read the articles and answer the questions.

100 Years of Oppression

Life on the nation's largest Indian reservation is as harsh as its stark, forbidding landscape. Some 160,000 Navajos live on 16 million acres—an area slightly larger than West Virginia—in the Four Corners area where Arizona, New Mexico, Colorado and Utah meet. It is a land of high desert plateau broken by weathered sandstone buttes and rocky canyons. Strewn across this barren territory—miles from neighbors, schools and stores—are the homesteads of the Navajo: small western-style houses, mobile homes or hogans, the traditional one-room, eight-sided log home with a sod roof. The dwellings often lack electricity and plumbing.

There are few towns. The most common signs of community life are handfuls of cafes, general stores and filling stations clustered at some crossroads.

Persistently high unemployment means the *Dine*—or "Navajo people," and pronounced "Dih-NAY"—eke out an existence from a few head of sheep or cattle and, if they are lucky enough to have adequate water, a small garden.

Dependence on federal dollars is pervasive. Approximately 80 percent are jobless. The three out of four who are employed work for the government, which pays for everything from health care and education to law enforcement and job training.

Indian spokesmen are quick to assert that such aid is not a handout, but rather an obligation under treaties between their tribes and Washington.[2]

1. Look at a map of the United States and locate the Four Corners area discussed in the article. Why was the Navajo reservation established there?

2. To what extent does the government have an obligation to pay for health care, education, and job training for tribal members? Explain your answer.

3. Why is the unemployment rate so high in the Four Corners?

[2] K.M. Chrysler, "100 Years of Oppression," *U.S. News and World Report*, May 23, 1983, 71–72. Copyright 1983, U.S. News and World Report.

People Never See Us

"The desolation of reservation life sends thousands of Indians trekking to the city looking for a decent-paying job and a better life.

Often lacking job skills and adequate education, what they frequently find is the same poverty they left behind. But now they have to cope in an unfamiliar urban environment cut off from friends, family and the special federal aid available to reservation Indians.

Compounding their dilemma is that the nearly 627,000 Indians living in cities—about half the country's total—usually blend in with the rest of the urban poor rather than congregate in recognizable Indian neighborhoods.

'People never see us or our plight,' observes Lyman Pierce, a Seneca from New York State and director of the Indian Center of Los Angeles. 'We are not only invisible but ignored.'

Although the Los Angeles area has the most native Americans of any city—more than 48,000—they constitute only 0.6 percent of the region's population. Other cities with sizable numbers of Indians, Eskimo and Aleut residents include Boston, New York, Chicago, Dallas, Denver, Seattle, San Francisco and San Diego.

'My people are very shy, very private,' explains Jonathan Wilson, a Choctaw from Oklahoma and pastor of the First Indian Baptist Church in the blue-collar Los Angeles suburb of South Gate. 'They just suffer silently. You have to learn how to spot that suffering and do something about it without being asked.'

Help comes from private and public sources. Those among the 120 members of Wilson's church who can afford it give food and clothing. The Indian Center gets three million in federal, state and local funds for job training, emergency shelter, alcoholism rehabilitation, day care and other programs.

Besides facing economic obstacles, urban Indians must adjust to bewildering changes in culture. 'City life is fast and reservation life is slow,' notes Wilson. His advice to any Indian thinking of coming to the city: 'First, make absolutely certain there is nothing for you on the reservation.'

Many Indians, says one expert, arrive from the reservation with 'an institutional mentality, like they had just been freed from prison.'

In cities, they often run into people with stereotyped ideas. 'One view is the lazy, shiftless, drunken Indian,' says Pierce of the Indian Center. 'The other extreme is the noble savage of the Boy Scouts and the movies. If we had had better immigration laws in 1500, we would be the ruling class in America today, instead of being beggars in our own land.'

Whites' ignorance about Indians and tribal life cause grief for the newcomers. David Ridenour, a Pasadena lawyer who is half Apache, says social workers sometimes accuse Indian parents of child neglect because the home may be dirty, with little furniture and only a mattress for sleeping. 'The trouble is, they have never been on a reservation and seen life there,' he adds.

Another example: Doctors suspected an Indian baby had been abused. The mother was charged after she reacted stoically to word that the girl could die. 'They charged this woman because she did not react correctly in the modern American context of things,' says Ridenour. Investigators found that the girl's white stepfather had harmed her.

No. 1 problem. As on the reservation, alcohol is solace to many Indians living in the nation's cities. 'Every Indian I know has at least one alcoholic in his family, and some have two or three or more,' says an Indian pastor.

'When you face racism, poverty and powerlessness, you drink to forget,' explains Robert Sundance, a Sioux, a recovered alcoholic and director of the Los Angeles Indian Alcoholism Commission. Liquor is one of the top causes of death among Indians, he says, warning: 'We will be annihilated as a race within the next century if we don't solve the alcoholism problem. Then the Indian problem is settled—genocide without firing a single bullet.'"[3]

4. Why do Native Americans leave the reservation for the city? What do they find there?

5. Compare life on a Native American reservation with a Japanese resettlement camp.

6. When Native Americans move to the city, they tend to congregate with other urban poor, rather than settle in Native American areas. Why?

7. Why are Native Americans shy, very private, people?

8. "Many Indians arrive from the reservation with an institutional mentality." How might this affect their social development?

9. Why is alcoholism a major problem for Native Americans?

[3] Joseph L. Galloway, "People Never See Us" *U.S. News and World Report,* May 23, 1983, 72. Copyright 1983, U.S. News and World Report.

Part C.

To conclude this lesson, assume that the incoming president has asked you to be his "idea person." To him, the statement in the Declaration of Independence that "all men are created equal" should, of all people, apply to Native Americans. He recognizes that little has changed in recent years to improve living conditions for Native Americans. He visualizes going down in history as the president who took seriously the problems of this important minority, and he plans to undertake a ten-year program to achieve real progress. (Just as President Kennedy believed that, with effort, we could put a man on the moon by the end of the 1960s, the new president believes this country *can* solve the problems of Native Americans within a decade.)

As he prepares his first State of the Union message, the new president wants you to write a compelling introduction to dramatize the urgency of reform, an outline of a ten-year program to address the problem, your rationale for the proposal, and an appropriate two-word "sound bite" that television reporters will be likely to pick up to label his administration.

Lesson 28
The Crimes of Watergate

Objective

- To understand the forced resignation of Richard Nixon as a result of the accumulated crimes and scandals of his administration

Notes to the Teacher

At this point in time, many students make only a vague association between President Nixon and Watergate. Some students may recognize that "Watergate" refers on one level to the 1972 break-in at Democratic National Headquarters at the Watergate apartments in Washington to steal campaign secrets and bug offices, and, later, to cover up the administration's involvement. Fewer understand the complex and multifaceted crimes and scandals, known collectively as the "Watergate Affair," that destroyed the Nixon presidency and forced Nixon to become the first President in U.S. history to resign.

In dealing with Watergate, Theodore White goes beyond a mere list of crimes to describe Richard Nixon's most serious offense:

> "The true crime of Richard Nixon was simple: he destroyed the myth that binds America together, and for this he was driven from power.
>
> The myth he broke was critical—that somewhere in American life there is at least one man who stands for law, the President. That faith surmounts all daily cynicism, all evidence or suspicion of wrongdoing by lesser leaders, all corruptions, all vulgarities, all the ugly compromises of daily striving and ambition. That faith holds all men are equal before the law and protected by it; and that no matter how the faith may be betrayed elsewhere, at one particular point—the Presidency—justice will be done beyond prejudice, beyond rancor, beyond the possibility of a fix. It was that faith that Richard Nixon broke, betraying those who voted for him even more than those who voted against him."[1]

In this lesson, students consider the crimes with which Richard Nixon was charged. They will be asked to analyze document-based questions and to complete a mix-and-match chart on Watergate. To conclude the lesson, students assume the perspective of a historian charged with the task of composing an advanced placement essay question on the significance of Watergate to mark the twenty-fifth anniversary of President Nixon's resignation.

Much of the information used in this lesson was taken from "The Offenses of Richard M. Nixon: A Guide for the People of the United States of America" by William A. Dobrovir, et al., Quadrangle/The New York Times Book Co., 10 East 53 St., New York, NY 10022, 1973.

Procedure

1. Introduce the topic using material in the Notes to the Teacher or by showing the class the videotape or sound filmstrip *All the President's Men* (Warner Home Video, 1976, 138 mins., color).

2. Distribute **Handout 31**, part A. Have students complete it individually. Conduct a discussion based on their responses. Allow students to speculate. Answers are clarified in part B.

3. Distribute **Handout 31**, part B. Have students complete the assignment in pairs. Remind them that there will be more than one answer for most offenses. Correct the assignment in class, having students justify their choices in oral arguments.

---

[1] Theodore H. White, *Breach of Faith, The Fall of Richard Nixon* (New York: Atheneum Press, 1975), 322.

Suggested Responses:

1. *b, g, k*   9. *c, e*
2. *b, d, f, g*   10. *e, c, f, o, p*
3. *a, b*   11. *b, c, l*
4. *g*   12. *c, e, k*
5. *b, k*   13. *o, p*
6. *a, b, g*   14. *m*
7. *b, f, k*   15. *f*
8. *e*

4. To conclude, have students assume the role of a historian who has been asked to draft an essay question on the long-range importance of Watergate. Allow them to work in pairs to write an interpretive essay question that might be used to mark the next anniversary of President Nixon's resignation.

5. As a follow up to this lesson, have students read and report on selections from the following bibliography:

Bernstein, Carl and Bob Woodward. *All the President's Men*. New York: Simon and Schuster, 1974.

Dean, John W. *Blind Ambition*. New York: Simon and Schuster, 1976.

Lukas, J. Anthony. *Night-Mare, The Underside of the Nixon Years*. New York: Viking Press, 1973.

Rather, Dan and Gary P. Gates. *The Palace Guard*. New York: Harper & Row, 1974.

Schell, Jonathan. *The Time of Illusion*. New York: Random House, 1975.

White, Theodore H. *Breach of Faith, The Fall of Richard Nixon*. New York: Atheneum Publishers, 1975.

Wills, Gary. *Nixon Agonistes*. New York: Houghton Mifflin, 1971.

The Crimes of Richard Nixon

Part A.

Read the handout and answer the questions that follow.

Counts 1–9 charge a single plan or scheme, i.e., a conspiracy headed by the President, to deprive political opponents of their constitutional rights by various methods, some of which were themselves illegal. The plan began in 1969 when the President ordered domestic wiretaps without court order and the IRS was ordered to harass political enemies. The President himself ordered an admittedly illegal plan for domestic surveillance by means of wiretaps and burglaries and personally approved the creation of a new interagency intelligence unit to gather the same kind of information on political opponents. He personally approved the creation of the "plumbers," an extra-legal, private, White House operation headed by White House staff aide Egil Krogh. The President also personally approved the trip by two of the "plumbers," Liddy and Hunt, to "case" the office of Daniel Ellsberg's psychiatrist for an illegal entry and was to receive any information obtained by the entry. The President himself ordered his chief domestic aide, John Ehrlichman, to approach the trial judge, Judge Byrne, in the midst of the Ellsberg trial (which was of great importance to the President) about a promotion to the Directorship of the FBI.

All of the activities of the campaign group were directed by and known to the President's closest aides, Haldeman and Mitchell. The espionage plan that led to the Watergate burglary was approved by Mitchell, then Attorney General, and Colson, Special Counsel to the President, and was presumably known to Haldeman. Their illegal acts of wiretapping and burglary were intended to benefit Richard Nixon by ensuring his reelection.

Following the burglary, the effort to cover up White House involvement by (a) buying silence with promises of money and executive clemency, (b) suborning the perjury of campaign officials Jeb S. Magruder and Herbert Porter, and (c) restricting the FBI's investigation (by invoking CIA involvement) deeply involved Mitchell, Haldeman, Herbert Kalmbach (the President's lawyer and long-term political associate, who raised the hush money) and White House Counsel John Dean. The President by his own admission participated in (c) (trying to hamstring the FBI) and by John Dean's testimony, contradicted by others, participated in a decision to make offers of money and executive clemency to keep the burglars quiet. And of course the President, whose reelection was at stake, was the principle beneficiary of the cover-up effort.

Counts 10–25 charge a second plan or scheme, created and carried out by the same persons, with the addition of others like Maurice Stans and Murray Chotiner, to collect a political campaign fund without precedent in history by the use of methods known to be in violation of law, including the corrupt bargaining of governmental benefits for cash.

The finance operation was first headed by Kalmbach, who was designated by Haldeman, speaking for the President, in January, 1971. Mitchell and Haldeman were involved and were kept informed from then on. Maurice Stans became finance chairman in February, 1972, but there is no indication that reports to the White House ceased, and the White House gave advice to Stans about funding problems. The President oversaw the whole operation; his private secretary, Rose Mary Woods, maintained a list of over-$1000 campaign contributions. And, of course, the fund raising operation had as its sole purpose the support of President Nixon's reelection campaign—he was its chief, if not sole, beneficiary.

In the course of this operation Kalmbach and Stans solicited and obtained campaign contributions from corporations and unions and they and other fund raisers were able to trade immensely valuable government decisions for campaign contributions from powerful and interested economic interests.

Thus Robert Vesco paid $200,000 for promises by Mitchell and Stans to divert the SEC from investigating his financial dealings. A Greek oil dealer paid $25,000 and received a $4.7 million contract to fuel the Sixth Fleet in Piraeus. McDonald's hamburger chain chairman paid $200,000 and received permission from the Price Commission to raise the price of their cheeseburger. Carpet manufacturers paid $200,000 and obtained a meeting with Colson and Commerce Department officials—set up by Stans—that resulted in the killing of proposed new, stricter safety/flammability standards for carpets.

Dwayne Andreas paid $25,000 (in cash, used to finance the Watergate burglary) and received approval of a national bank charter application in record time. Robert Allen paid $100,000, likewise used to finance the Watergate burglary, and obtained the dropping by the government of action against his company's pollution. The Seafarers Union paid $100,000 and obtained the dropping by the government of a prosecution for illegal campaign gifts the Union made in 1968. Howard Hughes paid $100,000 to C.G. Rebozo, Nixon's closest friend and obtained (a) approval by the President of his purchase of Air West and (b) approval by the Justice Department of his proposed purchase of another casino in Las Vegas.

President Nixon was personally involved in several of these transactions. Dairy interests wrote him a letter promising $2 million for his reelection campaign and asked for quotas on dairy product imports—which the President promptly imposed. When the Secretary of Agriculture refused to increase the 1971 price support for milk, long-time Nixon associate Murray Chotiner set up the channels for a flow of dairy money. After the flow began, dairy leaders met with Nixon and two days later the Secretary of Agriculture reversed himself. The dairy groups eventually paid $427,500 (of which $5,000, delivered virtually in Nixon's presence, financed the Ellsberg psychiatrist's break-in) for a decision that cost consumers $500 million.

ITT paid $100,000 (it had promised more) to help the Republicans hold their 1972 convention in San Diego. The company obtained, from the Antitrust Division of Justice, the dropping of a suit to stop ITT from acquiring the Hartford Fire Insurance Company, with the President telling Justice not to oppose bigness-as-such and to treat ITT "fairly." Nixon, Colson wrote, was "directly involved," he discussed the ITT case with Mitchell and personally ordered Deputy Attorny General Kleindienst to delay the case.

Counts 26–28 charge the President with using his office to enrich himself personally by causing the government to spend money on his private estates and by taking an unallowable tax deduction. He knew what physical improvements were being made to the property, and could veto them; indeed the work was usually ordered or approved by Kalmbach or Haldeman. Like all other citizens he assuredly signed his own tax returns, in which he declared taxable income of around $7000 on a salary of $200,000.

There are a number of points of overlap and intersection among these various acts. For example, the Watergate burglary, the last known overt act in pursuance of the plan to suppress dissent and opposition to the administration, was financed in part by campaign contributions apparently contributed out of corporate funds and "laundered" through foreign bank accounts, which funds appear to have been contributed in exchange for the dropping by the government of enforcement action against the corporate giver's polluting smelter in Idaho. Likewise, the burglary of the office of Daniel Ellsberg's psychiatrist carried out by the "plumbers," directed and employed by the White House, was in part financed by money contributed by dairy cooperatives who obtained a price support increase for dairy products with promises of contributions of $2,000,000 (less than 25% of which was actually delivered).

Of course the two organizations that carried out these acts—the White House staff and the Committee to Re-Elect the President—were under the overall direction of and were ultimately responsible only to one man—President Nixon. Indeed, he has admitted "responsibility" for the acts of his subordinates. Moreover, the various acts were carried out directly by and under the direct supervision of the President's closest official and unofficial advisers. The President's personal attorney, Herbert Kalmbach, a political and personal associate of Mr. Nixon for twenty years, handled much of the campaign contribution solicitation personally and directed the entire operation until February, 1972, when Maurice Stans resigned as Secretary of Commerce to take formal charge. Kalmbach ordered and supervised installation at government expense of improvements at the President's estate in San Clemente, California, and his partner Frank DeMarco handled the President's tax avoidance device. Kalmbach was in charge of making payoffs to some of the burglars and wiremen who served as the White House "plumbers" and then were employed by the Committee to Re-Elect the President to burglarize the Democratic National Committee, and raised money to pay their legal fees and living expenses—or to buy their silence—after they were apprehended.

H.R. Haldeman, the President's chief of staff and the effective guardian of the President's time, appears to have supervised and was kept informed of campaign contribution affairs, likewise ordered property improvements at San Clemente, and was generally involved in the various devices used in efforts to suppress dissent. John Mitchell, the President's 1968 campaign manager, law-and-order Attorney General and then 1972 campaign manager, approved illegal domestic wiretaps and the Liddy campaign espionage plan, was part of the campaign contribution collection operation and in furtherance of it made decisions at the Justice Department that favored big contributors.

All three of these men were the President's chosen instruments—his agents. As we shall see, he is criminally liable under the law for all the acts carried out in the conspiracy which he headed.[2]

[2] William A. Dobrovir, *The Offenses of Richard M. Nixon: A Guide for the People of the United States of America* (New York: Times Book Co., 1973), 11–15.

Questions

1. List and define the constitutional rights that Nixon violated.

2. What did the president hope to gain by sending Ehrlichman to talk to Judge Byrne? What law was broken when that happened?

3. Why did the president attempt to interfere with the FBI's investigation following the burglary? What law did he break?

4. Define the concept of influence peddling.

5. What Nixon aides solicited and obtained campaign funds from corporations and unions? What did the corporations and unions get in exchange for their contributions?

Part B.

Read the list of statutes Nixon violated and match them with the specific Watergate violation on the following pages (Section B). Note: Some incidents may represent more than one violation.

Section A—Violations of Statutes

a. Violation of limits on gifts president may accept

b. Bribery, federal

c. Aiding and abetting criminal acts

d. Offering, giving, soliciting, or receiving bribes

e. Conspiracy against the civil rights of any citizen

f. Conspiracy to commit any federal offense

   Conspiracy to defraud the United States

g. Political campaign contributions by corporations and labor unions

h. Political campaign contributions by foreign nationals

i. Conversion and embezzlement of public monies, property or other things of value belonging to the United States

j. Extortion

k. Fraud and false statements

l. Obstruction of justice in court proceedings

m. Perjury

n. Suborning perjury

o. Wiretapping

p. Burglary

Section B—Offenses

_____ 1. **Bunker Hill Case**

Robert Allen, President of Gulf Resources and Chemical Corporation, contributed $100,000.00 to C.R.P. (The Committee to Re-Elect the President). Gulf Resources' principal asset is a lead and zinc mining and smelting operation in Idaho, the Bunker Hill Company.

In March 1972, the EPA said it was going to impose stiffer air pollution control standards. After April 3, the EPA dropped its stiffer standards. Bunker Hill profits that year were 86 million dollars.

_____ 2. **Quarter Pounder Case**

In November 1971, McDonald's raised its price for the Quarter Pounder cheeseburger from 59 cents to 65 cents without authorization from the Price Commission. In May 1972, the Commission ordered McDonald's to reduce its price of its Quarter Pounder. Between May and September 1972, Ray Kroc, owner of McDonald's, contributed over $200,000.00 to C.R.P. In September 1972, the Price Commission reversed its decision and granted McDonald's price increase.

_____ 3. **Vesco Case**

Robert Vesco, a financier, was being investigated by the SEC on charges of impropriety in business practices. Vesco contributed $200,000.00 to C.R.P. The SEC investigation was postponed. Later, the SEC filed suit against Vesco and he demanded that the contribution he made to C.R.P. be returned to him. It was.

_____ 4. **Carpet Case**

The Department of Commerce planned to require a stricter product safety flammability test for carpets. Several leading carpet industry executives contributed $200,000.00 to C.R.P. Shortly afterward the Department of Commerce dropped all plans to use a new instrument to test for carpet safety.

_____ 5. **Seafarer Case**

The Seafarers International Union was indicted in June 1970, for violation of the Federal Corrupt Practices Act. The gist of the indictment was that SPAD, the Seafarers Political Activity Donation Committee, was a sham and that through SPAD, the union made political contributions to Nixon totalling $750,000.00 of union funds. The indictment also charged extortion of contributions from union members and from foreign sailors. In September 1970, the District Court dismissed the indictment for lack of prosecution. In October 1972, the Department of Justice abandoned the case.

_____ 6. **Greek Case**

Thomas Pappas, a wealthy Greek/American businessman, held dual citizenship. Pappas was a Nixon fundraiser and a co-chairman of C.R.P. (Finance Department). He made eleven round trip flights to Greece on company business. Less than twelve days before the 1972 election, two Greek Nationals contributed $25,000 each to C.R.P. One of the men owns an oil company in Greece. In December, his oil company was awarded a $47 million contract for the refueling of the United States Sixth Fleet, based in Greece.

_____ 7. **The Milk Case**
The three largest dairy cooperatives established political action committees to make political contributions. A representative of one of the dairy P.A.C. wrote the president to discuss a matter of some delicacy and of significant political impact. The dairy P.A.C. contributed about $135,000 to Republican candidates in the 1970 election. The dairy representative agreed to establish appropriate channels for contributing $2 million to C.R.P. The remainder of the letter contained a plea for immediate imposition of revised dairy import quotas. Two weeks later, dairy import quotas were revised according to industry wishes.

_____ 8. **Eavesdropping**
In May 1969, Nixon ordered the illegal wiretapping of thirteen government officials and four newsmen.

_____ 9. **Enemies List**
In the summer of 1969, Nixon requested the I.R.S. to move against leftist organizations and to have them audited and harassed by its agents.

_____ 10. **Plumbers**
In June 1971, Nixon personally approved the creation of a special investigation unit within the White House, later called the Plumbers. Nixon ordered them to find out all they could about Daniel Ellsberg. Later, the group was ordered to go to California and break into Ellsberg's psychiatrist's office and photograph Ellsberg's psychological file. They did this. The Plumbers were paid from C.R.P. funds.

_____ 11. **Judge Case**
President Nixon met with the United States District Judge Byrne during the final stages of the trial of Daniel Ellsberg for turning over the Pentagon Papers to the New York Times. The President's aides then had several subsequent meetings with the judge. Ehrlichman later interviewed the judge for a job as possible F.B.I. Director. The judge eventually declared a mistrial when confronted with the questionable propriety of his discussing a federal appointment during the case.

_____ 12. **Dirty Tricks Case**
In 1972, a committee chaired by a Nixon aide, Don Segretti, operated a campaign to sabotage the campaigns of Nixon's Democratic rivals in the primaries. The Segretti campaign used forged Muskie stationery to charge Senators Humphrey and Jackson with sexual misconduct.

_____ 13. **Watergate Break-in—Culprits Caught**
The break-in and wiretapping of the Democratic National Committee's Watergate offices occurred on May 27, 1972. On June 17, 1972, five agents of the Nixon campaign were apprehended.

_____ 14. Officials of C.R.P. lied under oath when asked about Nixon's activities.

_____ 15. **Gifts**
Nixon donated his presidential papers and, later, claimed false tax deductions in the amount of $570,000.

Lesson 29
Evaluating Recent Presidents

Objectives

- To analyze criteria for evaluating presidential performance

- To evaluate recent administrations in the light of those criteria

Notes to the Teacher

This lesson asks students to use evaluations of past presidents as a starting point for generating a list of criteria for presidential evaluation. They then apply the criteria to recent presidents. You will want to emphasize that the class's evaluation is, at best, provisional; still, responsible citizenship entails an alert and educated awareness of presidential activity.

Even advanced placement students sometimes bring much naivete to their study of historical figures, leading to a tendency to apply Savior or Satan generalizations. The lesson should lead to realistic awareness of the very difficult job of the United States presidency. Before the lesson, students should have completed **Handout 32**.

In this lesson, students read historians' evaluations of twentieth-century presidents through the Nixon administration. They establish their own criteria for an effective president, apply those criteria to an informal evaluation of the Reagan administration, and locate similar informal evaluations of recent presidents since Nixon and try to account for these assessments. This lesson provides an effective way to study recent presidents, but the lesson will take more than one day to complete.

Procedure

1. Review **Handout 32**. Encourage students to express their intuitive evaluations of the presidents. Ask them to account for any differences between their assessments and those of the professional historians.

2. Point out that professional evaluations often include a list of specific responsibilities. Have small groups brainstorm lists of specific United States presidential responsibilities.

3. Have each small group read aloud the results of the brainstorming. Encourage groups to add new ideas to their own lists.

4. Have the class compose a "Presidential Evaluation Checklist," incorporating the results of their brainstorming in a clear, concise, useful evaluation tool. Write the list on the board.

Sample Criteria:

1. *Establishment of a cooperative relationship with Congress*

2. *Selection of a cooperative, competent, effective administrative staff*

3. *Projection of an attractive, responsible American image*

4. *Just interaction with leaders of other nations for the best interests of the United States*

5. *Recognition of domestic and international problems as they arise*

6. *Avoidance of unnecessary engagement in military combat*

7. *Knowledge and understanding of history*

   (Alert students to avoid redundance and to try to incorporate all general aspects of presidential responsibility.)

5. Have students complete part A of **Handout 33** by recording their list of criteria for an effective president.

6. Have students read the evaluations of President Reagan in part B of **Handout 33** and rate his administration in terms of the criteria they established. Then have the class decide on one general grade for the Reagan Administration.

7. Point out that a number of factors can tend to bias an evaluation. Ask students to identify some. (*Political party, sensitivity to specific issues, socio-economic group, etc.*)

8. Divide the class into groups equal to the number of presidents since Nixon (excluding Reagan). For homework, ask each group to find similar informal evaluations of their assigned president and be prepared to share their assessment, explain major events in the administration that account for the evaluation, and relate that assessment to their own evaluation using the criteria they established in the rating sheet.

Evaluating Presidential Greatness

In 1948, Professor Arthur M. Schlesinger, Sr., polled fifty-five experts on the issue of presidential greatness. He followed with a poll of seventy-five in 1962. Participants used standard academic grades (A, B, C, D, F) to vote the performance of the presidents. Schlesinger published the results, classifying each president as great, near great, average, below average, or failure.

Less structured presidential evaluation takes place continuously through historical writings, newspapers, magazines, and other media. Particularly in the case of recent presidents, the evaluation may change as new perspectives emerge.

Consider the following evaluations of some twentieth-century presidents. As you read, make marginal notes with criteria you believe essential in determining a president's effectiveness.

President	Poll, 1948	Poll, 1962	Bailey, 1966	Hargrove and Nelson, 1984
Theodore Roosevelt 1901–1909	Near great #7/29	Near great #7/31	" . . . the masses loved him. . . . A consummate politician, he was also a great opportunist and a great leader. Yet, on balance, Roosevelt fell short of being a Grade-A President; at best he was a B plus . . ."[1]	" . . . his major innovation as president was to enliven a long dormant enumerated power of the presidency . . . to recommend legislation to Congress."[2]
Woodrow Wilson 1913–1921	Great #4/29	Great #4/31	" . . . spectacular successes at home are substantially cancelled out by his failure abroad . . . He belongs with the Greats, where the experts put him, if we consider his first six years. He rises no higher than Near Great, if that high, when we consider all eight years . . ."[3]	"Wilson's success as 'chief legislator' marked a milestone in the history of the presidency."[4]

[1] Thomas A. Bailey, *Presidential Greatness* (New York: Appleton-Century-Crafts, 1966), 308.

[2] Erwin C. Hargrove and Michael Nelson, *Presidents, Politics and Policy* (New York: Alfred A. Knopf, 1984), 50.

[3] Bailey, *Presidential Greatness*, 312.

[4] Hargrove and Nelson, *Presidents, Politics and Policy*, 50.

President	Poll, 1948	Poll, 1962	Bailey, 1966	Hargrove and Nelson, 1984
Calvin Coolidge 1923–1929	Below Average #23/29	Below Average #29/31	" . . . acclaimed a highly successful president when he left office . . . The myth of the strong, silent President must be discarded: he was neither strong not silent . . ."[5]	"Weak"[6]
Herbert Hoover 1929–1933	Average #20/29	Average #19/31	"Hoover offered active leadership but not effective leadership . . . I would regard him as in many ways a remarkable man but a Below Average President."[7]	"Weak"[8]
Franklin D. Roosevelt 1933–1945	Great #3/29	Great #3/31	" . . . lived greatly in great times, but he made many mistakes . . . On the basis of impact alone, Roosevelt can hardly be denied a place in the highest echelon of American Presidents."[9]	"His greatest capacity was for moral leadership, and his greatest moments were in the crises of depression and war, when he could lead by inspiration . . . Roosevelt's greatness was in his understanding of both the possibilities for and limits to achievement."[10]

[5] Bailey, *Presidential Greatness*, 317.

[6] Hargrove and Nelson, *Presidents, Politics and Policy*, 51.

[7] Bailey, *Presidential Greatness*, 320.

[8] Hargrove and Nelson, *Presidents, Politics and Policy*, 51.

[9] Bailey, *Presidential Greatness*, 321–322.

[10] Hargrove and Nelson, *Presidents, Politics and Policy*, 96.

President	Poll, 1948	Poll, 1962	Bailey, 1966	Hargrove and Nelson, 1984
Harry Truman 1945–1953	———	Near Great #9/31	" . . . his greatness lies largely in having done greatly better than anyone had any reason to anticipate . . . I would say that this seemingly average man turned out to be no better than an average President."[11]	" . . . his own self-image as one who could make decisions. He drew the inference that his capacity would be enhanced by orderly arrangements . . . Truman's most effective efforts at reorganization came when Congress gave its assent to specific recommendations of the Commission on the Organization of the Executive Branch of Government . . ."[12]
Dwight D. Eisenhower 1953–1961	———	Average #23/31	"Historians will almost certainly never give him as high a mark as the voters did, but perhaps we ought to be grateful that this national soldier and popular idol turned out to be an eminently respectable and respected President, remembered for his dignity, decency and dedication . . . In my opinion, he belongs at least several notches higher [than the Schlesinger poll results] . . ."[13]	"Although Eisenhower was not a professional politician, he seems to have understood, as did Roosevelt, both the possibilities for and limits to action, and, also like Roosevelt, he knew that his standing with the public was his chief political resource."[14]

[11] Bailey, *Presidential Greatness*, 325.

[12] Hargrove and Nelson, *Presidents, Politics and Policy*, 251.

[13] Bailey, *Presidential Greatness*, 328.

[14] Hargrove and Nelson, *Presidents, Politics and Policy*, 97.

President	Poll, 1948	Poll, 1962	Bailey, 1966	Hargrove and Nelson, 1984
John F. Kennedy 1961–1963	———	———	"He will be remembered perhaps more for what he championed than for what he achieved: The obligation to public service, the welfare of the underprivileged . . . His tragic death shocked the nation and the Congress into greater movement . . ."[15]	"Kennedy was an effective president of preparation because his strategic sense of what was politically possible in domestic policy matched the reality of the times . . . Criticism of him for being too cautious or for not getting his major program ideas passed by Congress is unjustified. Kennedy understood what was possible."[16]
Lyndon B. Johnson 1963–1969	———	———	"The tall Texan has displayed an almost pathological desire to be judged great, and if he does not suffer another heart attack or break himself down with overwork, he may well attain his goal . . . If crisis times make great men, he is well on his way to greatness."[17]	"The war brought Johnson down in 1968. The public had turned against him . . . his failure to choose between domestic reform and war, when combined with his mistakes in judgment about the war itself, give (sic) us a picture of a political leader who was so determined to be great that he overreached himself and brought about his own downfall."[18]

[15] Bailey, *Presidential Greatness*, 331.

[16] Hargrove and Nelson, *Presidents, Politics and Policy*, 105.

[17] Bailey, *Presidential Greatness*, 331, 335.

[18] Hargrove and Nelson, *Presidents, Politics and Policy*, 108, 111.

President	Poll, 1948	Poll, 1962	Bailey, 1966	Hargrove and Nelson, 1984
Richard M. Nixon 1969–1974	————	————	————————	"Nixon's tragedy, and the actions he took that destroyed him, ultimately sprang from weakness rather than strength. Nixon could have been a brilliant president of consolidation in both foreign and domestic policy . . . But, like Lyndon Johnson, he ultimately and fatally lost his sense of political reality."[19]

1. Do you agree with the evaluations? Why or why not?

2. For each presidency, cite one or two specific events that you find most crucial in evaluating the president's achievements.

[19] Hargrove and Nelson, *Presidents, Politics and Policy*, 114.

A Presidential Evaluation

Part A.

Record the Presidential Evaluation Checklist here:

❑

❑

❑

❑

❑

❑

❑

❑

❑

❑

Part B.

Below are two more informal evaluations of the Reagan Administration. Notice that the basic character of the Administration was clear before his term ended. Recognize that later information may change the evaluation of a president years after he leaves office. Read these paragraphs and rate President Reagan using the criteria you established in your presidential evaluation checklist.

The Reagan administration does have a foreign policy, in the sense that it has a number of complementary aims which are clearly discernible and which it has pursued, if not with intelligence, then at least with considerable consistency and vigor. It has been engaged in a systematic effort to shape the world in a certain way. Yet for the most part, and especially within the United States itself, the consistency and coherence of this effort have been little understood—as is witnessed by the prevalence of the view that the administration's conduct in foreign affairs has been rather chaotic and desultory. To some extent this is a result of the frequent disarray within the administration caused by factional squabbling over questions of means; but it is also a tribute to the effectiveness with which the administration had propagated the official lies about its aims and activities. For it is primarily the divergence between the administration's stated aims and its actual behavior which has given rise to the impression that it is confused, inconsistent, and ineffectual.[20]

Reagan also moved quickly to assert the authority of the presidency within the executive branch. Presidential appointments were used to put Reagan loyalists into the top positions of the departments and agencies. Being a Republican was not enough; one also had to share Reagan's conservative ideology and give evidence of personal support for the president before Inauguration Day. The intention was to compose an administration of such like-minded people that the managerial authority of the president would be exercised automatically. The creation of cabinet councils, each guided by White House aides, manifested the Reagan principle of collegiality through central oversight and control. To be sure, it was easier to find people to serve in departments and agencies whose mission was compatible with Reagan's ideology, such as deregulation of business, than it was to fill positions in agencies whose purposes clashed with Reagan goals, such as the Environmental Protection Agency. In some cases, posts were not filled for months, and when they were filled, conflict ensued between presidential and career appointees, usually in the form of press leaks. However, with a few exceptions, the administration established control over such agencies by moving aside unsympathetic members of the Senior Executive Service and replacing them with allies. Also, much more attention was paid to middle-level civil service appointments and promotions than in past administrations. Reagan showed that it is possible for a determined president to achieve bureaucratic compliance with administration policy through infiltration rather than hierarchical control.[21]

[20] Jeff McMahon, *Reagan and the World* (New York: *Monthly Review Press*, 1985), 9.

[21] Erwin C. Hargrove and Michael Nelson, *Presidents, Politics, and Policy* (New York: Alfred A. Knopf, 1984),

Lesson 30
Social History and Contemporary Art

Objectives
- To view postwar American art as a reflection of contemporary social history
- To become acquainted with Abstract Expressionism, Pop Art, and Op Art

Notes to the Teacher

Art, like literature, reflects contemporary social history. American artists, active since colonial times, had long worked in the traditions of the great European movements. After World War II, U.S. artists for the first time assumed an individual leadership role in world art development. Abstract Expressionism, represented by Jackson Pollock, Franz Kline, and others, is characterized by very large canvases, improvisation, and sometimes chaotic energy. The Pop Art movement in the 1950s, on the other hand, takes a strongly representational approach to elements of mass culture, often leading the viewer to skeptical detachment. Op Art uses optical illusions to create a sense of continual motion.

This lesson leads to an understanding of contemporary art as a barometer to social and cultural history. Students begin by finding and photocopying at least four examples each of Abstract Expressionism, Pop Art, and Op Art. They share their findings in small groups and try to relate the works of art to values of contemporary society. They conclude by writing an essay illustrating how contemporary art reflects American social and cultural history.

Procedure
1. Point out that art, like literature, reflects history in interesting ways. Add that after World War II, American artists assumed a strong leadership role in world art development.

2. Write on the board: Abstract Expressionism. Ask:

   a. What does "abstract" mean? (You may want to prompt students' thoughts by asking for antonyms as well as synonyms.)

   b. What does it mean to "express" something? How does "expression" differ from "suggestion"?

   c. What do you expect in art representative of Abstract Expressionism?

3. Show students prints or slides of Abstract Expressionist art.

4. Point out the Abstract Expressionism led to a reaction called Pop Art. Then show representative slides or prints. Students will recognize the contrast in styles immediately.

5. Tell them that Op Art is sometimes called "art of the roving eye." Again show them representative slides or prints.

6. Point out that although there is much diversity in contemporary art, there are also characteristics that make it relatively easy to distinguish it from other periods.

7. Distribute **Handout 34**, part A and have students complete it for homework.

8. On the day of discussion of this lesson, divide the class into small groups to share their collections of photocopied art works.

9. Give them part B of **Handout 34** and ask them to write their own definitions of the three terms and make their personal rankings of the values expressed by the art by marking the continuum on the handout.

10. Have them share conclusions. (Students will probably observe contemporary art's energy, tension, freedom, improvisation, alienation, subjectivity, physicality, power, invention, and disruption.)

11. To conclude this lesson, have students work in pairs to write the short essay indicated in item 3 of **Handout 34**, part B. Students may gain greater insights working in pairs for this activity than writing individually.

Social History and Contemporary Art

Part A.

For homework, locate, photocopy, and mount at least four examples of each of the following three styles of contemporary art. After each, write a brief statement of your reaction to the painting.

1. **Abstract Expressionism**

   Abstract Expressionism avoids all attempt at representation and relies on color, texture, and shape to express emotions. American Abstract Expressionists became the first artists from this country to lead rather than follow a movement. Artists painting in this style include Jackson Pollack, Franz Kline, Willem de Kooning, Arshile Gorky, Mark Rothko, and Robert Motherwell.

2. **Pop Art**

   Pop Art, sometimes called "the art of the commonplace," is often highly realistic and often ridicules products of mass culture. Artists painting in this style include Robert Rauschenberg, Roy Lichtenstein, Andy Warhol, and Robert Indiana.

3. **Op Art**

   Op or Optical Art includes optical illusions, striking juxtapositions of color, and moire patterns. In your search for this style, look for works of artists such as Frank Stella, Keith Noland, Josef Albers, and Julian Stanczak.

Part B.

Use your completed collection of modern art as a resource in doing the following activities.

1. Write your own personal definition of each of the following terms:

    a. Abstract Expressionism

    b. Pop Art

    c. Op Art

2. Express your general ideas about contemporary art by using the following continuum chart. Place a check on each line to indicate where you believe contemporary art falls on the continuum between the two qualities.

Energy	Inertia
Tension	Serenity
Structure	Freedom
Improvisation	Planning
Alienation	Social commitment
Objectivity	Subjectivity
Intellectuality	Physicality
Power	Fragility
Tradition	Invention
Disruption	Complacency

3. Write a short essay showing how contemporary art reflects a response to nuclear capability, social protest, prosperity, disillusionment with institutions, or some other aspect of American history after World War II.

Part 3
The Grand Review—
Mastering American History

The goal of an Advanced Placement course is not merely to pass the Advanced Placement examination but to equip students with a commanding sweep of information and skills which will enable them to understand and appreciate the whole process of civilization. The experience of this course should help students comprehend literature, the arts, and politics in a new light and thus afford them a sense of personal satisfaction and enjoyment that comes from opening the world of the mind.

Passing the Advanced Placement examination is, of course, a major goal. The preparation for this experience should help a properly-prepared student solidify the work of the whole year and in doing so meet the challenge posed by the exam. In order to do this, the student must have an articulate command of American history. This review unit will provide not only preparation for the examination, but also a solid basis for further cultural and intellectual growth.

In order to achieve these goals, it is essential to build into the course a lengthy review to insure mastery of the material. During the year, reviews should be built in gradually to help students piece together the stream of history. However, at least four to six weeks should be reserved before the Advanced Placement examination for a comprehensive review of American history. It is in this setting that students can have the opportunity to master the material and develop a sense of accomplishment that comes from an understanding of the survey. As a result, the review is not merely an addendum to the course but the single most important part of it. Students have to be directed to the importance of this since many of the exercises place substantial demands on their time and energies and require a sustained ability to think historically. Since a competent review is a massive enterprise, students need each other's support in group activities to accomplish the task at hand; the reviews must be closely monitored to insure that they are done accurately and completely. It is therefore prudent to grade at least some of the exercises.

The following review exercises demand both accuracy and creativity and are designed to cover the main themes of American history. They are further constructed to approach similar topics from different directions and therefore assist the students in grasping both the depth and sweep of history as they continuously weave the information into a comprehensive sense of the subject.

Lesson 31   Continuity and Change in American History

Lesson 32   Turning Points in American History

Lesson 33   Remember Your Ps and Qs—Presidential Promises and Quotable Quotations

Lesson 34   Where in the U.S.A. Did It Happen, Carmen?

Lesson 35   The Power of the Printed Word

Lesson 36   Points of Conflict—The Focus of History

Lesson 37   Our Inheritance—A Legacy of Reform

Lesson 38   The Secretary of State Hall of Fame

Lesson 39   The Individual in History

Lesson 40   The Confidence Builder—Tackling the Essay

Lesson 31
Continuity and Change in American History

Objective
• To review American history by tracing key themes

Notes to the Teacher

In preparation for the Advanced Placement Examination in U.S. History, it is critical that students organize the major themes of American history lest the major threads are lost in an avalanche of data. Since many courses are taught in a chronological sequence, students need to return to the subject to trace continuity and change from a different vantage. Tracing continuity and change as part of a review of key themes in our nation's history provides a useful way to begin a comprehensive review of the course.

In this lesson, small groups research and become experts in one of three major areas of American history. They complete thematic time lines, note trends, detect cause-effect relationships, and try to find connections between events on related time lines, for example business and labor or wars and threats to civil liberties. At this point they should feel confident to teach their time lines to student groups who have been working in other areas. Such cooperative learning activities help to lighten the burden of the review and have the added benefit of helping students learn the material more effectively since they have to "teach" it to their classmates.

Procedure
1. Divide the class into three groups, and distribute **Handout 35**.

2. Have each group complete the required handout activities for one of the three time line groupings. Tell students that they will later have to teach their section to their classmates and be prepared to field questions from the class.

3. Insist on student note taking during group presentations.

4. After individual group presentations, take time to clarify misunderstandings, answer questions, and encourage further insights on patterns, trends, generalizations, relationships, and continuity and change over time.

This time line activity should be extended as much as time permits since a careful analysis of completed time lines may lead to insights students never had in their first encounter with the material earlier in the year.

Suggested Responses, Time Lines:

Colonial history—*Jamestown; Virginia House of Burgesses and first African Americans in Virginia; Mayflower Compact; Harvard; Fundamental Orders of Connecticut; Massachusetts Education Law; Maryland Act of Toleration; Bacon's Rebellion; Zenger Trial; beginning of French and Indian War; Treaty of Paris*

American Revolution—*Treaty of Paris; Stamp Act; Townshend duties; Boston Massacre; Boston Tea Party; Lexington and Concord; Declaration of Independence; Battle of Saratoga; alliance with France; surrender at Yorktown*

Confederation to Constitution—*Articles of Confederation into effect; Treaty of Paris; Shays' Rebellion; Northwest Ordinance and Constitutional Convention; Constitution into effect; Rhode Island, the last of the original thirteen states, ratified the Constitution; Bill of Rights ratified*

National period—*Constitution into effect; Proclamation of Neutrality; Virginia and Kentucky Resolutions; Louisiana Purchase and Marbury v. Madison; Embargo; War of 1812; Treaty of Ghent; Missouri Compromise; Monroe Doctrine; Tariff of Abominations; Bank War and election of Andrew Jackson*

Sectionalism, Civil War, and Reconstruction—*Missouri Compromise; Tariff of 1832 and resulting controversy; Tariff Compromise of 1833; Wilmot Proviso; California's application for statehood; Compromise of 1850;* Uncle Tom's Cabin; *Ostend Manifesto and Kansas-Nebraska Act; Dred Scott decision; Lincoln-Douglas debates; John Brown's raid; Election of Lincoln; secession and Fort Sumter; Emancipation Proclamation; surrender at Appomattox Court House and assassination of Lincoln; impeachment of Johnson; withdrawal of last troops from the South*

Intolerance and threats to civil liberties—*Alien and Sedition Acts; Know-Nothing Party; suspension of habeas corpus; black codes and Ku Klux Klan; literacy tests, poll taxes, residence requirements, and Jim Crow laws; Red Scare; Ku Klux Klan, Sacco and Vanzetti trial, and Immigration Act of 1924; internment of Japanese-Americans; McCarthyism*

Wars in American history—*Beginning of the French and Indian War; Treaty of Paris; Lexington and Concord began American Revolution; Treaty of Paris; War of 1812; Treaty of Ghent; outbreak of Mexican War; Treaty of Guadalupe Hidalgo; beginning of Civil War; surrender at Appomattox Court House to end Civil War; Spanish-American War and Treaty of Paris; United States' entry into World War I; armistice to end World War I; Pearl Harbor; end of World War II; beginning of Korean Conflict; armistice to end Korean War; beginning of U.S. involvement in Vietnam; Paris Peace Accord*

Development of political parties—*First split into political parties, the Federalist and Democratic-Republican parties; beginning of Era of Good Feeling after Federalists died out; controversial election, which led to split into Whig and Democratic parties; first electoral victory of modern Republican party; Democrats became the majority as a result of the new Democratic coalition forged by Franklin Roosevelt after a long Republican rule*

Immigration—*Chinese Exclusion Act; Gentlemen's Agreement with Japan; Literacy Test; Immigration Act of 1924 established the first national origins quota; Immigration Act of 1929 made the quota permanent and drastically curtailed the quota; McCarran-Walter Act; Immigration Act substituted national needs and family priorities for the more discriminatory quota based on national origins*

Business enterprise in America—*First Bank of the United States; Clay's American System, which included the first protective tariff; Tariff of Abominations; controversy over reestablishment of the Bank of the United States; Lincoln's pro-business platform enacted by Congress;* Munn v. Illinois; Wabash v. Illinois; *Interstate Commerce Act; Sherman Anti-Trust Act; Roosevelt's intervention in the anthracite coal strike; Elkins Act; Hepburn Act, Pure Food and Drug Act, and Meat Inspection Act; Federal Reserve Act and Underwood-Simmons tariff; Clayton Anti-trust Act and Federal Trade Commission; Hawley-Smoot tariff; Fair Labor Standards Act*

Agriculture in American history—*First black indentured servants arrived in Jamestown; cotton gin; McCormack reaper; Homestead Act, Morrill Act, and Bureau of Agriculture; Grange;* Munn v. Illinois; *Bland-Allison Act;* Wabash v. Illinois; *Interstate Commerce Act; Sherman Silver Purchase Act; Populists organized; high point of prosperity for American farmers; falling sales after World War I, with resulting early depression for farmers; Agriculture Adjustment Act; Omnibus Farm bill*

Labor in American history—*Knights of Labor organized; Haymarket Riot; Homestead Strike; Pullman Strike; anthracite coal strike; Clayton Anti-trust Act; Wagner Act and Social Security; Fair Labor Standards Act; Taft-Hartley Act*

As an example of the trends or change over time on the colonial time line, students might recognize that over time the colonists' experiences gave them some of the institutions and skills necessary for success as an independent country. In relating colonial experiences to later ones, students might recognize that this background in self-government prepared the colonists both to feel ready for independence and to handle it successfully when it came. However, their strong reliance on, and preference for, local government led to the short-lived attempt to create a confederate form of government. Experience with the Articles of Confederation proved quickly the wisdom of having a national government with real authority. Earlier experiences, as well as a broad knowledge of political philosophy, led the Founding Fathers to the truly inspired federal form of government under the Constitution.

Making similar generalizations and tracing continuity and change in other areas of American life should help students to recognize the broad outlines of American development, a useful first step in reviewing for the Advanced Placement U.S. History Examination.

Continuity and Change in American History

To this point much of your study of American history has probably been chronological. Many Advanced Placement questions require you to make generalizations, note trends, and trace continuity and change over time. For this reason, creating time lines is a useful review strategy. The key, of course, is not merely identifying an event to match the date, but to state its significance and its relationship to the theme and to what came before and what follows. To make effective use of the time lines, do several tasks. First, create time lines with the dates indicated. Second, identify the event and its significance for each date on the time lines assigned to your group. Third, try to state at least one generalization or one trend over time. Finally, try to state a connection between events on one time line and the time line below it. This is important to help you start drawing connections between areas of American life. Here, the more, the better applies. Work cooperatively! It eases the burden and makes greater insights possible.

Group 1

Colonial history

    1607, 1619, 1620, 1636, 1639, 1647, 1649, 1676, 1735, 1754, 1763

American Revolution

    1763, 1765, 1767, 1770, 1773, 1775, 1776, 1777, 1778, 1781, 1783

Confederation to Constitution

    1781, 1783, 1786, 1787, 1789, 1790, 1791

National period

    1789, 1793, 1797, 1803, 1807, 1812, 1814, 1820, 1823, 1828, 1832

Group 2

Sectionalism, Civil War, and Reconstruction

    1820, 1832, 1833, 1846, 1849, 1850, 1852, 1854, 1857, 1858, 1859, 1860, 1861, 1863, 1865, 1867, 1877

Intolerance and threats to civil liberties

    1798, 1853, Civil War, Reconstruction, end of nineteenth century, 1919, 1920s, WWII, 1950s

Wars in American history

    1754, 1763, 1775, 1783, 1812, 1814, 1846, 1848, 1861, 1865, 1898, 1917, 1918, 1941, 1945, 1950, 1953, 1954, 1973

Development of political parties

    approx. 1792, 1816, 1824, 1860, 1936

Group 3

Immigration

    1882, 1907, 1917, 1924, 1929, 1952, 1965

Business enterprise in America

    1791, 1816, 1828, 1832, Civil War, 1877, 1886, 1887, 1890, 1902, 1903, 1906, 1913, 1914, 1930, 1939

Agriculture in American history

    1619, 1793, 1834, 1862, 1867, 1877, 1878, 1886, 1887, 1890, 1892, WWI, 1920s, 1933, 1961

Labor in American history

    1869, 1886, 1892, 1894, 1902, 1914, 1935, 1938, 1947

Lesson 32
Turning Points in American History

Objective
• To review American history through critical events

Notes to the Teacher

An Advanced Placement U.S. history student should have a sense of the broad sweep of events and personalities that dot the landscape of our nation's history. Within the context of the sweep, students should be able to identify easily contemporaneous movements, trends, and personalities across a wide variety of human endeavors. This skill is essential to handle free-response questions on the Advanced Placement U.S. History Examination. In addition, it is an obvious tool of individuals who are conversant with the discipline.

In this lesson, students begin the first of several quick reviews of significant data commonly required on either the objective or free-response section of the Advanced Placement examination. The assumption is that several encounters with the same material in different contexts will cement this information in their memory. Students are likely to become more adept at recall during the course of the several reviews. For this reason this lesson is purposely kept short. Students are given dates of major turning points. They identify the implied event and its long-range significance. They also identify important contemporaneous movements, trends, and events in literature, science, art, and economics. One purpose of this exercise is to help students understand the process of initial brainstorming necessary to have a broad grasp of the breadth and depth of the period. Later reviews progress to a higher and more specific level of brainstorming.

Procedure

1. Distribute **Handout 36** and have students complete it individually.

2. Discuss their responses. Contemporaneous events and trends students cite will be wide-ranging and reflect the focus of their particular course.

Suggested Responses:

1763—*The Treaty of Paris ended the French and Indian War. The British won control of all land west to the Mississippi River, including Florida. This British victory left the colonists with no foreign enemies on their immediate borders. It was at this moment that the British, in need of money to pay for past wars and the costs of administering new lands, chose to impose new taxes on the colonies. The colonists saw no reason to pay taxes for protection they felt they did not need. Thus began the clash that ended in the American Revolution.*

1776—*The Declaration of Independence marked the first time in history that a colony had boldly asserted independence from a mother country. Winning the war was necessary, however, to make independence a reality. The Declaration of Independence, as a document, justified the separation on the grounds of violations of the colonists' natural rights and asserted that "all men are created equal." This statement, also not reality at the time, has served as a standard by which we judge how far we have come and how far we have to go to achieve real equality in America.*

1789—*Ratification of the Constitution gave the United States a "more perfect union" than had been possible under the state-dominated Articles of Confederation. The document, based on the principles of federalism, separation of powers, representation, and flexibility, created a firm foundation for the growth and development of the United States.*

1800—*In the "Revolution of 1800," the Democratic-Republicans, after a heated struggle, won the presidency and control of Congress. The new nation survived this critical change of power from the business-oriented, aristocratic Federalists to the more-agrarian and democratic party of Jefferson without violence.*

1803—Both the Louisiana Purchase and the Supreme Court decision in Marbury v. Madison had major importance for the future. Acquisition of Louisiana gave the United States control of the Mississippi River, which it needed for commercial reasons. More important, it doubled the size of the country, assured the downfall of the Federalists, strongly suggested that the country would one day extend from sea to sea, and required Jefferson, who had previously opposed use of the elastic clause, to take a step toward a loose interpretation. The Marbury case set a precedent for judicial review and raised the Supreme Court to a position of equality with the president and Congress.

1814—The Treaty of Ghent, ending the War of 1812, resulted in a return to the status quo ante bellum. While it did not represent a victory for the United States, as many later assumed, it did have important consequences, among them an increase in nationalism, a chance to pursue westward expansion relatively unhampered by Native American resistance, encouragement of American manufacturing, disappearance of the Federalist party, and a strengthening of isolation that kept the country out of major foreign wars for a century.

1848—The Treaty of Guadelupe-Hidalgo, which ended the Mexican War, gave the United States control of the vast Mexican Cession. Acquisition of this territory revived the slavery issue that shortly played an important role in the Civil War. The Treaty also created lasting resentment of the powerful United States among Latin American countries.

1861—The outbreak of the Civil War ended any chance to settle the slavery issue peacefully. In dividing the Union, it also threatened to destroy credibility of government under the Constitution. What other country would model a government that could not survive its first major crisis?

1865—The end of the Civil War and the death of Lincoln had major consequences. Lincoln, in his Second Inaugural Address, had pledged a lenient peace when the war ended. President Andrew Jackson and Radical Republicans in Congress had other ideas. Republicans in Congress knew that their own majority would be threatened when southern states returned. They hoped to secure their own programs and African-American political support before agreeing to southern readmission. Tensions between North and South increased rather than abated.

1877—After Hayes won the disputed election of 1876, he agreed to withdrawal of the last remaining Union troops from the former Confederacy. This official end of Reconstruction and of northern supervision of the South (1877) left the new freedmen at the mercy of vengeful southerners.

1914—The outbreak of World War I in Europe brought to an end almost a century of peace on the Continent. Promising steps toward Progressive reform in the United States came to a halt as President Wilson focused his attention on foreign affairs and how best to influence the course of the war and eventual peace.

1919—The Treaty of Versailles, based in part on Wilson's Fourteen Points, included plans for a League of Nations. This controversial organization proved to be the sticking point that prevented the Senate from ratifying the treaty. The United States never joined the League, thus reducing its potential impact, and instead returned to relative isolation.

1929—The Stock Market Crash (1929) brought to an end a long period of prosperity for American business and started the worst depression in American history. In the course of dealing with the Depression, the United States, under Franklin Roosevelt, introduced a welfare state with government taking increasing responsibility for the interests of a variety of less fortunate groups in American society.

1941—*The Japanese attack on Pearl Harbor brought the United States into active participation in the worst war in the history of the world.*

1945—*The end of World War II ushered in the Atomic Age, the creation of the United Nations, the Cold War, and the beginning of the end of colonialism.*

1954—*The year was significant both for this country's first involvement in the war in Vietnam and for the historic Supreme Court decision in* Brown v. Board of Education of Topeka *(1954), which overturned the 1896 "separate but equal" decision and began the change in American treatment of African Americans.*

1960—*The first sit-ins in Greensboro, North Carolina (1960), marked the beginning of a new activism of African Americans in protest against segregation. The election of John F. Kennedy later that year, in a close election in which African Americans made a difference, led to a "revolution of rising expectations" among African Americans and a new support for civil rights legislation within the federal executive branch.*

1964—*Passage of the historic Civil Rights Act outlawed segregation in public accommodations and public facilities and banned discriminatory practices in hiring, voting, and education.*

1968—*The assassination of both Martin Luther King, Jr. and Robert F. Kennedy effectively brought the Civil Rights Movement of the 1960s to an end.*

1973—*The Paris Peace Agreement marking the end of the longest war in American history forced Americans to realize that they were not invincible and could not solve all the problems of the world. Congress took steps to limit presidential options in the War-Powers Resolution in an effort not to be drawn into another undeclared war.*

1989—*The dismantling of the Berlin Wall, the election of Solidarity in Poland, and the fall of the Eastern European economies in Hungary, East Germany, Czechoslovakia, Bulgaria, and Romania signaled the impending collapse of the former Soviet Union and ushered in a new era in U.S. diplomatic relations.*

1994—*The Republican landslide in the November elections gave the party its first control of both houses of Congress in many years. The election brought into question the public's satisfaction with long-standing welfare legislation and suggested a return of significant authority to state governments.*

Turning Points in History

Listed below are major turning points in American history. In each case, identify the implied event, comment on its significance, and then list at least three contemporaneous movements, trends, or activities in literature, science, art, or economics. This brainstorming activity will help you to develop the skills to put your free-response essays in historical context. For purposes of this activity, define "contemporaneous" as any event within a five-year period of the event.

Turning Points:

1763

Event:

Significance:

Related events:

a.

b.

c.

1776

Event:

Significance:

Related events:

a.

b.

c.

1789

Event:

Significance:

Related events:

a.

b.

c.

1800

Event:

Significance:

Related events:

a.

b.

c.

1803

Event:

Significance:

Related events:

a.

b.

c.

1814

Event:

Significance:

Related events:

a.

b.

c.

1848

Event:

Significance:

Related events:

a.

b.

c.

1861

Event:

Significance:

Related events:

a.

b.

c.

1865

Event:

Significance:

Related events:

a.

b.

c.

1877

Event:

Significance:

Related events:

a.

b.

c.

1914

Event:

Significance:

Related events:

a.

b.

c.

1919

Event:

Significance:

Related events:

a.

b.

c.

1929

Event:

Significance:

Related events:

a.

b.

c.

1941

Event:

Significance:

Related events:

a.

b.

c.

1945

Event:

Significance:

Related events:

a.

b.

c.

1954

Event:

Significance:

Related events:

a.

b.

c.

1960

Event:

Significance:

Related events:

a.

b.

c.

1964

Event:

Significance:

Related events:

a.

b.

c.

1968

Event:

Significance:

Related events:

a.

b.

c.

1973

Event:

Significance:

Related events:

a.

b.

c.

1989

Event:

Significance:

Related events:

a.

b.

c.

1994

Event:

Significance:

Related events:

a.

b.

c.

Lesson 33
Remember Your Ps and Qs—
Presidential Promises
and Quotable Quotations

Objective

• To review U.S. history through presidential mottos and memorable quotations

Notes to the Teacher

Frequently two-word designations of presidential administrations or recognizable quotations from speeches, documents, court decisions, and writings act as a shorthand key to complex themes. For the student of American history, the real importance is not in identifying the source but in explaining the motto or quotation's significance among the larger themes of American history.

During the course of the year, Advanced Placement students cover a multitude of ideas in relatively rapid fashion. Review, preferably in a variety of contexts different from the original presentation, is essential. In this lesson, students review the course of American history through presidential administrations and significant quotations. For each, they identify the presidential administration or source of the quotation and its larger importance in explaining a key theme in American history.

Procedure

1. Distribute **Handout 37** and have students attempt to complete the handout individually.

2. Go over responses in class and answer questions that students may have. Insist that students explain major accomplishments of each presidential administration, as well as the larger importance of the idea presented in each quotation.

Suggested Responses, Part A:

1. *Theodore Roosevelt's domestic program tried to give equal opportunity to business executives, farmers, laborers, and consumers. It included attempts to break "bad" trusts, Meat Inspection Act, Pure Food and Drug Act, forced arbitration of the anthracite coal strike, and conservation measures.*

2. *Taft endorsed the Roosevelt Corollary and expanded America's role as police officer by substituting dollars for bullets in promoting loans to business executives in Latin America and the Far East.*

3. *Although Eisenhower did not extend the welfare state begun by Franklin Roosevelt and Harry Truman, he did not tamper with programs already in place.*

4. *Wilson's progressive reform agenda sought to strengthen democracy through programs such as the Underwood Tariff, Clayton Act, Federal Reserve Act, and Federal Trade Commission.*

5. *Franklin Roosevelt's New Deal included a variety of relief, recovery, and reform acts designed to get the country out of the Great Depression and avoid a similar catastrophe in the future. During FDR's administration, the country first adopted the concept that the government has a responsibility to "promote the general welfare."*

6. *Polk promised to complete the country's expansion to the Pacific Ocean through acquisition of the Oregon Country, Texas, and what became the Mexican Cession.*

7. *Hoover believed that the country's prosperity and greatness to date had stemmed from rugged individualism rather than government action and that this philosophy would work again in the Great Depression.*

8. *Lyndon Johnson believed the country could eliminate poverty and racial injustice, improve education for all, and revitalize city slums to create a truly "great society." Programs included the Civil Rights Act, "war on poverty," Voting Rights Act, Medicare, Immigration Act, and Elementary and Secondary Education Act.*

9. Truman's Fair Deal aimed to preserve and extend the New Deal but met considerable Congressional opposition.

10. Kennedy's New Frontier sought to find opportunity in space, medicine, technology, and social relations. Many of his proposals for civil rights, poverty programs, Medicare, and education became law after his assassination.

Suggested Responses, Part B:

1. Abraham Lincoln set the tone for the Lincoln-Douglas debates by expressing concern that a nation divided by slavery could not exist half slave and half free, but would become one or the other. His aim was to preserve the Union.

2. In McCulloch v. Maryland, the Supreme Court ruled that a state could not take measures that would destroy the Union, so Maryland's tax on the Baltimore branch of the Bank of the United States was unconstitutional. This established the principle that the national government is dominant.

3. Booker T. Washington's Tuskegee Institute operated on the principle that African Americans would be well-advised to seek training in the trades rather than strive immediately for social equality and the "opportunity to spend a dollar in the opera house."

4. Earl Warren ruled "separate but equal," established in 1896 by Plessy v. Ferguson unconstitutional in the 1954 Brown v. Board of Education of Topeka decision.

5. This goal established in the Declaration of Independence has remained an American standard for judging progress toward equality since 1776.

6. Wilson's unrealized goal in the "Great War" was to end war for all time.

7. At the time of the Civil War, the Confederate States of America sought the right to leave the Union and fought for that right.

8. In Franklin Roosevelt's War Message to Congress, he made this memorable reference to the Japanese attack on Pearl Harbor.

9. Martin Luther King, Jr.'s dramatic speech at the Lincoln Memorial during the 1963 March on Washington was a major factor in the passage of the Civil Rights Act of 1964.

10. John Marshall's statement in Marbury v. Madison (1803) established a precedent for judicial review.

11. This provision in Article I of the Constitution gave Congress the authority to use implied powers.

12. The Mayflower Compact (1620) became the first document of self-government in the English colonies.

13. Polk's campaign theme suggested that this country might demand all the Oregon territory to the southern border of Alaska, but this left him room for negotiating and compromising with the British later.

14. These were key issues in the American decision to go to war in 1812.

15. William Jennings Bryan made a passionate attack on the gold standard at the Democratic nominating convention in 1896 with his "Cross of Gold" speech.

16. Franklin Roosevelt sought, for economic reasons if no others, to end the Roosevelt Corollary and establish friendlier relations with Latin America.

17. Kennedy's inspirational message in his 1961 Inaugural Address set the theme for a new commitment to America.

18. Franklin Roosevelt used this rationale in calling for the Lend-Lease Act prior to our involvement in the military aspects of World War II.

19. In his Second Inaugural, Lincoln called for a lenient peace and a quick return to the Union of the Confederate States after the Civil War.

20. Washington set a long-standing policy of United States' foreign affairs in his Farewell Address.

21. Andrew Jackson made the retort in response to John Marshall's decision in support of the Cherokee Nation in Worcester v. Georgia in 1832.

22. At the time of the South Carolina threat to nullify the Tariff of Abominations, Daniel Webster, the Massachusetts Senator, suggested this should be the motto of the United States.

23. This became the Federalist rallying cry after the French made demands for a bribe, a loan, and an apology from President John Adams in 1797 in the XYZ Affair.

24. Lincoln's primary objective in the Civil War was the preservation of the Union.

25. Wilson's idealistic plan for a negotiated settlement of the war before either side achieved a victory was unacceptable to Germany in January 1917, and Germany instead resumed unrestricted submarine warfare, a step that led to U.S. entry into the war.

26. This became the rallying cry of those favoring war against Spain in 1898.

27. This became the rallying cry of Texans in their war for independence from Mexico in 1836.

28. As President, Theodore Roosevelt pursued a vigorous foreign policy based on this old African saying. Taking the Canal Zone and pursuing the Roosevelt Corollary in Latin America are two examples.

29. The Truman Doctrine offering peacetime aid to Greece and Turkey in 1947 marked a significant break with Washington's advice in his Farewell Address to pursue a more isolationist foreign policy.

30. In his Inaugural speech in 1933, Franklin Roosevelt tried to inspire confidence in his ability to lead.

31. The Declaration of the Sentiments of Women issued at the 1848 Seneca Falls Convention based the claims of women on the Declaration of Independence.

32. Monroe's 1823 State of the Union address issued this warning, now a cornerstone of American foreign policy, against European expansion in this hemisphere.

33. Lincoln's 1863 Emancipation Proclamation committed the United States to freeing the slaves and, at the same time, helping gain British support for the Union in the Civil War.

34. The Preamble of the United States Constitution, written in 1787, promised an effort to create a more effective government than the state-dominated Articles of Confederation had provided.

35. In one of her published newspaper columns, Eleanor Roosevelt, ever the human rights activist, wrote this reassuring and inspiring statement.

36. Andrew Carnegie's "Gospel of Wealth," written in 1889, celebrated the benefits that great amounts of accumulated wealth could do for the public. Not all were convinced that his treatment of workers was justified by this philosophy of philanthropy.

37. Frederick Jackson Turner, in his famous 1890 "Significance of the Frontier in American History," helped Americans to understand this neglected factor in American development.

38. This first telegraph message sent in 1837 introduced a revolution in communication.

39. Ronald Reagan's philosophy of government in the 1980s was based on this motto.

40. Betty Freidan, in The Feminist Mystique published in 1963, touched a responsive chord among many women and essentially started the women's rights movement.

Remembering Your Ps and Qs—
Presidential Promises and Quotable Quotations

Names given to presidential administrations and significant quotations from speeches, documents, Supreme Court decisions, and writings often serve as shorthand keys to conveying larger themes of American history. Recalling these ideas can be one of many effective strategies in a comprehensive review of the course in preparation for the Advanced Placement examination.

Part A.

Presidential Administrations

In this section, identify the president associated with each designation, key policies of his administration associated with the motto, and the motto's importance in conveying a major theme of our history at the time.

1. Square Deal

2. Dollar Diplomacy

3. Modern Republicanism

4. New Freedom

5. New Deal

6. Manifest Destiny

7. Rugged Individualism

8. Great Society

9. Fair Deal

10. New Frontier

Part B.

Quotable Quotations

In this section, identify the source of the quotation, when and in what context it was used, and its larger significance in illuminating a theme of American history.

1. "A house divided against itself cannot stand."

2. "The power to tax involves the power to destroy."

3. "It is at the bottom of life we must begin, not at the top."

4. "Separate educational facilities are inherently unequal."

5. "We hold these truths to be self-evident: that all men are created equal."

6. "A war to end all wars."

7. "All we ask is to be left alone."

8. "December 7, 1941—a date that will live in infamy."

9. "I have a dream that my four children will one day live in a nation where they will not be judged by the color of their skin but by the content of their character."

10. "A law repugnant to the Constitution is void."

11. "To make all laws which shall be necessary and proper for carrying into execution the foregoing powers."

12. "We . . . covenant and combine ourselves into a civil body politic."

13. "Fifty-four forty or fight."

14. "Free trade and sailors' rights."

15. "You shall not crucify mankind upon a cross of gold."

16. "God made us neighbors. Let justice make us friends."

17. "And so, my fellow Americans: Ask not what your country can do for you, but what you can do for your country."

18. "We must be the great arsenal of democracy."

19. "With malice toward none, with charity for all. . . ."

20. "It is our policy to stay clear of permanent alliances."

21. "John Marshall has made his decision; now let him enforce it."

22. "Liberty and Union, now and forever, one and inseparable."

23. "Millions for defense, but not one cent for tribute."

24. "My paramount object in this struggle is to save the Union."

25. "Peace without victory."

26. "Remember the Alamo."

27. "Remember the Maine."

28. "Speak softly and carry a big stick, you will go far."

29. "The ideals and traditions of our nations demanded that we come to the aid of Greece and Turkey and that we put the world on notice that it would be our policy to support the cause of freedom wherever it was threatened. . . ."

30. "The only thing we have to fear is fear itself."

31. "We hold these truths to be self-evident: that all men and women are created equal; that they are endowed by their Creator with certain unalienable rights."

32. "The American continents, by the free and independent condition which they have assumed and maintain, are henceforth not to be considered as subject for future colonization by any European powers."

33. "And, by virtue of the power and for the purpose aforesaid, I do order and declare that all persons held as slaves within these said designated States and parts of States are, and henceforward shall be free."

34. "We the people of the United States, in order to form a more perfect Union, ..."

35. "No one can make you feel inferior without your consent."

36. "Surplus wealth is a sacred trust which its possessor is bound to administer in his lifetime for the good of the community."

37. "The advance of the frontier has meant a steady movement away from the influence of Europe, a steady growth of independence on American lines. And to study this advance . . . is to study the really American part of our history."

38. "What hath God wrought!"

39. "Government is not the solution to our problem. Government is the problem."

40. "Women of the world unite! You have nothing to lose but your vacuum cleaner."

Lesson 34
Where in the U.S.A. Did It Happen, Carmen?

Objective
• To review U.S. history through geography

Notes to the Teacher
Students—even the best of them—often "learn" history without having a clear idea of where key events took place. In so doing, they develop incomplete or even inaccurate concepts of critical issues. In this review lesson, students first identify the state or states implied in a descriptive phrase and then go on to review the larger significance of the event. This review offers an opportunity to clarify points students may have missed when they originally studied a topic. Of course, it is this discussion of the importance of the event in the scheme of American history that is crucial as students attempt to prepare for the Advanced Placement examination, particularly the objective portion.

Procedure
1. Distribute **Handout 38** and have students complete it either individually or in small groups.

2. Review their responses, and take time to clarify points on which students have questions.

   Suggested Responses:

   1. 2—*The Convention developed the Constitution to replace the Articles of Confederation. It was based on principles of federalism, separation of powers, representation, and flexibility.*

   2. 27—*After Andrew Jackson's 1818 military expedition into Florida to crush hostile Seminole Indians, Spain sold Florida to the United States rather than risk losing it by force. This eliminated border problems with pirates and runaway slaves. The United States gave up claims to Texas, and Spain accepted the 42nd parallel as the border between Mexico and the Oregon Country.*

   3. 10—*Virginia wanted representation in Congress under the new Constitution to be based on population. This suggestion became the basis of the House of Representatives.*

   4. 3—*New Jersey wanted representation in Congress to be based on equality of states, as it was under the Articles of Confederation. This became the basis of the Senate.*

   5. 5—*The Great, or Connecticut, Compromise on representation called for a popularly-elected House of Representatives based on population and a Senate with two representatives per state chosen by the state legislatures. This compromise settled the most pressing conflict at the Constitutional Convention.*

   6. 28—*Tyler suggested Congress admit Texas by joint resolution after Polk had campaigned successfully on an expansionist platform. Annexation was a major cause of the Mexican War in 1846.*

   7. 22—*Muscle Shoals was the site of a federal project which set out to harness the power of the Tennessee River to produce electricity and nitrates for the poverty-stricken farmers of the Tennessee River Valley. After a long struggle between public and private interests over control of the project and vetoes by both Coolidge and Hoover, President Roosevelt signed a bill for federal control and expanded the project to become the Tennessee Valley Authority.*

   8. 46—*When the last remaining territory of the continental United States was opened to white settlers in 1889, the legal homesteaders found the land already occupied by illegal "Sooners," who had "jumped the gun" to establish claims. The 1890 Census revealed that, for practical purposes, the frontier of the United States was gone—The Turner Thesis.*

9. 45—After facing persecution in several eastern states, the Mormons settled near Salt Lake City and used irrigation and progressive farming techniques to make the desert bloom.

10. 38—Gold discoveries, the Homestead Act, and transcontinental railroads made Colorado ready for statehood in 1876, the centennial of the Declaration of Independence.

11. 23—Maine was admitted as a free state to counterbalance the slave state, Missouri. The line 36° 30´ would divide slave and free territory in the rest of the Louisiana Purchase.

12. 31—After the outbreak of the Mexican War, John C. Fremont and settlers set up the Bear Flag Republic in California. The United States took control of it in the Mexican War. Discovery of gold in California made the territory ready to apply for statehood in 1849, and it was subsequently admitted to the Union as part of the Compromise of 1850.

13. 48—Arizona was admitted to the Union during the Taft administration.

14. 44—Teapot Dome, Wyoming, was one of two government oil reserves that Secretary of the Interior Albert Fall leased to private interests in return for gifts and a loan. This scandal landed Fall in jail and discredited the Harding administration when it became public shortly after Harding's death.

15. 4—Georgia was meant to be a charity colony and a buffer against Spanish intrusion. James Oglethorpe's colony was the least prosperous of the original thirteen colonies.

16. 8—South Carolina had been the leader of southern radicalism since the days of John C. Calhoun and the tariff controversy in the Jackson administration.

17. 20—The Union victory at Vicksburg in the Civil War gave the Union control of the Mississippi River and effectively cut the Confederacy in half. This was a key measure in the Union strategy to win the war.

18. 14—Ethan Allen's Green Mountain boys captured British cannons from Fort Ticonderoga and dragged them overland to use in the successful colonial strategy to take the important port of Boston from the British at the start of the Revolution.

19. 6—These incidents in 1775 marked the first battles of the Revolution, in which the American colonies became the first ever to win independence from a mother country.

20. 5—Some colonies, including Connecticut, had charters extending "from sea to sea." One requirement for unanimous approval of the Articles of Confederation was that these states give up their western lands so that large states, such as Virginia, did not dominate the Union.

21. 2—When farmers in western Pennsylvania refused to pay Alexander Hamilton's whiskey excise tax, George Washington sent 15,000 federal troops to demonstrate the power and authority of the new national government under the Constitution.

22. 6—Daniel Shays led a rebellion of Massachusetts farmers in 1886 to protest mortgage foreclosures. The lack of a national force to put down such uprisings convinced many that a more powerful federal government than the Articles of Confederation provided was needed to preserve the peace and protect private property.

23. 19—Chicago demonstrators in support of an eight-hour day in 1886 faced brutal treatment by police. When the demonstration turned violent, the public turned against the Knights of Labor, who had been blamed erroneously for the bloodshed. This incident effectively doomed the Knights of Labor.

24. 34—"Bleeding Kansas" resulted from conflicts between pro-slavery and anti-slavery settlers in Kansas after the Kansas-Nebraska Act of 1854 introduced the concept of popular sovereignty in the two territories. The bloodshed was a precursor of the Civil War.

25. 25—When Arkansas Governor Orval Faubus opposed implementation of the Supreme Court decision in Brown v. Board of Education of Topeka, President Dwight Eisenhower had to send in the National Guard to guarantee the rights of black students to attend Central High School in Little Rock and preserve the authority of the federal government against states' rights advocates.

26. 36—Discovery of silver in Nevada in 1859 led to a stampede of fortune seekers in the territory. More than 300 million dollars worth of silver came out of the lode in the first twenty years after its discovery.

27. 35—The northwestern counties of Virginia chose to remain loyal to the Union, and their secession from Virginia helped the Union to keep control of the Ohio River.

28. 17—The Northwest Ordinance of 1787 had provided for eventual statehood rather than perpetual subordination, as the British expected of their colonial territories. Ohio became the first state to enter the Union under this "enlightened colonial policy."

29. 10–The first representative colonial legislature was started in Virginia in 1619. It became the model for other colonies.

30. 49–This bold claim by James Polk in his presidential campaign allowed room for compromise with the British over disputed claims to the Oregon Country. The two settled on 49° as the eventual border.

31. 9—Theodore Roosevelt mediated an end to the Russo-Japanese War in 1905 (for which he received the Nobel Peace Prize). The treaty, signed in New Hampshire, alienated the Japanese, who believed they were entitled to land as a result of their victory. This slight was the start of tensions between Japan and the United States. Pearl Harbor was the eventual result.

32. 10—The raid to capture the federal arsenal and arm the slaves took place in the state of Virginia. (The area is in the part of Virginia that seceded several years later to become West Virginia.) The raid convinced southerners that the north would stop at nothing to abolish slavery.

33. 8—The fort, located in Charleston harbor in South Carolina, was the site of the first battle between the North and South. President Lincoln, who hoped to preserve a Union fort in Confederate territory as a symbol of national authority, sent food and medical supplies to the fort. When Confederates prevented provisioning the fort, Lincoln claimed that this was an act of aggression on their part and put the blame for the start of the war on the South.

34. 31—The 1945 San Francisco Conference guaranteed that the United Nations, unlike the earlier League of Nations, would have the full cooperation and support of the United States.

35. 13—Roger Williams's colony of Rhode Island became the model for the rest of the country when it guaranteed religious freedom for all.

36. 7—Maryland, originally settled by Catholics, passed this legislation in order to guarantee religious rights for Catholics, who had by then become a minority.

37. 2—Andrew Carnegie's steel plant in Homestead, Pennsylvania, was the site of a bloody battle between strikers and the state militia, who had been called to protect property rights. The strike reaffirmed the position of the government on the side of business rather than labor.

38. 48–The purchase of this strip of land from Mexico in 1853 gave the United States access to a favorable route for a southern transcontinental railroad. Some viewed it, too, as "conscience money" for the Mexican War.

39. 40—This was the sight of the last of the Indian battles in 1890 and also of the 1973 takeover of the Oglala Sioux Pine Ridge Reservation by the radical American Indian Movement. In 1975, Congress passed the American Indian Self-Determination and Education Act to give Native Americans greater authority on their own reservations.

40. 24, 25, 7, and 1—Although in some instances it was not a free choice, the retention of the border states of Missouri, Kentucky, Maryland, and Delaware in the Union helped the United States keep control of the Mississippi and Ohio rivers and prevent the capital from being surrounded by Confederate territory.

41. 49—Secretary of State Seward's purchase of Alaska in 1867 later proved to be a wise move, for both strategic and economic reasons.

42. 50—The December 7, 1941, attack on Pearl Harbor led to a Congressional declaration of war against Japan on the following day.

43. 2—The Confederate attempt to disrupt the railroad center at Harrisburg, Pennsylvania, was derailed when the Union fought and won the battle at Gettysburg. This proved to be a turning point in the war for the Union.

44. 23—Settlement of a lingering border dispute between Britain and the United States over Maine gave this country the fertile Aroostook Valley and paved the way for compromise on the Oregon Country.

45. 22—Booker T. Washington's Tuskegee Institute, a vocational training facility for African Americans, typified the gradualist approach to progress for African Americans that W. E. B. DuBois found so objectionable.

46. 31, 36, 45, and 48—Loss of these lands, as well as parts of New Mexico and Colorado, caused Mexico and other Latin American countries to view the United States with suspicion for decades after the war. Acquisition of these lands also revived the slavery issue that led to the Civil War.

47. 31—Riots in the Watts section of Los Angeles touched off a summer of urban violence and led to white backlash against the progress achieved in the Civil Rights Movement. Too, it called attention to the views of radical African American leaders and their proposed solutions for problems of African Americans in America.

48. 24—John Brown and his sons murdered five proslavery men in their beds to avenge an earlier proslavery sacking of Lawrence, Kansas, during the "Bleeding Kansas" episode after passage of the Kansas-Nebraska Act. The incident incited passions on both sides and contributed to the outbreak of the Civil War.

49. 30—Robert LaFollette's Progressive reforms, including the direct primary and state commission to regulate railroad rates, became the model of Progressivism for other states.

50. 42 and 43—The Oregon Compromise with Britain established the 49th parallel as the northern border of these states and part of Montana. Settlement of this issue freed Polk to focus on his campaign promise to secure what later became known as the Mexican Cession.

Where In the U.S.A. Did It Happen, Carmen?

Beside each item, write the number of the state on the map on the following page to indicate where the event occurred or the state (or states) implied in the statement. Be prepared to state the larger significance of each of the items.

_____ 1. The Constitutional Convention was held here.

_____ 2. The Adams-Onis Treaty dealt with this state.

_____ 3. The author of the large-state plan came from here.

_____ 4. The author of the small-state plan represented this state.

_____ 5. Roger Sherman, author of the Great Compromise, represented this state.

_____ 6. The United States annexed this area in 1845.

_____ 7. Muscle Shoals is in this state.

_____ 8. This state is known as the "Sooner State."

_____ 9. The Mormons finally settled here.

_____ 10. This is the Centennial State.

_____ 11. This state was admitted as a free state in 1820.

_____ 12. This state was originally the Bear Flag Republic.

_____ 13. This was the last of the continental forty-eight states to be admitted to the Union.

_____ 14. This is the site of Teapot Dome.

_____ 15. This colony was originally set up for debtors.

_____ 16. This was the first state to secede.

_____ 17. Vicksburg is in this state.

_____ 18. The Green Mountains are in this state.

_____ 19. Lexington and Concord are located here.

_____ 20. Ohio's Western Reserve was originally a part of this state.

_____ 21. The Whiskey Rebellion took place here.

_____ 22. Shays' Rebellion took place here.

_____ 23. This was the site of the Haymarket Riot.

_____ 24. This future state experienced a small civil war in 1856.

_____ 25. The National Guard was called here to facilitate school integration in 1957.

_____ 26. The Comstock Lode is in this state.

_____ 27. This area separated from an existing state in 1863.

_____ 28. This became the first state in the Northwest Territory to become a state.

_____ 29. The House of Burgesses sits in this state.

_____ 30. The line implied in "Fifty-four forty or fight!" is the southern border of which state?

_____ 31. The Treaty of Portsmouth was signed here.

_____ 32. John Brown's famous raid at Harper's Ferry was in this state.

_____ 33. Fort Sumter is located in this state.

_____ 34. The conference to start the United Nations was held in this state.

_____ 35. This was the first colony to grant complete freedom of worship and separation of church and state.

_____ 36. This colony passed an Act of Toleration in 1649.

_____ 37. This state was the site of the Homestead Strike.

_____ 38. Most of the Gadsden Purchase is in this state.

_____ 39. This state is the location of Wounded Knee.

_____ 40. These four border states remained loyal to the Union.

_____ 41. Seward's Folly referred to this area.

_____ 42. This was the site of the attack on Pearl Harbor.

_____ 43. The Battle of Gettysburg took place here.

_____ 44. The Webster-Ashburton Treaty established the border of this eastern state.

_____ 45. Tuskegee Institute is located here.

_____ 46. The Mexican Cession included all of these four states.

_____ 47. The area known as Watts is located in a large city in this state.

_____ 48. The Potawatomie Massacre took place here.

_____ 49. This state's Progressive governor made it "the laboratory of democracy" and a model for others interested in reform.

_____ 50. The Oregon Compromise set the northern border of these two states.

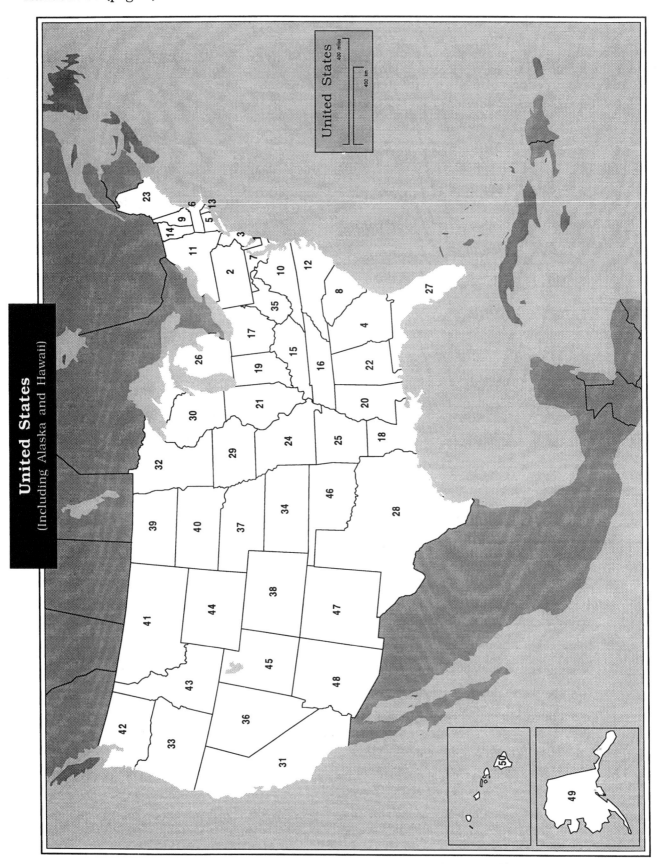

Lesson 35
The Power of the Printed Word

Objective

- To review the impact of critical books, pamphlets, and documents in the evolution of American society

Notes to the Teacher

A few books, documents, and pamphlets have had a far-reaching impact on the political, economic, and social development of American society. These writings have stood the test of time in that they have shaped American society for good or ill since 1776. Some have also influenced the thinking of individuals in other countries or the actions of other governments. Other writings might have been included, but those selected provide students with a foundation for understanding major themes in American thought.

Students review these classics by stating the main idea and the impact of each work and then organizing the writings by centuries and discussing the extent to which they shaped the character of the century in which they were written. They conclude by attempting to rank the works in importance for the development of American thought.

Procedure

1. Distribute **Handout 39** and have students complete part A as a small-group activity.

2. Review their responses. Use students' responses as a springboard for discussion.

    Suggested Responses, Part A:

    1. *Stowe's* Uncle Tom's Cabin *(1852), a best seller, serves as an indictment of the evils of slavery and the laws that supported it. Lincoln once referred to Stowe as "the lady who started this great war" and termed the novel the most powerful argument offered for the Emancipation Proclamation.*

    2. *The Declaration of Independence, written largely by Thomas Jefferson, announced the colonies' separation from Britain and justified independence on the grounds of British violations of the colonists' natural rights. The statement that "all men are created equal" has served since 1776 as a standard by which to judge America's progress toward the ideal of equality.*

    3. *Mahan's study of sea power, especially that of England, convinced him that a country's strength on the sea largely determined its prosperity and position in the world. The book prompted many countries, including the United States, Germany, and Japan, to begin naval expansion in the pre-World War I years.*

    4. *Paine's influential pamphlet, "Common Sense," attacked monarchy and inherited privilege. In a brilliant statement of the colonists' cause, he demanded complete independence from England and establishment of a strong federal union. Both influential leaders and thousands of ordinary colonists became converted to the cause of independence.*

    5. *The novel,* The Jungle, *exposed the evils of early twentieth-century Chicago meatpacking plants and led to the 1906 Meat Inspection Act, one of the first pieces of Progressive legislation to regulate industries.*

    6. *Hamilton's report to Congress argued persuasively the advantages of a diversified economy with both industry and agriculture to insure the country's economic as well as political independence. He called, in particular, for a high protective tariff, a measure finally enacted in 1816.*

    7. *Turner's famous essay, published just after the Census Bureau announced the end of the frontier, outlined how the frontier experience had shaped American development and focused historians' attention on a previously-overlooked factor in explaining America's past.*

    8. *The* Feminist Mystique *argued that the media had convinced American women that they could be completely fulfilled through a life as a wife and mother. The book launched the women's rights movement and led to the establishment of the National Organization for Women (NOW).*

9. The Liberator, *which began publication in 1831, became the leading abolitionist newspaper and helped create the climate of public opinion necessary for success in the antislavery movement.*

10. *Helen Hunt Jackson's expose of the government's treatment of Native Americans detailed a long list of broken promises and treaties with Native Americans and led to the Dawes Act, often called the "Indian Emancipation Act," giving the president authority to distribute Native American lands among the tribes.*

11. The Federalist, *a collection of essays, was meant to persuade New York to ratify the Constitution. The essays have since become the classic interpretation of the Constitution.*

12. *Drawing on the philosophy of Social Darwinism, Carnegie argued that unbridled competition had brought order and efficiency to chaos in the business world, but the wealth it created obligated the rich to spend some of their wealth to help their "poorer brethren." His own large-scale philanthropy created a model for others to follow although some questioned whether his cruel treatment of workers was justified by the philanthropy.*

13. *Thoreau's essay, based on his own protest against paying taxes to support the war in Mexico, became an inspiration for others, including Martin Luther King, Jr.*

14. *Steinbeck's Nobel Prize-winning novel chronicled the plight of migrant workers during the Depression. The popular social-protest novel suggested the perfectibility of humanity and the possibility of improved conditions.*

15. *Steffens's muckraking expose of municipal corruption in numerous cities led to a variety of changes in the form of urban government and other municipal reforms during the Progressive Era.*

16. *Harrington's moving expose of rampant poverty, particularly among the "invisible poor"—the elderly, uneducated, and low-paid workers—inspired Lyndon Johnson's "war on poverty."*

17. *"The Atlanta Compromise" aimed to cement relations between the black and white races by suggesting that African Americans should work their way up by starting with vocational training and proving their worth before striving for social integration and the right to "spend a dollar at the opera house." This gradualist approach was popular among many whites but probably set the Civil Rights Movement back several decades.*

18. The Promise of American Life *outlined a "New Nationalism," a philosophy on which Theodore Roosevelt based his 1912 campaign for the presidency. According to the philosophy, a strong government would act as "steward of the public welfare" to guarantee the rights of the people.*

19. *George proposed a "single tax" on the unearned increment in land values to break up landholding monopolies and finance a better life for all. Henry George's faith in the people's ability to effect change created a climate for reform efforts rather than inaction later, during the Progressive and New Deal periods.*

20. *Locke's* New Negro *focused on black contributions to American culture and civilization. The book made him the "Father of the Harlem Renaissance," the movement of the 1920s that contributed to African Americans' sense of self-esteem and whites' recognition of the value of African American culture for both races.*

21. *Adam Smith's* A Wealth of Nations, *published in England the year the colonists declared their independence, launched an assault on the principles of mercantilism. Smith's contention that enlightened self-interest, competition, and a laissez-faire approach of government provided a better basis for an economy suited conditions in America and became the foundation of the new U.S. economy.*

22. *Bellamy's Utopian novel predicted how class divisions and relentless competition would give way to a caring, cooperative, classless, socialistic state by the year 2000. This manifesto for social and economic reform won many adherents and helped set the stage for new philosophies in the Progressive and New Deal eras.*

23. *Twenty Years at Hull House describes Jane Addams's settlement house experiences in early twentieth-century Chicago. Her work provided a model for the kind of services settlement houses everywhere could offer the urban poor.*

24. *Rachel Carson's book revealed the depletion and pollution of America's resources, both by government actions and by the use of toxic chemicals and pesticides. The book raised environmental consciousness and inspired the ecology movement.*

25. *Taylor showed factory managers how to use efficient plant organization and time-motion studies to lower production costs per unit and increase production per worker.*

26. *Woodward and Bernstein, reporters for the Washington Post newspaper, painstakingly tracked numerous leads to unravel the story of the Watergate cover-up. Their book was a major factor in forcing the resignation of President Nixon.*

27. *DuBois predicted that race relations would be the critical issue of the twentieth century. Unlike Booker T. Washington, he advocated an immediate end to segregation and prompt steps to introduce quality education and voting for African Americans. His impassioned plea for unconditional equality set the agenda for the Civil Rights Movement.*

28. *Defense analyst Daniel Ellsberg leaked to the New York Times a secret account of American involvement in Vietnam. The papers allowed Americans to read the lies and faulty assumptions that led to this country's increasing involvement in the War. The Supreme Court*

denied the Nixon administration an injunction to halt publication. Thus, the public's right to know took precedence over the Defense Department's claim of secrecy in the name of public security. As a result, protests over American involvement increased until the government promised to end the war without fighting on to victory.

29. *Martin Luther Kings's response to white leaders who criticized his willingness to go to jail rather than obey an unjust segregation law became the classic interpretation of the Civil Rights Movement. It prompted President Kennedy to make an important television address supporting civil rights legislation.*

30. *Jacob Riis, a reform-minded photojournalist, included grim pictures of New York City tenements along with his accounts of life in the poorer neighborhoods. His work led to the first housing reforms and other education, social welfare, and health care legislation during the Progressive Era.*

3. Have students group the writers by centuries as indicated in part B. Then conduct a discussion of how this grouping of influential writers might help to suggest a labor for each century.

Suggested Responses, Part B:

Eighteenth century—*Paine, Jefferson, Smith, Hamilton, and Hamilton, Madison, and Jay*

Nineteenth century—*Garrison, Thoreau, Stowe, George, Hunt Jackson, Bellamy, Carnegie, Mahan, Turner, Booker T. Washington, Riis*

Twentieth century—*DuBois, Steffens, Sinclair, Croly, Addams, Taylor, Locke, Steinbeck, Harrington, Carson, Freidan, King, Woodward and Bernstein, Ellsberg*

4. Raise the following points in a concluding discussion: What three works in each of the following categories have had the greatest long-range impact: political, economic, and social? Have students justify their choices. What other writings should have been included on the list? Why?

The Power of the Printed Word

Part A.

On your own paper, write the main idea and significance of each of the following books, pamphlets, or documents which had important consequences for American development.

1. Harriet Beecher Stowe, *Uncle Tom's Cabin.* 1852.

2. Thomas Jefferson, Declaration of Independence. 1776.

3. Alfred Thayer Mahan, *The Influence of Sea Power upon History, 1660-1783.* 1890.

4. Thomas Paine, "Common Sense." 1776.

5. Upton Sinclair, *The Jungle.* 1906.

6. Alexander Hamilton, "The Report on Manufactures." 1791.

7. Frederick Jackson Turner, "The Significance of the Frontier in American History." 1893.

8. Betty Friedan, *The Feminine Mystique.* 1963.

9. William Lloyd Garrison, *The Liberator.* 1831.

10. Helen Hunt Jackson, *A Century of Dishonor.* 1881.

11. Alexander Hamilton, James Madison, and John Jay, *The Federalist* Papers. 1787.

12. Andrew Carnegie, "The Gospel of Wealth." 1889.

13. Henry David Thoreau, "On Civil Disobedience." 1849.

14. John Steinbeck, *The Grapes of Wrath.* 1939.

15. Lincoln Steffens, *The Shame of the Cities.* 1904.

16. Michael Harrington, *The Other America.* 1961.

17. Booker T. Washington, "The Atlanta Compromise." 1895.

18. Herbert Croly, *The Promises of American Life.* 1909.

19. Henry George, *Progress and Poverty.* 1879.

20. Alain Locke, *The New Negro.* 1925.

21. Adam Smith, *A Wealth of Nations.* 1776.

22. Edward Bellamy, *Looking Backward.* 1888.

23. Jane Addams, *Twenty Years at Hull House.* 1910.

24. Rachel Carson, *Silent Spring.* 1961.

25. Frederick Taylor, *Principles of Scientific Management.* 1911.

26. Bob Woodward and Carl Bernstein, *All the President's Men.* 1974.

27. W.E.B. DuBois, *The Souls of Black Folk.* 1903.

28. Daniel Ellsberg, *The Pentagon Papers.* 1971.

29. Martin Luther King, Jr., "Letter from Birmingham Jail." 1963.

30. Jacob Riis, *How the Other Half Lives.* 1890.

Part B.

First group the writers by centuries. Using these groupings and your completed part A, try to assign a label to each century based on the intellectual breakthroughs of its great minds.

Eighteenth century

Writers

Label

Nineteenth century

Writers

Label

Twentieth century

Writers

Label

Lesson 36
Points of Conflict—The Focus of History

Objective

- To review the course of American history through its major conflicts

Notes to the Teacher

Conflicts that have highlighted an age have often had long-range implications for the course of history. Reviewing these critical conflicts helps students gain an understanding of chronology and main characters and movements that have shaped America's development. At this stage in their review, this activity should be a confidence builder as students recognize that they understand main currents in American thought.

In this lesson, students identify the characters, conflict, time, issues, and impact of fifteen major conflicts in American history.

Procedure

1. Distribute **Handout 40** and have students complete the outline individually.

2. Review their responses, and answer any lingering questions students have about these critical issues.

Suggested Responses:

1. *President Woodrow Wilson, a Democrat, and Senator Henry Cabot Lodge, the Republican chairman of the Senate Foreign Relations Committee, battled over ratification of the Treaty of Versailles in 1919. At issue, in particular, was U.S. entry into the League of Nations, which was part of Wilson's Fourteen Points peace proposal that he managed to salvage at the Versailles negotiations. Lodge was angry with Wilson for not consulting him or other key Republicans during the negotiations and sought to add a list of "reservations" to the League of Nations. Wilson, who was unwilling to compromise, was adamant about retaining Article X, which called for member nations to go to the assistance of any nation which suffered acts of aggression. Lodge's protests and stalling, coupled with Wilson's intran-*

sigence and crippling stroke at the height of the battle, led to defeat of the Treaty and U.S. membership in the League. This country retreated from obligations of world leadership until World War II and, in so doing, may have crippled the League.

2. *Hamilton, secretary of the treasury in Washington's cabinet, and Jefferson, Washington's secretary of state, clashed over Hamilton's proposed financial program and Jefferson's support for France in foreign relations. Jefferson disagreed with Hamilton's plans to fund the state debt, plans to create a Bank of the United States, his whiskey excise tax, and his proposal to impose a protective tariff to encourage manufacturing. Representing different constituencies, the two men soon headed different factions with Hamilton representing the business elite and Jefferson, the agrarian elements in society. Congressional acceptance of Hamilton's funding plans, Bank of the United States, and whiskey excise tax put the country on a firm foundation financially and set a precedent for a strong national government, but it was Jefferson's less aristocratic faction which in the end garnered greater political and public support and set the country on a path toward democracy.*

3. *President Richard Nixon clashed with the Supreme Court in July, 1974, over his claim of executive privilege in objecting to release of critical portions of the Watergate tapes. Special prosecutor Leon Jaworski obtained a court order directing Nixon to turn over the tapes. Nixon's appeal to the Supreme Court to support his decision resulted in an 8-0 decision against him. Release of the tapes, which contained damaging evidence that the president had lied about his knowledge of the Watergate cover-up, was a key factor in forcing the Nixon's resignation the following month.*

4. In 1937, Franklin Roosevelt, frustrated by the Supreme Court's invalidation of key New Deal legislation, sought the right to add six new justices to the Court to "assist" the older judges over 70 years old. Even though Congress was of the president's party, it refused to allow this "packing of the Court" because it would have upset the balance of power among the three branches of government.

5. Rutherford B. Hayes, a Republican, and Samuel Tilden, a Democrat, clashed in the very close presidential election in 1876. Voters, apparently tired of the corruption of the Grant administration, voted in large numbers for Tilden. Election results hinged on twenty key electoral votes in states submitting disputed returns. Tilden needed only one of the votes, Hayes needed all twenty to win. An electoral commission, which was created with seven members of each party and one Independent, was upset in favor of the Republicans when the independent, a Supreme Court justice, resigned and President Grant replaced him with a Republican. Democratic claims of the "stolen election" quieted when Hayes agreed to remove the last remaining troops from the South and officially end Reconstruction. This action left newly-freed African Americans at the mercy of southern whites intent on retaliation.

6. Gloria Steinem, feminist founder of Ms. magazine, and Phyllis Schlafly, leader of a nationwide movement in opposition to the women's rights movement, clashed in the 1970s over the Equal Rights Amendment and a variety of other feminist issues. Steinem argued the necessity of reform to gain equal rights while Schlafly countered that these moves would deprive women of separate restrooms, exemption from the draft, alimony, and the right to attend single-sex colleges. Division within the ranks of the women's movement may have doomed the ERA.

7. During the Korean Conflict, President Truman, the Commander-in-Chief, and MacArthur, the general in charge of the UN's operation in Korea, argued over whether or not to pursue North Korean troops beyond the 38th parallel into their own territory. Fearing an all-out war with the Chinese, Truman argued against the move and had no choice but to fire MacArthur when MacArthur's public statements in support of a more vigorous policy became too loud. Many Americans found the concept of limited war and United Nations's policy of merely stopping aggression to be frustrating. Removal of MacArthur did, however, preserve the constitutional power of the president as Commander-in-Chief with final authority over the military.

8. In 1896, William Jennings Bryan, representing both the Populist and Democratic parties, lost to William McKinley, the Republican. The election dealt largely with the silver issue and Bryan's determination to support inflation beneficial to farmers. Results of the election made clear the waning influence of farmers and the rising control of American business interests.

9. Abraham Lincoln and Stephen Douglas first clashed in the Senate race in 1858 in Illinois. The Lincoln-Douglas debates focused on the slavery issue and served as a prelude to the 1860 presidential election. Lincoln's question asking Douglas how he reconciled his support for popular sovereignty with the recent Dred Scott decision of the Supreme Court turned out to be critical. In making his response, Douglas alienated both the proslavery advocates and the antislavery interests. By trying to take a neutral stand on the issue, Douglas hoped to preserve the Union. Lincoln's strong stand in opposition to the spread of slavery cost him all hope of gaining southern support but gained him solid support in the North. Although Douglas won the Senate seat, he lost the bigger campaign for the presidency in 1860. Lincoln's election was totally unacceptable to slave interests and led to southern secession.

10. In the American Revolution, Tories questioned giving up the stable government and protection of the British in return for an unknown American government. Fears of a possible move to remove the elite from office further disquieted them. Patriots, on the other hand, approved the reasoning of Thomas Paine in "Common Sense" and Jefferson in the Declaration of Independence and supported war with Britain in an effort to gain independence.

11. Federalists and Anti-Federalists argued over ratification of the Constitution in 1789. Anti-Federalists feared a strong central government, physically far removed from their sight. Federalists saw the need for a stronger national government that could solve pressing problems, such as trade wars, financial problems, threats to private property, and difficulties with Native Americans. Federalist victories led to ratification of the Constitution to replace the weaker Articles of Confederation and set the country on a firm foundation for progress in the future.

12. In 1832, President Andrew Jackson and Nicholas Biddle, president of the Second Bank of the United States, argued over the wisdom of rechartering the Bank. Jackson argued that it was an institution of the rich and was both undemocratic and unconstitutional. Biddle argued that it had served a critical role in preserving the stability of money. In the presidential election, in which the Bank was the key issue, Jackson, the popular war hero and incumbent president, won over Henry Clay, who supported the Bank. Killing the Bank meant that the national government lost control of the money supply.

13. In 1932, Herbert Hoover, the incumbent Republican president, and Franklin Roosevelt, the Democratic governor of New York, opposed each other in the presidential election. Hoover was convinced that the country could ride out the deepening depression without significant changes in government responsibilities. Franklin Roosevelt, unsure exactly how to proceed, promised bold experimentation to bring the country back to prosperity. Roosevelt's election in that year and in the succeeding three elections set the nation on the path to becoming a welfare state with broad federal obligations to help those unable to help themselves.

14. In the mid-1960s, Martin Luther King, Jr., who had preached and practiced nonviolence and cooperation with whites in his successful campaign to gain civil rights legislation, clashed with Malcolm X, radical and articulate spokesperson for "any means necessary to fight racism." Malcolm X spoke for the needs of urban poor in particular and insisted that violence would gain attention and help the cause. Although he was assassinated in 1965, his thinking dominated the Civil Rights Movement for the next several years.

15. W. E. B. DuBois, founder of the National Association for the Advancement of Colored People, took issue with Booker T. Washington's strategy of gradualism and accommodation with whites to prepare African Americans for eventual equality and social acceptance by whites. Washington, founder of the Tuskegee Institute in Alabama, suggested that blacks start at the bottom and gain economic strength before insisting on equality. DuBois insisted that voting, an end to segregation, and advanced education for the "Talented Tenth" were reasonable requests in the early 1900s and that adherence to Washington's philosophy would put the Civil Rights Movement back decades.

Points of Conflict—The Focus of History

Review the following conflicts that set the tone for the ages by identifying the main characters and the conflict, time, issues, and impact.

1. Woodrow Wilson v. Henry Cabot Lodge

   Characters

   Conflict

   Time

   Issues

   Impact

2. Alexander Hamilton v. Thomas Jefferson

   Characters

   Conflict

   Time

   Issues

   Impact

3. Richard Nixon v. Supreme Court

   Characters

   Conflict

   Time

   Issues

   Impact

4. Franklin Roosevelt v. Supreme Court

   Characters

   Conflict

   Time

   Issues

   Impact

5. Rutherford B. Hayes v. Samuel Tilden

   Characters

   Conflict

   Time

   Issues

   Impact

6. Gloria Steinem v. Phyllis Schlafly

   Characters

   Conflict

   Time

   Issues

   Impact

7. Harry S Truman v. Douglas MacArthur

   Characters

   Conflict

   Time

   Issues

   Impact

8. William Jennings Bryan v. William McKinley

   Characters

   Conflict

   Time

   Issues

   Impact

9. Abraham Lincoln v. Stephen Douglas

   Characters

   Conflict

   Time

   Issues

   Impact

10. Tories v. Patriots

   Characters

   Conflict

   Time

   Issues

   Impact

11. Federalists v. Anti-Federalists

Characters

Conflict

Time

Issues

Impact

12. Andrew Jackson v. Nicholas Biddle

Characters

Conflict

Time

Issues

Impact

13. Herbert Hoover v. Franklin D. Roosevelt

Characters

Conflict

Time

Issues

Impact

14. Martin Luther King, Jr. v. Malcolm X

Characters

Conflict

Time

Issues

Impact

15. Booker T. Washington v. W. E. B. DuBois

Characters

Conflict

Time

Issues

Impact

Lesson 37
Our Inheritance—A Legacy of Reform

Objective

- To review progress toward equality in American society through a look at six key reform movements

Notes to the Teacher

When various groups in American society protest injustices today, it is easy to lose sight of the substantial progress that this country has made toward making a reality the concept that "all men are created equal." Certainly, the optimism characteristic of Americans, the belief in the perfectibility of man (and woman), and acceptance of the idea that it is possible to hasten evolution by taking positive actions to effect change all play a role in setting a climate for reform. Perhaps no other country has so frequently undergone a periodic self-evaluation with a resulting campaign to right the wrongs of society as has America. The reform eras of the 1830s and 1840s, Progressivism, the New Deal, and the 1960s are obvious examples. In addition, wars and other major stresses have brought significant social change as well.

Students review progress toward democracy by focusing on six key reforms: abolitionism, the twentieth-century Civil Rights Movement, labor reform, the women's rights movement, steps toward political democracy, and education reform. Students begin by brainstorming at least ten major steps toward progress in each of these areas. Then small groups take a closer look at the movements by preparing short reports on the movement's progress from its inception until today and developing a thesis to account for its relative success or failure.

Procedure

1. Introduce the lesson with information in the Notes to the Teacher.

2. Put the names of the six reform movements—abolition, women's rights, twentieth-century Civil Rights Movement, labor reform, education reform, and steps toward political democracy—on the chalkboard. Ask students to list individually on their own paper as many key steps in each

movement as they can. Then create a composite list on the board for each reform.

3. At this point, divide the class into six groups and assign each group one of the reform movements. Distribute **Handout 41** and have each group prepare the required short history and analysis of the movement for presentation to the rest of the class. Since this "divide and conquer" strategy is meant to make lighter the monumental task of a comprehensive review, be sure that students take notes during the presentations of their classmates.

Suggested Responses:

Abolition—*Students might point to accounts of Frederick Douglass or descriptions in Stowe's* Uncle Tom's Cabin *to illustrate evils of slavery. Steps toward reform will be varied, but might include the early Quaker protests that the practice violated the Declaration of Independence, the British example in ending the practice, the early abolitionist societies, the* Liberator, *Frederick Douglass's work and autobiography, the Underground Railroad, the work of Wendell Phillips, writings of Emerson and others, and the Emancipation Proclamation. The thesis might focus on varied efforts to create a climate of acceptance for abolition among a variety of groups in society.*

Twentieth-century Civil Rights Movement—*The century began with restrictions on voting, segregation, and sharecropping—Jim Crow laws. Steps toward progress might include the formation of the NAACP and Urban League, migration to the North during the world wars, Harlem Renaissance, work experiences during the wars, integration of the armed forces, the 1954* Brown v. Board of Education of Topeka *decision, the Montgomery bus boycott, sit-ins and freedom rides, Civil Rights Act of 1964, and the Voting Rights Act. The thesis might deal with disagreements among African Americans themselves about appropriate goals and strategies for success.*

Women's rights movement—*The Declaration of the 1848 Seneca Falls Convention is a good statement of the status of women at the start of the movement. Steps toward progress might include the Seneca Falls Convention, work in women's clubs, the suffrage campaign, the Nineteenth Amendment, changing conditions of education and work for women, women in significant political positions, the Civil Rights Act of 1964, the ERA campaign, women's liberation movement, National Organization for Women (NOW), and Roe v. Wade. The thesis here, too, might focus on divisions within the movement.*

Labor reform—*Initially, laborers did not bargain collectively and suffered low wages, long hours, poor working conditions, child labor, and other unsatisfactory conditions. Steps might include* Commonwealth v. Hunt *(1842), the Knights of Labor, American Federation of Labor, Wagner Act, Congress of Industrial Unions, Social Security, Fair Labor Standards Act, AFL-CIO merger, Landrum-Griffin Act, and the Civil Rights Act of 1964. Thesis might deal with the changing position of the government toward labor organization.*

Education—*Before the 1830s, one-room schools, untrained teachers, short school terms, and a focus on basics were characteristic of schools. Steps might include actions of Horace Mann and Henry Barnard, the public school movement, the development of technical schools, the Morrill Act, Charles Eliot's elective system at Harvard, state universities, the GI Bill of Rights, 1954* Brown v. Board of Education of Topeka *decision, adult education programs, affirmative action decisions, college scholarship programs, Head Start and Upward Bound. The thesis might deal with public support for extensions of educational opportunity in this country for all who want it.*

Steps toward political democracy—*Initially, only wealthy, white, male landowners voted. Since the early 1800s, the religious and property qualifications have ended; the Fifteenth, Nineteenth, Twenty-fourth, and Twenty-sixth amendments extended suffrage; nominating conventions, the secret ballot, direct election of Senators, direct primary, initiative, referendum, and recall made voting more fair; Native Americans now vote;* Baker v. Carr *decreed voting districts of equal size; literacy tests, the grandfather clause, and residence requirements are illegal; and the Voting Rights Act of 1965 made voting easier for African Americans. The thesis might deal with determination to erase inequities or the significant progress made in this area to give the opportunity for all Americans to vote (whether they exercise it or not).*

Name_____

Date_____

Our Inheritance—A Legacy of Reform

Six key reform movements in American history have made significant steps toward bringing equality for all Americans. These are the abolition movement, the twentieth-century Civil Rights Movement, education reform, the labor movement, the women's rights movement, and moves toward political democracy. Your initial brainstorming gave you a start toward a more thorough study of the reform. Complete the following guide to your assigned reform in preparation for a presentation to your classmates.

Reform _____

Describe as completely as you can the situation at the start of the movement.

Given further research since your brainstorming, what do you now see as the ten most significant steps in progress toward equality in this area?

1.

2.

3.

4.

5.

6.

7.

8.

9.

10.

What is your thesis to explain the relative success (or lack of it) in this movement?

Lesson 38
The Secretary of State Hall of Fame

Objective

- To review all of American diplomatic history through the eyes of the "best" and the "worst" secretaries of state

Notes to the Teacher

This lesson is partially based on an article written in the *American Heritage Magazine*, Vol. 33, No. 1, December, 1981, pages 78–80. David L. Porter of William Penn College in Oskaloosa, Iowa, sent a questionnaire to fifty historians that asked them to rate the best and the worst secretaries of state in U.S. history. Their choices are surprising and controversial; therefore, the activities in this lesson challenge their conclusions and their criteria.

Foreign policy is a key theme of both the objective and essay sections of the Advanced Placement Examination. In this lesson, students research fifteen secretaries of state and their accomplishments in order to create their own Secretary of State Hall of Fame. The activity provides a convenient summary of major foreign policy decisions—especially valuable just before the Advanced Placement Examination.

Procedure

1. A few days prior to discussion of this lesson, assign each student (or pair of students) one of the names on the list in part A of **Handout 42**. The task is twofold: preparation of a written presentation (to be duplicated for the entire class) and a short "Hall of Fame" nominating speech. A sample written presentation is provided in part B of **Handout 42**. Students should prepare a three-minute nomination speech for the Secretary of State Hall of Fame. The speech should address the criteria listed in part A and present the secretary in the best light but not distort historical reality.

2. In class distribute written reports to other students in the class and have students present their nominating speeches. After each speech, ask the class to rate the Secretary on the ranking sheet in part A of **Handout 42**. At the conclusion of the speeches, have students turn in their ratings. Ask one or more students to compile a composite ranking and report back to the class on the following day. At that time you may wish to compare your students' ranking with that of Professor Porter's poll. It is included in **Handout 43**. A poster-size chart with your class rankings would spark interest and provide a handy tool for review just prior to the Advanced Placement Examination.

   Because of his brinkmanship policy, John Foster Dulles will probably prove to be highly controversial.

3. To conclude the lesson, have the class consult their completed scorecards and consider the following issues:

   a. Speculate about turning points in American foreign policy.

   Suggested Responses:

   > *a. Isolation and the Monroe Doctrine*
   >
   > *b. Expansion and the Open Door*
   >
   > *c. Containment and the Truman Doctrine*
   >
   > *d. The Reagan imprint on foreign policy*

   b. The results of the poll should provoke many disputes but one may puzzle why some secretaries were not mentioned. Have students make a list and suggest why some prominent names were omitted (e.g., *James Madison, James Monroe, James G. Blaine, Henry L. Stinson, Cordell Hull*). Students may recognize that these men served presidents who chose to be their own secretaries of state.

Secretary of State Scoreboard

As you listen to nominating speeches, decide on a ranking and mark the chart below accordingly.

Name	Dates Served	A	B	C	D	E	Total
Thomas Jefferson	1789–93						
John Quincy Adams	1817–25						
Daniel Webster	1841–43 and 1850–52						
William H. Seward	1861–69						
Hamilton Fish	1869–77						
John Hay	1898–1905						
Elihu Root	1905–09						
William J. Bryan	1913–15						
Charles Evans Hughes	1921–25						
George Marshall	1947–49						
Dean Acheson	1949–53						
John Foster Dulles	1953–59						
Henry Kissinger	1973–77						
George P. Shultz	1982–89						
James A. Baker III	1989–92						

Criteria for Judging

A. Ability to achieve diplomatic goals

B. Political and moral leadership on foreign affairs

C. Impact on American history

D. Ability to communicate

E. Other _____

Points

Superior	21–25
Excellent	16–20
Good	11–15
Below Average	6–10
Failure	0–5

Sample Presentation

Rusk

(David) Dean (1961–1963, 1963–1969)

February 9, 1909–December 20, 1994

Education

(Highest Degree) M.A. International Relations, St. John's College, Oxford University, England, 1934. Studied law at U.C. Berkeley from 1937–40.

Qualification to be secretary of state

Worked in the State Department under George Marshall (1947). Served as Dept. of State representative to the United Nations from 1947–49. Appointed Assistant Secretary of State for War Eastern Affairs in March, 1950 to 1952.

What problems did he face while in office?

    a. Communist rebels advancing in Laos

    b. Independence of South Vietnam was threatened

    c. Friction between United States and Castro

    d. Revolution in the Republic of the Congo

    e. Maintain our position in Berlin

How did he solve these problems?

Rusk was appointed by John F. Kennedy in an effort to counteract the criticism leveled at Dean Acheson. Kennedy asked Rusk to remain behind the scenes since the president wanted to conduct foreign affairs himself. Consequently, Rusk became an advisor rather than a formulator of policy.

What influence did he have on the office?

Rusk served as an international negotiator but under strict directions from the White House. He was unable to divert some of the criticism leveled against the Department.

How does he rank in history?

Despite a fine background and a wealth of experience, Dean Rusk was a minor Secretary of State and does not rank in the top ten.

The Ten Best Secretaries of State

Read the samples. They are provided to help you write your nominating speech.

1. John Quincy Adams, who served (1817–1825) under President James Monroe, was the first choice of over 80 percent of the respondents. Stern, cerebral, conscientious and articulate, he negotiated the acquisition of Florida from Spain in 1819 and collaborated with the president in formulating the Monroe Doctrine.

2. William H. Seward served (1861–1869) Presidents Abraham Lincoln and Andrew Jackson. He helped keep France and Britain from recognizing the Confederacy during the Civil War, persuaded France to withdraw her troops from Mexico after that war ended, and successfully engineered the purchase of Alaska from Russia in 1867.

3. Hamilton Fish served (1869–1877) President Ulysses S. Grant. Calm, judicious, and untainted by the corruption that permeated the Grant administration, he helped settle the thorny Alabama Claims controversy with Britain in 1871, directed negotiations that settled American claims against Spain, and signed a commercial reciprocity treaty with Hawaii in 1875, helping to pave the way for later annexation.

4. Charles Evans Hughes served (1921–1925) Presidents Harding and Coolidge. He presided over the Washington Conference for Limitation of Armament (1921–1922) that froze for a decade naval armament among the United States, Britain, and France, and he brought about the 1922 Nine Power Treaty, which called upon its signatories to maintain an Open Door policy toward China and respect her independence.

5. George C. Marshall served (1947–1949) President Harry Truman. The first professional soldier ever to become Secretary—and the man who held the post for the shortest time among the top ten—he helped establish the postwar policy of containment. He promulgated the Truman Doctrine that provided military aid for Greece and Turkey, developed the Marshall Plan for rebuilding postwar Europe, and helped foster the Organization of American States and the North Atlantic Treaty Organization.

6. Dean Acheson, Marshall's successor, also served (1949–1953) President Truman. He helped create NATO, brought West Germany into the European defense system, and implemented a policy of armed intervention in Korea.

7. Henry Kissinger, our only foreign-born Secretary of State, served (1973–1977) under Presidents Nixon and Ford. After four enormously influential years as Nixon's special advisor on national security affairs, he sought, as secretary, to relax tensions and promote trade with China and the Soviet Union and pioneered the art of "shuttle diplomacy," traveling 560,000 miles in search of peace.

8. Daniel Webster, one of only two Secretaries of State to hold nonconsecutive terms, served under three Presidents: William Henry Harrison and John Tyler (1841–1843) and Millard Filmore (1850–1852). He negotiated the Webster-Ashburton Treaty of 1842, averting war with Britain over Maine's boundary, and asserted America's right to recognize republican Hungary and other popular governments in Europe.

9. Thomas Jefferson served (1789–1793) President George Washington. As our first Secretary of State he established a host of diplomatic and administrative precedents and, when war broke out between France and Britain in 1793, subsumed his own sympathy for the French Revolution to successfully administer a policy of strict neutrality.

10. John Hay served (1898–1905) Presidents McKinley and Roosevelt. An expansionist, he urged annexation of the Philippines, called for an Open Door policy toward China, helped prevent partition of that country after the Boxer Rebellion, and negotiated the 1903 treaty with Panama granting the Canal Zone to the United States.

The Five Worst Secretaries of State

Read the short biographies which follow. Do you agree or disagree? Why?

1. John Sherman served (1897–1898) President McKinley. An Ohio senator (and the younger brother of General William Tecumseh Sherman), he was seventy-four at the time of his appointment—made purely in order to create a vacancy in the Senate for McKinley's mentor, Mark Hanna, to fill. In failing health and absentminded—he once forgot entirely that his department was engaged in annexing Hawaii—he resigned when an assistant secretary was invited to attend Cabinet meetings in his stead.

2. Robert Smith, a Pennsylvanian who had served as Secretary of the Navy under Jefferson, was appointed in 1809 by James Madison when a Senate cabal barred the President from appointing the man he really wanted, Albert Gallatin. Madison, who had himself been Secretary of State, planned to direct foreign policy in any case. Smith was inept and unschooled in diplomacy—Madison complained that he personally had to rewrite all the Secretary's papers—and was replaced in 1811 by James Monroe.

3. Elihu Washburn, President Grant's first Secretary of State, served the shortest term of all—just five days (March 5 to March 10, 1869). An Illinois congressman and long-time political ally of the new President, he was made Secretary out of gratitude for past favors—and perhaps to add luster to his new appointment: minister to France. His successor, Hamilton Fish, would prove one of the ablest Secretaries.

4. John Foster Dulles served (1953–1959) under President Eisenhower. A stern, pious lawyer and diplomat, he was ranked among the worst primarily because of his dangerous tendency toward overstatement—he was the champion of "brinkmanship" and "massive retaliation"—that caused distrust among America's allies and bewilderment among her potential adversaries.

5. William Jennings Bryan, three times Democratic candidate for President, was made Secretary of State in 1913 because he had thrown his support to Woodrow Wilson at the 1912 Democratic convention. Bryan knew little of foreign affairs: his chief concern when asked to take the job was whether he would be expected to serve intoxicants. Assured that he would not, he accepted, only to find his unbending pacifism increasingly out of favor with the growing interventionist spirit of the President and public. He resigned in 1915, charging that Wilson's notes to the Germans following the sinking of the *Lusitania* were too belligerent.[1]

[1] David L. Porter, "The Ten Best and The Ten Worst Secretaries of State," *American Heritage Magazine*, Vol. 33, No. 1 (December 1981), 78–80.

Lesson 39
The Individual in History

Objective

- To review the role of the individual in American history

Notes to the Teacher

One of the most controversial topics in history involves the role of the individual in history. Does an individual shape an era, or is the individual a reflection of the times? In this lesson, students attempt some mental gymnastics designed to test their own competence in quickly assessing major characters from the entire scope of American history. Competent students who are able to grasp the methods needed to select heroic figures based on an understanding of history and historical forces will find this a valuable tool to focus the whole course. This activity can be both enjoyable and profitable as a strategy of review.

Procedure

1. Distribute **Handout 44** and have students complete part A individually.

2. Review their selections. Insist on a rationale for each choice because this discussion is the most important part of the activity. There is, of course, no "right" answer, but students should note that earlier centuries are more likely to produce consensus while more recent times will elicit varied selections. Discuss why this is so, stressing the more complicated nature of history in recent times.

3. Divide the class into small groups to complete part B.

4. Review their responses in a large-group activity. Again, insist on a rationale for their various choices.

5. Continue the discussion by raising the following points: Whom would you select as the outstanding individual of each century if you were a military historian? an intellectual? a writer of the history of science? an African-American historian? a feminist? Why, in each case?

6. Reassemble the small groups to complete part C. Have each group determine the criteria for its selection of the "Person of the Age."

7. As a concluding activity, discuss in a large group the rationale for each group's choice for "Person of the Age" and why different groups might make valid but different nominations for this award. Ask if the individual(s) chosen shaped the era or reflected the times. Finally, ask which students would like to revise their original selection and why.

Name_____
Date_____

The Individual in History—The Person of the Age

Part A. Begin a review of important individuals in U.S. history by identifying in each period who best fits the designation at the left.

	1750–1800	1801–1850	1851–1900	1901–1950	1951–Present
Most influential political figure					
Greatest intellectual					
Most important person in the arts					
Most influential woman					

Part B.

Identify the person in each century who best fits the labels at the left.

	1750–1800	1801–1850	1851–1900	1901–1950	1951–Present
Bad guy (or woman)					
Good guy (or woman)					

Part C.

Identify the individual you believe best represents the spirit of the age. Indicate your criteria for selection at the bottom.

My nomination for "Person of the Age" is _____

Criteria for selection

1. _____

2. _____

3. _____

4. _____

5. _____

6. _____

Lesson 40
The Confidence Builder—
Tackling the Essay

Objective
- To review the broad spectrum of American history through several questions from the Advanced Placement Examination

Notes to the Teacher
At this point in the review process, students should have a good grasp of the basic themes of American history. Practicing past Advanced Placement essays at this juncture should boost students' confidence that they can and will succeed on the Advanced Placement Examination.

In this lesson, small groups prepare in advance in-depth presentations on one of a series of questions covering major themes in American development. In class, they analyze for their classmates how to read, interpret, cover, and conclude the essay. Notetaking on the products of this investigation should be enormously useful to other students as they piece together threads of the past. The mutual sharing of expertise in particular aspects of history helps to lighten the burden of review for the many possibilities on the examination.

Procedure
1. Several days in advance of this lesson, distribute **Handout 45** and assign individual questions to small groups to prepare for presentation to the class.

2. To ensure quality, you might wish to critique student presentations before students teach their topic to the class.

3. On the day allotted for debriefing, have students critique—and applaud—each other's findings. Other students should take careful notes on these presentations to facilitate their own learning at this point.

Suggested Responses:
1. *Students will develop a thesis and put the issue in the context of new realities for workers in an age of huge factories and owners' desire to make big profits and command whole industries, Repub-lican control of government, and public antipathy to organized labor. The response requires approximately equal attention to the failures of organized labor and the unwillingness of the federal government to offer support for labor. Evidence of union failures might be allowing bloodshed in key strikes, putting all workers in a single union (Knights of Labor), failing to recognize the value of political pressure, inadequately organized strikes, putting too little emphasis on dues and organization of the union, the Knights of Labor focus on eliminating capitalism, and being associated—unjustly—with the Haymarket Affair. Samuel Gompers's organization of the American Federation of Labor, with its emphasis on "bread and butter unionism," was the one success story of the period. Government failures to support organized labor include failure to provide supportive legislation (e.g. outlawing blacklists or yellow dog contracts), ordering state or federal troops to protect the property interests of owners in the key strikes (B & O, Homestead, Pullman strikes), and issuing injunctions to forbid strikes, which might endanger property or threaten the national interest.*

2. *A good essay for this question will adopt a thesis, outline the social dislocations that typically result from wars, discuss the specifics of social change that resulted from wars of the twentieth century, including both world wars, Cold War, Korea, and Vietnam. Students may cite wartime migrations, changing employment patterns as women and African Americans take positions formerly held by white males, the tendency not to want to return to previous positions at the close of the war despite encouragement from government and employers to do so. Specifics for African Americans in World War I might include movement to northern and western cities during the wars; work in factories;*

racial tensions over housing and living conditions in the cities; race riots at the conclusion of the war; KKK; World War II might include Franklin Roosevelt's Fair Employment Practices Commission; segregated military; wartime jobs; later, military desegregation under Truman; the rise of the Civil Rights Movement; violence in the cities. For women, one might mention the Nineteenth Amendment, employment, wartime jobs, Rosie the Riveter, military services, NOW, the ERA struggle, women's liberation movement, and others.

3. Students could argue either in support or opposition to the suggested interpretation. Context includes Social Darwinist philosophy, traditional laissez-faire government, and Republican business-oriented control of government. Government intervention includes the tariff, Homestead Act, support for transcontinental railroads, Contract Labor Law, Chinese Exclusion Act, among others. The Interstate Commerce Act and Sherman Anti-Trust Act can be interpreted as promising precedents for government control of business or "window dressing" to give the illusion of government control while, in fact, providing vague or unenforced legislation. The efforts to inflate the currency, especially the Sherman Silver Purchase Act, had similar mixed results. State support for the railroads and the Granger laws can also support either position. Students should make clear the enormity of the economic transformation during the 1860-1900 period and its implications for the future of the government, business grants, and the working person.

4. Students need to develop a thesis, put the elections in historical context, and cite substantial evidence from the earlier (unsuccessful?) presidency and the (perhaps?) more hopeful promises of the winner in the current campaign.

1912—Election of Woodrow Wilson (Democrat, New Freedom) over Taft (Republican, too conservative (?), Progressive), and Theodore Roosevelt (Republican turned Bull Moose third-party candidate); issue was conservatism of Taft in view of public support for Progressive reform; Roosevelt's third party split the Republican vote and allowed a Democratic candidate to win. Wilson's Presbyterian College president image was hardly the attraction.

1920—Warren Harding (Ohio's Republican, "Normalcy") won over James Cox (Ohio Democrat); the issue was the failure of Woodrow Wilson's campaign to join the League of Nations; Harding promised a return to a more conservative (business-oriented?) domestic policy and more isolationist foreign policy. Harding was the candidate of the party regulars, rather than an attractive candidate with whom voters could identify.

1932—Franklin Roosevelt (Democratic governor of New York, polio victim) over Herbert Hoover (engineer, incumbent Republican). Issue was the failure of Hoover to deal with the Depression. Roosevelt was not at the time the popular candidate that he became in later years as his New Deal policies gained popular appeal (and hatred).

1952—Dwight Eisenhower (Republican war hero) won over Adlai Stevenson (bookish Democrat). Truman's difficulties with Congress and perhaps the public's tiring of years of New Deal/Fair Deal emphasis made them ready for a change. Truman's containment policies were not seen at the time as successful. Eisenhower's appealing personality and status as a genuine was hero predominated over his promises of Modern Republicanism.

1960—John F. Kennedy (rich, attractive, young, Democrat) won over Richard Nixon, Eisenhower's vice-president. Nixon's television personality did not match that of Kennedy in the 1960 debates. Kennedy's promises of new initiatives and a new generation of leadership were appealing. Eisenhower's record had brought modest results at best.

1968—*Richard Nixon (Republican comeback) won over Hubert Humphrey (Democrat) and George Wallace (Independent). The split Democratic vote and Lyndon Johnson's failure to end the Vietnam War despite massive financial and troop commitments were key to the Democratic loss. Too, the civil rights issue cost Humphrey the votes of conservatives within his own party.*

5. *Whether students agree or disagree with the statement in their thesis, they will want to put their answer in the context of a generation of conservative Republican control of the government and increasing demands for radical solutions to critical problems. They need to define liberalism and conservatism. If they agree with the statement, their evidence may focus on the relatively few trusts that were broken up during the period, the lack of enforcement of key legislation, the Supreme Court roadblocks to key laws to protect women and children, the fact that a variety of democratic forms did not bring real change or eliminate public apathy, and Roosevelt's support for labor in the anthracite was not repeated. Progressive reform only served to prevent more radical reforms. Students who disagree with this statement will cite the many more traditional democratic reforms (e.g. initiative, referendum, recall, direct election of Senators, Australian ballot), economic reforms (trust-busting, railroad controls, bringing the National Securities Company under federal control, utility laws, Meat Inspection Act, Pure Food and Drug Act, Clayton Act, among others), and social reforms at the state and local levels. Students may conclude that Progressive presidents set important precedents in strengthening the role of the national government in making government more democratic, business*

more competitive, and society more moral and just. Progressive presidents, especially Roosevelt and Wilson, set a new standard for presidents as leaders and popularizers of reform. Evidence for both groups should include national, state, and local levels and span the administrations of Roosevelt, Taft, and Wilson (prior to the outbreak of World War I).

6. *In responding to this question, students will develop a thesis and put the answer in the context of British mercantile philosophy and concept of a state church. Events in Britain exerted both an economic push (enclosure movement, unemployment in cities, debtors) and a religious push (persecution of Pilgrims, Puritans, Quakers, Catholics, and other dissenters) to drive individuals and groups from England. Other economic and religious factors pulled them to the colonies, in particular free land and a chance to practice their religion in an area isolated from discrimination. Evidence of economic motives might include the London Company in Virginia, settlers from Virginia in North Carolina, fortune seekers in North Carolina, James Oglethorpe in Georgia, and Thomas Hooher's congregation in Connecticut. The British attempt to oust the Dutch and Swedes in the Middle Colonies was rooted in a desire to control the rich river valleys of the area and develop a solid string of British colonies along the Atlantic coast. Religious motives dominated for the Pilgrims and Puritans in Massachusetts, Roger Williams in Rhodes Island, William Penn in Pennsylvania, and, applied to some extent, for Lord Baltimore in Maryland. Even in these instances, most of the groups, particularly later groups, coming for religious reasons were not unaware of possible economic satisfaction as well.*

The Confidence Builder—Tackling the Essay

The following questions appeared on previous American History Advanced Placement Examinations. They serve as a fair sample of the sort that you may expect when you take the examination. At this point in your study of United States history, your skills in history, critical thinking, and writing should have prepared you to do creditable work on questions such as these. Research your assigned question in preparation for "teaching" it to your classmates. Be prepared to offer a thesis, historical context, evidence, and a conclusion of the significance of the topic.

1. "Though organized labor could blame itself for many of its failures during the period 1865–1900, the unwillingness of the federal government to play an active role on labor's side was the major reason for the weakness of labor unions." Explain to what extent you agree with this interpretation.[1]

2. "Social dislocations resulting from wartime conditions frequently bring lasting change within a society." Evaluate the relevance of this generalization to American society in the twentieth century in view of the experiences of Blacks AND women.[2]

3. "Although the economic growth of the United States between 1860 and 1900 has been attributed to a governmental policy of laissez-faire, it was in fact encouraged and sustained by direct governmental intervention." Assess the validity of this statement.[3]

4. "A presidential election that results in defeat of the party in power usually indicates the failure of the party in power to have dealt effectively with the nation's problems, rather than indicating the positive appeal of the winning candidate and his party's platform." Assess the validity of this generalization with references to TWO of the following elections in which the party in power was defeated: 1912, 1920, 1932, 1952, 1960, 1968.[4]

5. "The Progressive movement of 1901 to 1917 was a triumph of conservatism rather than a victory for liberalism." Assess the validity of this statement.[5]

6. "Throughout the Colonial period, economic concerns had more to do with the settling of British North America than it did the religious concerns." Assess the validity of this statement with specific reference to economic and religious concerns.[6]

[1] *Advanced Placement Examination, United States History*, (Princeton, New Jersey: Educational Testing Service, 1961).

[2] *Advanced Placement Examination, United States History*, (Princeton, New Jersey: Educational Testing Service, 1987).

[3] *Advanced Placement Examination, United States History*, (Princeton, New Jersey: Educational Testing Service, 1988).

[4] *Advanced Placement Examination, United States History*, (Princeton, New Jersey: Educational Testing Service, 1980).

[5] *Advanced Placement Examination, United States History*, (Princeton, New Jersey: Educational Testing Service, 1987).

[6] *Advanced Placement Examination, United States History*, (Princeton, New Jersey: Educational Testing Service, 1990).

Acknowledgments

For permission to reprint all works in this volume, grateful acknowledgment is made to the following holders of copyright, publisher, or representatives.

Lessons 2, 10, 40; Handouts 3, 12, 45

Advanced Placement (test questions or other material) selected from College Entrance Examinations Board. Reprinted by permission of Educational Testing Service, the copyright owner of the test questions.

Permission to reprint AP test materials does not constitute review or endorsement by Educational Testing Service or the College Board of this publication as a whole or of any other testing information it may contain.

Lesson 10, Handout 12

Cartoon by J. N. "Ding" Darling. Reprinted with the permission from The J.N. "Ding" Darling Foundation.

Lesson 13, Handout 15

A Diplomatic History of the American People, 10th Edition, by Bailey, Thomas A., © 1980. Reprinted by permission of Prentice-Hall, Inc., Upper Saddle River, NJ.

Lesson 14, Handout 16

The Puzzle of Pearl Harbor by Paul Burtness and Warren U. Roin. Copyright © 1962, Peterson & Company.

Lesson 16, Handout 18

Adapted from *Bill of Rights in Action*, Constitutional Rights Foundation, Los Angeles, California.

Lesson 17, Handout 20

6 pages from *Encyclopedia of American History* by Richard B. Morris. Copyright © 1953, 1961, 1965, 1970, 1976 by Harper & Row, Publishers, Inc. Reprinted by permission of HarperCollins Publishers, Inc.

Lesson 27, Handout 30

"America's Indians: Beggars in Our Own Land," May 23, 1983, *U.S. News & World Report*. Copyright © 1983, U.S. News & World Report.

Lesson 29, Handout 32

Excerpts from *Presidential Greatness* by Thomas A. Bailey, 1966. Copyright by Thomas A. Bailey, Stanford, California.

Lesson 29, Handouts 32, 33

From *Presidents, Politics and Policy* by Erwin C. Hargrove and Michael Nelson. Copyright © 1984 by Alfred A. Knopf, Inc. Reprinted by permission of the publisher.

Lesson 38, Handout 43

Excerpt from "The Ten Best and the Ten Worst Secretaries of State" by David L. Porter. Reprinted with permission from David L. Porter.

Social Studies Series

Advanced Placement

Advanced Placement U.S. History, Book 1
(Teacher and Student Editions)

Advanced Placement U.S. History, Book 2
(Teacher and Student Editions)

Advanced Placement Economics

Advanced Placement European History, Book 1
(Teacher and Student Editions)

Advanced Placement European History, Book 2
(Teacher and Student Editions)

Advanced Placement U.S. Government and Politics
(Teacher and Student Editions)

Basic Skills

Basic Skills, Geography

Basic Skills, Government

Basic Skills, United States History

Basic Skills, World Cultures/World History

Economics

Economics, Book 1:
Microeconomics and the American Economy

Economics, Book 2:
Macroeconomics and the American Economy

Government

U.S. Government, Book 1: We, the People

U.S. Government, Book 2: Government of the People
and by the People

Issues

American Social Issues

Contemporary Issues

Current Issues in Global Education

Issues in Our Changing World

Special Topics

Supervisor/Student Teacher Manual

Peer Mediation:
Training Students in Conflict Resolution

Primary Sources in U.S. History

Colonization: 1521–1763*

Revolution and Constitution: 1763–1791

Early Nation: 1791–1820*

Jacksonian America: 1820–1840*

Antebellum America and Civil War: 1840–1865*

Reconstruction: 1865–1877

Expansive America: 1877–1898*

America in the Age of Imperialism: 1898–1920*

Interwar America: 1920–1940

America in World War II: The 1940s

Consensus and Conformity: The 1950s

America in Upheaval: The 1960s

Disillusioned America: The 1970s*

America's Turn to the Right: The 1980s*

Technological Revolution: The 1990s*

Senior High Electives

Anthropology

Psychology

Sociology

Social Issues

The American Family

The Deficit and National Debt

The Environment

Issues in the Workplace

Juvenile Justice: In the Hands of the Law

Teens and Alcohol

United States History

U.S. History, Book 1: Beginning–1865

U.S. History, Book 2: 1866–1920

U.S. History, Book 3: 1920–1960

U.S. History, Book 4: 1960–1990

World History

World History, Book 1: Beginning–1200 A.D.

World History, Book 2: 1201–1814

World History, Book 3: 1815–1919

World History, Book 4: 1920–1992

 The Center for Learning

To be published

The Publisher

All instructional materials identified by the TAP® (Teachers/Authors/Publishers) trademark are developed by a national network of teachers whose collective educational experience distinguishes the publishing objective of The Center for Learning, a nonprofit educational corporation founded in 1970.

Concentrating on values-related disciplines, the Center publishes humanities and religion curriculum units for use in public and private schools and other educational settings. Approximately 500 language arts, social studies, novel/drama, life issues, and faith publications are available.

While acutely aware of the challenges and uncertain solutions to growing educational problems, the Center is committed to quality curriculum development and to the expansion of learning opportunities for all students. Publications are regularly evaluated and updated to meet the changing and diverse needs of teachers and students. Teachers may offer suggestions for development of new publications or revisions of existing titles by contacting

The Center for Learning

Administrative/Editorial Office
21590 Center Ridge Road
Rocky River, OH 44116
(440) 331-1404 • FAX (440) 331-5414
E-mail: cfl@stratos.net
Web: www.centerforlearning.org

For a free catalog containing order and price information and a descriptive listing of titles, contact

The Center for Learning

Shipping/Business Office
P.O. Box 910
Villa Maria, PA 16155
(724) 964-8083 • (800) 767-9090
FAX (888) 767-8080